beats Muskie, who is virtually eliminated. Now leads in delegates and becomes the front-runner.

May 2 • Loses tight race with Humphrey in Ohio, but demonstrates strong support among blue-collar voters. Jackson fails to win any delegates and is written off as contender.

May 9 • Wins Nebraska primary, defeating Humphrey's charges of radicalism.

May 15 • Wallace shot while campaigning in Maryland. Eliminated from further serious contention and from third-party race.

May 16 • Finishes second behind Wallace in Michigan and third behind Wallace and Humphrey in Maryland.

May 23 • Sweeps Oregon and Rhode Island primaries.

May 28 • First debate with Humphrey in California.

June 5 • Cool reception from Democratic Governors, meeting in Houston.

June 6 • First candidate to win four primaries on one day— California, New Jersey, New Mexico, South Dakota. Margin in California narrower than expected, but moves ahead of Wallace in total popular vote.

June 9 • After indications that he might withdraw, Muskie balks, fueling anti-McGovern effort.

June 20 • Strong victory in New York primary.

June 29 • Credentials Committee strips McGovern of 151 California delegates as anti-McGovern forces reach high point of strength.

July 12 • Nominated candidate of the Democratic Party.

July 13 • Selects Eagleton of Missouri as running mate.

July 25 • Eagleton tells press of hospitalization for depression and of shock treatments.

July 31 • Eagleton leaves Democratic ticket at McGovern's request.

Aug. 8 • Shriver is nominated to replace Eagleton as Vice Presidential nominee.

Aug. 16 • Incident in which confused communications lead McGovern to deny that he asked Pierre Salinger to meet North Vietnamese in Paris.

Aug. 29 • Speech on Wall Street on broad tax and welfare reform proposals.

Oct. 10 • "Presidential"-style address to nation on Vietnam.

Nov. 7 • Defeated by President Nixon. Margin ranks with Landon and Goldwater losses. Says he will seek to remain in Senate.

THE LONG SHOT

A valuable and most
insightful book by a man best
qualified to write it.

George McGovern
July 22, 2009

It was a great honor of my life to
work with and for Sen. McGovern
and to remain his friend. This
book was an early remembrance
of the campaign

Gordon L. Weil
7-22-2009

Books by *Gordon L. Weil*

The European Convention on Human Rights
A Foreign Policy for Europe?
The Benelux Nations
Trade Policy in the 70's
The Gold War (with Ian Davidson)
The Long Shot—George McGovern Runs for President

THE
LONG SHOT

George McGovern Runs
for President

GORDON L. WEIL

W · W · Norton & Company · Inc ·
New York

First Edition

Copyright © 1973 by Gordon L. Weil. All rights reserved. Published simultaneously in Canada by George J. McLeod Limited, Toronto. Printed in the United States of America.

Library of Congress Cataloging in Publication Data
Weil, Gordon Lee.
    The long shot: George McGovern runs for President.
     1. Presidents—United States—Election—1972.
2. McGovern, George Stanley, 1922–   I. Title.
E859.W44   329'.023'730924   73–6856
ISBN 0-393-05498-5

1 2 3 4 5 6 7 8 9 0

TO
Roberta, Anne, and Richard
and to my *mother*

CONTENTS

PREFACE

I believe that the outcome of the 1972 Presidential election was determined by the careful incumbency campaign of Richard Nixon and the mistakes and misfortunes of the McGovern campaign. In my opinion, the result cannot be seen as a rejection by the American people of George McGovern's appeal to shift our resources and attention from the works of war to the building of a better America.

Throughout the campaign, I had the rare opportunity of working at Senator McGovern's side and of witnessing the role that the candidate played in his own campaign. I have tried to depict as accurately as possible some of the major events of the campaign to help McGovern supporters and others understand what happened.

In the last analysis, George McGovern was responsible for his campaign—just as much for the outstanding and unprecedented successes of the primaries as for later developments. Some matters—Nixon's campaign and Eagleton's deception—were beyond his control; others—campaign organization and positions on the issues—were under his supervision. I have tried to make a careful and honest appraisal of his role in hopes that later candidates and campaigns may learn from McGovern and his campaign.

I thank those people who worked for the success of the campaign and to make it an effort of which we could be proud. Without them there would have been no campaign and no book.

Most of these people I do not know by name. But I have seen them all across the country working with great dedication and skill. And there are those, many mentioned in this book, with whom I worked at the national level.

I thank George McGovern, who gave me such a unique opportunity and who tried so hard to do what he thought right. Eleanor McGovern deserves more credit for her major role in the campaign than this book gives her. She was a pleasure to work with as a colleague, one with considerable wisdom.

Among the campaign staff people with whom I worked most closely were the schedulers and the advance men and women. Under the most trying circumstances, they performed admirably and professionally. I was proud to have been associated with them.

The Secret Service was not part of the campaign; it worked closely with us. Rarely have I seen an organization, either in or out of government, that performed its duties with such skill and success. The professional standards so well maintained by the detail assigned to Senator McGovern helped us all to achieve standards of performance we might not otherwise have reached. In particular, I would express personal appreciation to Larry Short, George Hollendersky, Woody Taylor, and Dale Wunderlich.

I also greatly appreciated the friendship of the many objective and hard-working reporters, too numerous to mention here, who covered the McGovern campaign. We share the memory of Michele Clark of CBS News, an excellent newswoman, who lost her life tragically during the course of the campaign.

In connection with this book, I owe particular appreciation to Robert Sam Anson, McGovern's biographer; Peter Shepherd, my agent; Richard E. Burns, my lawyer; George Brockway, Evan Thomas, and Rose Franco of Norton.

Michael Lloyd Carlebach photographed much of the campaign for leading American and foreign publications. He has provided many of the illustrations for this book. Stuart Bratesman, whose pictures also appear here, was on the McGovern Campaign staff. I am grateful to both, to NBC's "Meet the Press," and to all of the others who helped me gather photographs.

Roberta M. Weil and our children Anne and Richard made great sacrifices. Our family life was totally disrupted during the 1970–72 period. Their forbearance and support was unlimited and a very real contribution to the McGovern campaign.

G.L.W.

Washington, D.C.
February 1973

THE LONG SHOT

I

---◆◆---

VIETNAM AND THE McGOVERN CANDIDACY

"A policy of moral debacle and political defeat."
—George McGovern, September 24, 1963.

At ten minutes before ten on the morning of Tuesday, September 1, 1970, the floor of the United States Senate was crowded. Some 94 Senators, an unusually large number, were in their places. Although they already knew the outcome of the roll call that morning, they all wanted to be recorded on the first congressional vote to legislate an end to American military involvement in Vietnam.

William Spong, a first-term Senator from Virginia, enjoyed the momentary prominence of presiding over the assembly. He recognized a Senator standing in the back row of the Democratic half of the floor to make the closing statement prior to the vote.

George McGovern rose at his place. As he began to speak, he felt a surge of emotion. Months of effort to engage public support and to convince his colleagues to support the so-called

McGovern-Hatfield Amendment to the Military Procurement Authorization bill were coming to a climax. Just before McGovern had risen to speak, Kentucky's Republican Senator John Sherman Cooper, an opponent of the war and a respected leader in his party, had told him that he could not break with the President on this matter. To the South Dakota Democrat, Cooper's action was a clear case of putting party before country. McGovern was angry.

The quiet Senator, who had never sought acceptance in the Senate "club," felt inspired to address his colleagues as they had seldom been lectured before. Copies of the brief speech that he had labored throughout the night to write had already been distributed to the press. As he began to speak, McGovern looked up at the press gallery, jammed with newsmen who understood the significance of the moment.

> Mr. President, the vote we are about to cast could be one of the most significant votes Senators will ever cast.
> I have lived with this vote night and day since last April 30—the day before the Cambodia invasion—the day this amendment was first submitted. . . .
> What is the choice it presents us? It presents us with an opportunity to end a war we never should have entered. It presents us with an opportunity to revitalize constitutional government in America by restoring the war powers the Founding Fathers obliged the Congress to carry.

As he proceeded, the Senators on both sides of the aisle could see he was speaking with an unusual intensity. The cavernous room was silent; for a change. There were no whispered conversations on the edge of the floor. Yet the Senators and the press recognized that McGovern was saying nothing new. Many times he and others had argued that the President had usurped congressional powers over war and peace. They had admitted that the Congress itself had cooperated in the gradual shift of power. Then, suddenly, McGovern turned that admission into an accusation.

> Every Senator in this Chamber is partly responsible for sending 50,000 young Americans to an early grave. This Chamber reeks of blood.

It was as though 93 Senators had drawn in their breaths at once. To McGovern's right, in the Republican ranks, several faces were clouded with anger and fury. Many Senators on both sides stared down at their desks. Others, those who supported the amendment, looked up at McGovern, intent now on every word.

> Every Senator here is partly responsible for that human wreckage at Walter Reed and Bethesda Naval and all across our land—young men without legs, or arms, or genitals, or faces, or hopes.
>
> There are not very many of these blasted and broken boys who think this war is a glorious venture.
>
> Do not talk to them about bugging out, or national honor, or courage.
>
> It does not take any courage at all for a Congressman, or a Senator, or a President to wrap himself in the flag and say we are staying in Vietnam, because it is not our blood that is being shed.
>
> But we are responsible for those young men and their lives and their hopes.
>
> And if we do not end this damnable war, those young men will some day curse us for our pitiful willingness to let the Executive carry the burden that the Constitution places on us.
>
> So before we vote . . .

Just then, Senator Spong's hand brought the piece of marble that serves as the Senate gavel down on his desktop with a sharp rap. "The Senator's time has expired," he said.

This was the customary warning to the speaker that he must finish the sentence he is then speaking and resume his seat.

Then, from the Republican side of the chamber, several Senators rose, calling out "Regular Order! Regular Order!" This was clearly not the Senate custom and it meant that the Republicans, angered by McGovern's tough talk, wanted Spong to cut McGovern off in mid-sentence and to resume the regular order of proceedings.

Fighting to make himself heard against the Republican chorus, McGovern concluded:

> So before we vote, let us ponder the admonition of Edmund Burke, the great parliamentarian of an earlier day: "A conscientious man would be cautious how he dealt in blood."

The vote itself was an anti-climax. McGovern's cause received 39 votes from those attending and the support, on the record, of one absent Senator. The Nixon administration received 55 votes.

George McGovern had fought and lost one more battle in his war against the war. But he had come a long way from another Tuesday, September 24, 1963, when he had become the first Senator to attack the Vietnam war on the floor of the Senate. At that time, he had called American military intervention in Vietnam "a policy of moral debacle and political defeat." Now, instead of standing alone, he had forced the first vote in Congress to end that military intervention. He now found himself at the head of a growing anti-war movement that was well financed and politically sensitive.

Vietnam was never simply a political issue for McGovern. He saw it as an immoral war, an immoral act which was destroying much of what was innocent, hopeful, and unique in the American national character. He deplored the waste of American lives and resources that were so desperately needed at home. But, even more deeply, he believed that the United States had been drawn into a "senseless" involvement which could in no way serve our national interest. The unnecessary killing of hundreds of thousands of Vietnamese and the heaviest bombing in the history of the world were themselves an assault on the values of a nation founded on the principles of respect for human life, dignity, and property. McGovern was convinced that if the American people could only be made aware of what the war was doing to their heritage, they would put an immediate end to it.

Though he had been elected to the Senate by a margin of only 596 votes in 1962, McGovern was willing to risk everything to awaken public opposition to the war. It took great courage and foresight to make that speech in 1963, and it is a sad commentary that it still required great courage for McGovern to make the speech in 1970. In the intervening years, McGovern had become a historic figure in the Senate, a man whose patriotism was highly praised by many of the very men who opposed him the most.

I had been McGovern's Press Secretary for the past five

months and had worked closely with him on the McGovern-Hatfield Amendment. As I sat on the arm of one of the great leather couches that line the side of the Senate Chamber that September day, I knew that McGovern had long ago understood that he could not reach the American public from the back row of the Senate. He felt that he was as qualified to serve in the Presidency as many men who had. He felt he was better qualified to serve than many of the others who wanted to run because of his foresight on the war which he regarded as the pre-eminent issue of the 1960's. So I knew that George McGovern was already running for the Presidency. He would try to channel the anti-war forces into a bid for the Democratic nomination.

After first speaking out against the war, McGovern soon became known as one of the principal anti-war spokesmen. In the early 1960's, he believed that he was on the same side as Lyndon Johnson. He viewed the bellicose statements of Barry Goldwater as dangerous and enthusiastically campaigned for Johnson, who had promised to avoid full-scale military involvement. He backed Johnson on the Gulf of Tonkin resolution because he thought the Commander-in-chief should be given the limited authority to retaliate against attacks on our installations in Vietnam. This position in no way diminished his desire to see a complete pull-out of U.S. forces, although he soft-pedaled it.

In August 1964, only Senators Ernest Gruening and Wayne Morse voted against the Gulf of Tonkin resolution because they correctly saw it as a blank check for greater U.S. involvement. McGovern voted for the resolution, but warned the next day that his vote should not be construed as supporting any action beyond direct retaliation. Unfortunately the peace community would count votes, not intentions, and McGovern would be continually forced to explain his vote. It was one that he most bitterly regretted.

He continued his support for Johnson into early 1965. By bad luck an interview he had given in February to *The New York Times* in support of the restrained Johnson policy was not published until March, by which time Johnson had begun the bombing of North Vietnam. Thus it was made to appear that he favored the escalation of the war. Johnson regarded McGovern, and a few other Senators, as the jury to which he had to prove his desire for peace. But the jury remained unconvinced, and Johnson ceased trying. By 1966 McGovern felt free to criticize the administration without reservation.

Throughout the 1960's McGovern wanted the administration to pursue negotiations with the other side with as much vigor as it executed its bombing runs. After Nixon took office, he became the first Democrat to criticize Nixon's handling of Vietnam in a Senate speech in March 1969. Even the other leading Democrats told him that he had not given Nixon enough of a chance.

In 1970 he decided to introduce a piece of legislation that would express his anti-war sentiments. Charles Goodell, the New York Republican who was filling the unexpired term of Robert Kennedy, had submitted a resolution in late 1969 calling for the cut-off of funds for the Vietnam war. The resolution was never voted on, but instead was buried in committee because Goodell did not enjoy enough leverage with either Republicans or Democratics to push his case effectively.

On April 30, McGovern and Senator Mark Hatfield, the Oregon Republican and longtime opponent of the war, introduced to the Military Procurement Authorization Act an amendment designed to cut off appropriations for American military activities in Vietnam, Laos, and Cambodia. This amendment had certain advantages over the Goodell resolution. The amendment, drafted by John Holum, McGovern's legislative assistant, with the help of McGovern's academic friends at Harvard, contained very specific proposals. It called for the withdrawal of American forces and the end of U.S. military action in Indochina by December 31, 1971. It provided that the President could extend the deadline by 60 days and could ask the Congress to set a new withdrawal date. In short, the President would have to get new congressional authority if he wanted to continue the war, presumably because our prisoners had not been returned.

A second advantage of the proposal was that it was an amendment to a vital piece of legislation and, unlike the Goodell resolution, could not be bottled up in committee. It was certain to come to a vote.

Finally, and most importantly, the McGovern-Hatfield Amendment was introduced on the day before the President announced that U.S. forces had invaded Cambodia without any authorization from the Congress. The public outcry, which could be channelled into a lobbying movement dedicated to the passage of the McGovern-Hatfield Amendment, brought a sense of drama and urgency to the debate on the first congressional vote on the war.

By the following Tuesday, May 5, McGovern had decided that he would answer the President's Cambodia speech on television. I contacted the three major networks to see if they would give use a half hour for the response. But I knew they would turn us down on the grounds that McGovern was a self-appointed spokesman for the opposition, and there would be no way of telling how many others would ask for time. We immediately began trying to raise money to buy the time. We needed $60,000 just for the air time.

While two of the networks refused our request to buy the earliest available half hour of prime time, NBC told us they would give us the 7:30 P.M. time slot of "I Dream of Jeannie" on Tuesday, May 12, if we could find the money by 5 P.M. on Friday. On the Thursday evening news, David Brinkley mentioned that McGovern was trying to raise the money for the broadcast. Hardly had the news gone off the air than the phone in the Senate office started ringing with pledges. With the help of the Council for a Liveable Word, a peace organization, we were able to raise $25,000 from individual contributors by the following afternoon. I stayed at the phone most of that night taking pledges.

The next day, McGovern told a Washington columnist he would mortgage his house if necessary to make up the difference. But Stewart Mott, the young New York philanthropist known for his support of liberal causes, said he would contribute $5,000 and loan us the remaining $30,000. At 4:45 P.M. his representative walked into the NBC offices in New York and handed over the check. I was on the phone with NBC while we kept the vigil, and as soon as the money changed hands, we went to work.

Under pressure from his Senate colleagues, McGovern agreed to invited Frank Church of Idaho, Harold Hughes of Iowa, and Goodell to join him and Hatfield on the program. Charles Guggenheim, who had made all of McGovern's campaign films, produced the program on Sunday at a studio in Virginia. It went on the air Tuesday with a brief appeal for funds that Guggenheim had added at the end. We were genuinely afraid that we would not be able to repay Mott or cover the costs of production.

Within two days, we had received the $70,000 to cover the original investment, and the money kept flowing in. The revenue allowed us later to broadcast short television spots and to place newspaper advertisements. In the end, these and the original broadcast generated $480,000 to further the cause of the amendment.

Renamed the Amendment to End the War because some Senators were concerned about McGovern getting all the credit, the legislation was the object of a massive citizens lobbying operation. Several committees dedicated to its passage sprang up in Washington. The most important was the Congressional Committee for a Vote on the War, composed of members of the Senate and House and which was financed by the proceeds of the telecast. Thousands of anti-war lobbyists were channelled through these committees during the summer.

As an anti-war effort, the amendment succeeded in focusing public attention on the first meaningful vote in Congress on the war. The great surge of support for it undoubtedly pressured Nixon into setting an early date (June 30) for the withdrawal of all U.S. forces from Cambodia. And the amendment clearly established McGovern as the successor to Eugene McCarthy in the forefront of the anti-war effort.

There was some friction among the Senators because of the amendment's obvious benefit to McGovern. Goodell wanted credit for his role in the development of the proposal since his own Senate race was coming up that year. Hughes told me angrily that by handling the McGovern-Hatfield funds, supposedly under the supervision of the five Senators who had been on the program, I was really promoting McGovern, my employer. And none of the four other principal sponsors wanted to accede to McGovern's request to provide some funding for black groups supporting the amendment, undoubtedly because they saw it as a political move designed to further his own popularity in that community.

Less because of this kind of infighting than because of his impatience with the reluctance of most Senators to act against the war, McGovern remained angry. A few months after the McGovern-Hatfield vote, he reacted even more strongly than in his September 1 speech when I told him that Senator John Stennis, the chairman of the Armed Services Committee, seemed to be advocating the return to Vietnam of American forces that had already been withdrawn. McGovern told the Senate press corps: "I'm fed up to the ears with old men dreaming up wars for young men to die in."

In 1971 the McGovern-Hatfield Amendment was reintroduced. McGovern sought the same December 31, 1971, deadline, but provided that if no agreement on the return of prisoners was worked out within 60 days of enactment, the deadline would be extended by 60 days. This extension would, as in the first version, give the President the opportunity to ask the Congress to set a new deadline if the prisoners were not returned.

Lawton Chiles, the newly-elected Senator from Florida, urged us to water down the provisions of the amendment in order to give it a better chance of passage. On June 16, the day of the vote, McGovern, Hatfield, Chiles, and their staffs worked hurriedly in an antechamber of the Senate to come up with a new amendment. We agreed that Chiles should introduce it to prevent votes against McGovern (who was by then an announced candidate) from turning into votes against the amendment. The Chiles Amendment provided that the withdrawal date would be nullified if all prisoners were not repatriated some 60 days before the deadline. It seemed unlikely to me that the North Vietnamese would accept such an arrangement, but adoption by the Senate could serve as a warning to the President of harsher action. Some 45 Senators favored the Chiles Amendment; 43 supported McGovern-Hatfield. Only two Senators had defected on the second vote, because, as Republicans, they would not support a McGovern proposal.

The original McGovern-Hatfield Amendment, which contained no direct link between the return of prisoners and the complete withdrawal of American forces, was more in line with McGovern's thinking. He had been willing to try Chiles's approach, but when it failed, he saw no further chance for any congressional action that could actually bind the President.

The decisive votes against his own amendments, the obvious impossibility of gaining a majority in the House of Representatives for a tough anti-war measure, and Nixon's absolute refusal to accept even the mild Mansfield anti-war Amendment (which did not cut off funds) meant to McGovern that all hope was gone for effective congressional action to end the war and the only alternative was to elect a President who was willing to take decisive action to end American military involvement. What he had felt in September 1970 was now a certainty. McGovern wanted to be President. But he was realistic enough to know that some other Democrat might gain the nomination. In that case, he could draw satisfaction from knowing that all possible nominees, with the exception of Scoop Jackson, had lined up behind McGovern-Hatfield when he had forced a clear vote on the war. By that amendment he had virtually made it certain that the war would be a partisan issue in 1972—to be used by the Democrats against Nixon.

In August 1971, right after the Nixon announcement of his New Economic Policy, McGovern told a group of newsmen that he intended to talk more about the economy and less about the Vietnam war on which his position was far better known. When this statement was duly reported, McGovern's supporters in the anti-war movement reacted with shock and disappointment. At the same time, his Senate Nutrition Committee staff had boxed him into hearings on the possible relationship between consumption of dairy products and heart disease. These hearings could only hurt him in the farm states. Finally, on August 30, McGovern told me that he wanted to make a trip around the world in order to visit Vietnam. In this way, he would scotch the story about his abandoning the war, avoid the Nutrition Committee hearings and, hopefully, gain media coverage. The trip began on September 9, just a few days later.

McGovern and five staff members first met with both the Viet Cong and the North Vietnamese delegations in Paris. Our discussions centered on the link between two of their demands: setting the date for the withdrawal of U.S. forces from Vietnam and terminating support for Nguyen Van Thieu. We wanted to know whether setting the withdrawal date would be sufficient to insure the release of the prisoners. That was the position Mc-Govern had maintained about the prisoner release all along.

The other side was unwilling to separate the two points completely, although Le Duc Tho, the senior North Vietnamese negotiator, had done so in early July. Now our hosts told us President Nixon was supporting Thieu's re-election and matters had changed. But Dinh Ba Thi, the deputy chief of the Viet Cong delegation, implied that withdrawal of our forces would be one way of ending our support for Thieu. He added that military and economic aid would also have to be cut off. Then he shifted back and said: "We only say that the Thieu administration cannot remain in power if the United States does not give him such all-around support. But we do not relate this question to the release of the captured military men."

Xuan Thuy, the head of the North Vietnamese delegation, indicated that we were not posing the question in a practical way, because he was sure that Nixon would not let Thieu try to make it on his own. Thuy was sure that Nixon would maintain sufficient military capacity in Indochina to prop up Thieu. "You have good will, but I doubt that what you say is possible," Thuy told Mc-Govern.

McGovern agreed that Nixon would not be willing to let Thieu stand on his own. If he were elected President, he would not only be willing to do that, but would repudiate Thieu, who was a repressive dictator.

As a result of our discussion in Paris, McGovern would lay greater emphasis than previously on the complete withdrawal of support for Thieu. In fact, McGovern-Hatfield had never spoken of a cessation of economic aid. Coupled with setting a withdrawal date, he now recognized that this step would bring about the release of our prisoners and the safe withdrawal of our remaining forces. McGovern was convinced that the other side would meet its part of the bargain. I, too, was convinced from our talks that the other side had no incentive to keep the prisoners if those conditions were met.

I had the clear impression that the North Vietnamese had an excellent understanding of the domestic political scene in the United States. They told us that the McGovern-Hatfield Amendment would have no chance in the Congress. They would do nothing to help our cause, for they always refrained from intervening in American politics, probably in the belief that they would have to deal with their adversaries, not those who viewed the situation as they did, when the time came for a final settlement. Despite all our hopes, the North Vietnamese never even confirmed publicly the separation between their two demands in the degree they had discussed with us. McGovern was somewhat embarrassed when the Paris press corps picked up the discrepancy between the two versions of our talks.

The inescapable conclusion was that the North Vietnamese expected to deal with Nixon. They gave me the impression that they did not expect McGovern to have a chance at the Presidency. When he asked them about the possible release of some prisoners as a way of proving to the American people that they would keep their part of the bargain once a deadline was set, they declined. They were even reluctant to promise that they would provide him with a complete list of the prisoners held in South Vietnam, Cambodia, and Laos. They also shied away from accepting a list of American missing about whom there had been no information.

From Paris we made the long flight to Saigon. In Vietnam, we wanted to talk with the non-Communist opposition to the Thieu regime. McGovern was greatly interested in learning about the kind of government that might replace the dictator if he fell. On Tuesday night, September 14, McGovern, Holum, Frank Mankiewicz, and I climbed into two small Renaults to be driven to a Saigon church where a group of priests, lawyers, teachers, and students, who opposed the repressive prison system, were meeting. Gary Porter of Dispatch News Service would be there as well as an American expatriate, now teaching in Vietnam, who would serve as interpreter. The American Embassy was not informed of our plans.

We went directly to the church office building at the back of the courtyard. Those of us in the McGovern party sat with our backs to the large glass windows which covered the front of the building. What looked like it would be a dull and endless meeting got under way. Then, I noticed over my shoulder that there was a small fire in the courtyard. I went outside, immediately followed by Holum. It appeared that a piece of wood was burning under a truck parked in the courtyard. The fire was extinguished by a Vietnamese, and the truck was moved directly in front of the one-story office building. I felt that the situation was potentially dangerous, but all was quiet. Reluctantly, I went back into the building.

Within minutes, the truck was afire. Now we knew that the building was under attack. Fire bombs, presumably Molotov cocktails, were thrown at the building from a crowd in the street and along one wall of the courtyard. Porter panicked and the Vietnamese milled about without any sense of direction. The four of us in the McGovern party retired first to an office in the center of the building which unfortunately had glass walls. Mankiewicz and Porter began trying to call any Americans we knew, especially newsmen. They reached Iver Peterson of *The New York Times*.

Meanwhile the truck and the motorbikes parked in front of the building were ablaze, creating an impenetrable wall of fire. The only way out of the building was through the rear and then over a wall topped with barbed wire. We had no idea what was on the other side of the wall. The Vietnamese had found a makeshift wooden ladder and I told them to put it up against the wall. I asked McGovern and Mankiewicz to move to the rear of the building, as little exposed as possible, to be near this escape route. Holum and I went to the front room to discover most of the windows broken by large rocks and a roaring fire just inches away. I also thought I heard shots.

I did not think that the demonstrators had set out to kill us, but I thought that they might, by accident, if the building caught fire. No help had yet arrived.

I went back into the office to call Ambassador Bunker and to my relief found the phone still working. At the Embassy, I was told that he was at home. At his home, I was told he was out for the evening. I finally reached him.

"Mr. Ambassador, are you aware of the situation in which we find ourselves?" I asked.

"No."

"Could you please help us? We are at—what's the name of this church—can you send help from the Embassy?"

"I'll do what I can."

Just as we finished talking, the Saigon fire department arrived. They immediately began pouring water on the blaze. The rock throwing stopped. Holum was worried that, once the fire was out, the firemen would step aside and let the demonstrators at us. I could see they were close to us now. I asked our interpreter to tell the firemen to stay where they were to serve as a kind of barrier or at least discouragement to our tormentors.

"I won't do that," he said. "You can't do that. This is not your country and you can't tell them what to do."

"This may not be my country," I shouted in fury, "but this is my Senator and I want those firemen to stay." I shoved the interpreter all the way across the room into a pile of rubble. Then I discovered that some of the firemen could speak French and I asked them to stay. I was determined not to let any Vietnamese into the building, because I could not gauge their attitude toward us.

Just then a voice called McGovern's name. It was Peterson who had calmly walked through the demonstrators and the fire fighters. When he came into the room, McGovern stepped forward to meet him, his hand extended.

"Hello, I'm George McGovern." Just like on the campaign trail.

At last, the MP's arrived. The lieutenant in charge was at least as shaken as we were. McGovern and I piled into a police car where, to my surprise, there were two American police officers in Vietnam as part of the U.S. training program. Mankiewicz got into the MP jeep in front of us, together with a strange Korean who seemed to be dogging our steps in Saigon. When the Korean went to grab hold of the machine gun, Mankiewicz pushed him aside and seized it himself. We returned to the hotel without any further difficulty except for some talk by the police of gunning down anybody who blocked our way. McGovern overruled that idea. But, at the entrance to the hotel, he turned sharply on the Korean and told him that he could not enter with us. At my request, MP guards were posted outside the hotel. From my window, I could see them later engaged in earnest conversation with the local ladies of the night.

The next day, the Saigon police chief (who, coincidentally, was soon to be Thieu's son-in-law) claimed we had been meeting with known Communists. It was hard to understand why he had recently set some of them free if he knew they were Communists. He had arrested them all and, I was pleased to note, had taken into custody the American interpreter who wanted to be identified with the South Vietnamese in the church more than with his own countrymen. He also admitted that the "demonstrators" included a great number of auxiliary police, thus giving the impression that the Thieu government had ordered the attack, knowing we were in the building.

To us, the whole affair was one more piece of evidence of the corruption and lack of popular support of the Thieu regime. When McGovern met with Thieu a day later, he was unusually tough, criticizing Thieu's government and telling him that he could not count on continued American support.

While the American government was in no way responsible for the attack on the church, it was responsible for maintaining the Thieu regime in office. If we had needed any proof of the repressive nature of that regime, we got it that night in Saigon.

Back home, the press coverage did not do justice to the story. McGovern had played down the whole event. More important, the Attica Prison riot eclipsed our little adventure.

Once it became clear that McGovern would win the Democratic nomination in 1972, the North Vietnamese made contact with McGovern. Holum learned that they would welcome a visit to

Hanoi by McGovern or his representative. McGovern had not sought such a visit and, in fact, at the time of our talks with the North Vietnamese delegation in Paris ten months earlier, he had decided to turn down any such invitation since it could serve no purpose. McGovern could not negotiate with the other side. The best we could hope for was the immediate release of some prisoners as we had requested at our earlier meeting. (The State Department had been kept informed of this request and, of course, we did not seek to conduct our own negotiations.)

Pierre Salinger, who had been disappointed in hopes of appointment as Vice Chairman of the Democratic National Committee, decided to return to his home in France immediately after the Democratic Convention in July. McGovern asked him to discuss discreetly with the North Vietnamese the possibility of the release of some prisoners. No visit of a McGovern representative to Hanoi would be politically possible without such a step. Salinger met with North Vietnamese officials and asked for the release of as many as 40 prisoners. As before, the North Vietnamese refused to release prisoners, although they would shortly turn three over to the representatives of American peace organizations. In the course of his discussions with the North Vietnamese, Salinger repeated a well-known McGovern position that the candidate wanted peace as early as possible regardless of the effect an early settlement might have on his own chances for election.

Salinger was due in the United States in mid-August to take charge of the National Citizens Committee for McGovern-Shriver. Prior to his departure from Paris he briefed a wire service reporter on his contacts with the North Vietnamese. Unfortunately he had not briefed McGovern first. The wire services "bent" his report somewhat so as to say that McGovern had sent a message to the North Vietnamese that they should settle the peace with President Nixon rather than awaiting the possible election of McGovern.

At about noon on August 16, I received a call at Washington campaign headquarters from the *Washington Star* with the distorted wire service report. I denied that McGovern had sent any such message to the North Vietnamese. Only after I hung up did the probable cause of the misunderstanding occur to me.

At about the same time, McGovern was accosted by the press in Illinois, where he was campaigning. He was asked if he had sent Salinger to Paris to negotiate with the North Vietnamese and specifically to tell them to settle with Nixon on the peace terms. His initial reaction was the same as mine: denial of a story that had only the smallest grain of truth. Salinger had spoken with the North Vietnamese on behalf of McGovern, but only in response to their own initiative. He had not negotiated nor had he particularly advocated a settlement with Nixon.

McGovern spoke by phone with Salinger who had arrived in New York. Salinger confirmed our understanding of what he had done. But he was alarmed that McGovern had apparently denied having asked him to meet with the North Vietnamese. McGovern then issued a clarifying statement.

The press blew the matter out of all proportion. They made it appear that McGovern had sent Salinger to negotiate but did not want to admit it until he had no other choice. (News reports were so absurd that day as to say that McGovern was the only U.S. Senator to have met with the North Vietnamese. The slightest research would have shown that Indiana's Vance Hartke had met with the other side during the same period as our 1971 visit to Paris.)

The Vietnam issue was also soured by the adverse publicity surrounding the visit of former Attorney General Ramsey Clark to Hanoi. On August 13, after his return, he reported seeing extensive damage from American bombing of civilian facilities including schools and hospitals. He said that he had been told that American prisoners would be freed "if there is a change of administration." While in Hanoi, Clark had unwisely allowed himself to be interviewed by the North Vietnamese radio, which the Republicans charged amounted to aiding and abetting the enemy. Months earlier McGovern had said that Clark was the kind of man he would like to see serving as Attorney General or Director of the FBI. In addition, he agreed with Clark's appraisal of the Vietnam situation. Even though McGovern was restrained in his comments on the Clark visit to North Vietnam, the Republicans made it appear that McGovern would have to repudiate his friend or accept responsibility for his statements.

Despite the Salinger and Clark episodes, McGovern decided to reinvigorate his flagging campaign by making a major televised address on Vietnam in early October 1972. He hammered hard at continued American military involvement in Vietnam four years after Nixon's commitment to pull American forces out. In considerable detail, he reiterated his plan for setting a withdrawal date and leaving General Thieu on his own in return for the release of our prisoners.

But McGovern could gain little ground with this proposal. While Vietnam still ranked as the nation's top problem, a September Gallup Poll showed that 58 percent of Americans thought Nixon could do a better job ending the war than McGovern, and only 26 percent supported the Senator. Obviously the gradual withdrawal of ground troops had built public confidence in Nixon's ability to finish the job. Some voters remained unmoved by the moral and material costs of the war and feared the loss of face—"national honor"—that would result from meeting the conditions laid down by the other side.

On October 26, the North Vietnamese made a surprise announcement proving that the rumors about Kissinger's progress at the secret peace talks were true. The North Vietnamese outlined a settlement which, they claimed, should be signed by October 31. In a press briefing later in the day, Kissinger essentially confirmed the story that the other side had broken to the world. Clearly the North Vietnamese had experienced delay from the American side once the agreeement had been reached and hoped to use the pressure of the election campaign and world opinion to bring an early signature. On the American side, President Nixon apparently had some difficulty with Kissinger's agreement to the retention of North Vietnamese troops in the South and to a coalition mechanism for conducting new elections there. President Thieu could also be expected to oppose these terms, and it was now up to President Nixon to decide if he would proceed without Thieu's approval as McGovern had said he must.

McGovern, following his instincts, approved of the agreement and indicated that Thieu should not be allowed to stand in the way of a settlement which could bring the release of our prisoners. In the view of the entire staff, this was the most constructive approach to take, one on which the candidate could stress his own suggestion to do exactly what Nixon was now doing four years too late.

Clark Clifford, the former Defense Secretary who was a McGovern adviser, urged the candidate to attack the administration itself and not merely Thieu's intransigence. In a memorandum dated November 1, Clifford said:

> The simple fact is—there is no peace agreement. When the American people were told on Thursday, Oct. 26, that peace was at hand, we now know this to be a perversion of the truth. When President Nixon stated in Kentucky that we now had in our grasp a peace with honor instead of a peace with surrender, that statement constituted a fraud on the American people. . . . The fundamental factors and elements existing in Vietnam for many years and about which the war has raged interminably have not been settled. To tell the American people that peace is at hand when these major elements of controversy are still in violent dispute constitutes the bitterest kind of hoax.
>
> It is apparent now that President Nixon's strategy was to inform the American people that a peaceful disposition of the war had been reached and that minor details would be ironed out which would maintain the illusion of peace from Thursday, October 26, when Dr. Kissinger made his announcement, until Tuesday, November 7, when the American election would be held.

After a second memo and a late night conversation with Clifford, McGovern decided to criticize the administration directly. In a brief television address on the Sunday evening before the election, he took up the Clifford approach.

Nothing that McGovern could do during the general election campaign could make Vietnam "his" issue as he had hoped it would be. Perhaps more than on any other issue, McGovern had been able to draw the distinction between himself and President Nixon. But he was unable to convince the electorate that only his approach would work.

Despite this frustration, McGovern took some satisfaction from his efforts. He had succeeded in making sure, through the McGovern-Hatfield Amendment, that whoever ran against Nixon would raise Vietnam as an issue. He believed that his unrelenting pressure had pushed the Nixon administration to make concessions in the peace talks. Nixon and Kissinger agreed to set a withdrawal date before the prisoners were released. And, as McGovern had argued prior to his trip to Paris in 1971, the North Vietnamese were willing to agree to return American prisoners without an American commitment to end all support of Thieu. The ultimate agreement was just what McGovern had proposed: a withdrawal date was set; hostilities were to end; prisoners were to be released; and the rest was left to the Vietnamese.

In the end, the Vietnam issue could not win the election for George McGovern. But his stand might well have helped bring peace, and it certainly had helped bring him the nomination. Indeed it was the rock on which that nomination was founded.

2

ON WISCONSIN

"There is often to this campaign less than meets the eye."—Gary Hart, McGovern campaign manager.

On January 18, 1971, George McGovern walked into the studio of Sioux Falls television station KELO to announce his candidacy for the Democratic presidential nomination. He shattered precedent by announcing in his home state rather than in Washington where national media coverage would be better. But his campaign was designed to break precedent, so there was no more appropriate way to begin.

McGovern's announcement was greeted by expressions of respect for the man if not for his chances and, in some quarters, by outright derision. Jimmy "The Greek" Snyder, a Las Vegas publicist, who promoted himself by giving odds on everything from football games to political races, spotted McGovern at 200–1. He was a long shot.

The Gallup Poll showed McGovern fifth among the possible choices of Democratic voters to lead their party. He was less well known than most other potential Democratic candidates. McGovern's chances for overcoming these handicaps and seizing the nomination were not considered good since he started from so far behind.

The winning formula was simple—people and money. Mc-

Govern knew that he could win the nomination if he could put together a strong coalition, but not necessarily a majority of Democrats, and if he could find the financing to keep his campaign afloat before he began to be taken seriously.

Vital to success in attracting supporters and contributions was the early announcement of McGovern's candidacy. Never before had a candidate formally stated his intentions to seek the Presidency as much as two years before he might take office.

On July 25, 1970, McGovern had met with a few members of his staff at his home at Cedar Point, Maryland. He told them that he wanted to announce his candidacy immediately. He felt that he would be more believable in asking for support if he were an avowed candidate rather than a coy politician going to great pains to hide his ambition. Indeed, in late 1969, he had almost announced, but pulled up short when he realized that he had no staff, no financing, and no clear idea of what he would do after the announcement.

The Senator and his advisers measured the impact of an early announcement on other minor candidates in the liberal wing of the Democratic Party. McGovern would be moving around the country asking people directly for their support, while the other possible candidates would still be at the starting gate. Most people would turn him down, but he might then extract a commitment from many of them to keep their minds and pocketbooks open until they had been able to compare his campaign with the others'. In this way, McGovern could keep people who might otherwise have supported Hughes or Bayh or Harris or Lindsay or McCarthy or even Muskie from joining up with their favorites. They could be made to feel that they owed McGovern the first shot at the nomination.

In addition, the early announcement would, McGovern believed, force the media to pay more attention to him.

Despite his impatience to announce, his staff convinced him that he should wait until the 1970 congressional elections had passed. He agreed reluctantly.

When fall came, McGovern went out on the campaign trail. He had three objectives. First, he wanted to keep pace with Muskie and the others who were out campaigning for congressional candidates. Second, he wanted to gain greater visibility with the press and Democrats around the country. Third, he wanted to demonstrate to the progressive wing of the Party that he was a spokesman around whom they could rally.

McGovern was effective, especially in achieving the third goal. Fresh from the vote on the McGovern-Hatfield Amendment, he was able to assume the role of the leading anti-war spokesman in the Congress. Hundreds and occasionally thousands would come to hear him speak as a sign of their respect for his leadership. These people would soon form the core of the McGovern supporters. Preempting their allegiance was a major part of McGovern's strategy.

In addition, McGovern set himself apart from the other possible nominees and sharpened his appeal by speaking out forthrightly on a number of issues. In the next two years he intended to highlight the differences between himself and the more cautious Muskie by boldly staking out his positions. He was quick to seize an advantage. One day, for example, a sudden Senate vote condemned the report of the President's pornography and obscenity commission. McGovern had not read the report and, unlike other possible candidates, refused to vote against it. Then when he spoke at a Party dinner in Denver shortly afterwards, he quoted an old Ogden Nash ditty ("Smite, Smoot, be rough and tough. For smut, when smitten, is front-page stuff"). The Democrats roared their approval, and McGovern picked up some more supporters.

Almost as important as all of these measures to expand his base of support was McGovern's identification with party reform. Hubert Humphrey had had him appointed chairman of the Party's Commission on Party Structure and Delegate Selection in 1968. Although McGovern had not been one of the reform leaders at the Democratic Convention, Humphrey did not want Iowa Senator Harold Hughes, the logical choice, to have the post because he had been a McCarthy supporter.

McGovern began the active campaign for reform in February 1969, when the commission was established. Although he met active opposition and hostility from the AFL–CIO leadership and many Party leaders, especially in the South, he was convinced that reform was essential for the survival of the Democratic Party. Fortunately, most of his opponents sneered at the chances for reform and simply ignored the commission.

The commission's reforms that were adopted by the party dealt with two key problems. First, the party had discriminated against those it depended on for its vote: women, young people, and minorities. Therefore, a rule was written providing that delegates to the National Convention from each state must be in rough proportion on the basis of age, race, and sex to the population as a whole in that state. Some would wonder later why there had been no religious or occupational criteria, but the simple answer was that there had been no clear discrimination on those grounds in the past.

Second and probably more important was the requirement that state parties open up the delegate selection process. McGovern was fond of citing the changes brought about in the state of Arizona. In 1968 five men went into a room and emerged with the list of convention delegates. In 1972 an open convention system was used from the precinct up to the state level which resulted in some 30,000 Democrats taking part in the choice of the delegates.

McGovern knew that these guidelines would benefit him; the very groups that had been largely excluded in the past were those where his base of support was the broadest.

Later on opponents would say that McGovern, working behind the backs of the party fathers who showed no interest in reform, was able to tailor-make the guidelines to suit his needs. Though it was indeed true that labor and party chieftains opposed reform, other potential candidates stood to gain as much as McGovern did from the new guidelines. And certainly all party members were kept informed of the reforms. In fact, one of the first jobs I had when I joined McGovern in 1970 was advising on ways to obtain the maximum publicity for the Reform Commission report.

As the commission chairman and as a practical politician, McGovern took the guidelines seriously. He did not know if others intended to play by the new rules, but he was sure that the reforms gave him a fighting chance at the nomination.

His own commitment to reform was later mirrored by the action by Party Chairman Larry O'Brien requiring any delegation to adhere to the guidelines before it could be seated at the Convention. O'Brien felt that failure to enforce the guidelines would exclude much of the Kennedy-McCarthy wing of the party.

McGovern was encouraged by his early campaigning. At the end of October 1970, he wrote a memo about his view of the campaign:

> I think I'm much more philosophical about the whole question about whether we actually get the most votes for the nomination, although, of course, I want to win. What I now see is a great opportunity to know this country as you can know it in no other way, and that is by going out to deal with the people in every nook and cranny of this country, and God, what an exciting country it is . . .
>
> How . . . exciting it is to have an opportunity to educate an entire nation and to learn from an entire nation over the period of the next two years. That is its own reward.

Yet he would soon face a major setback.

On the Sunday before the congressional elections, Dick Goodwin, a former Kennedy speechwriter, called McGovern to tell him that there was a need for a Democratic answer to Nixon's campaigning, and that on election eve Muskie would deliver on television a speech written for him by Goodwin. Averell Harriman was footing the bill. The Muskie telecast was excellent, and McGovern deeply regretted that he had not had the idea. He felt that his chances for the nomination had been pushed perceptibly further away by the speech.

Despite this Muskie gain, the campaign leadership vowed never to show that we were daunted by this or any other setback and thus to cultivate the impression that there were hidden resources of strength behind the campaign. Eventually this self-confidence began to have its effect on the press. It also encouraged our supporters.

We also noticed that the Muskie campaign had not learned the lesson of our McGovern-Hatfield telecast: exploit your advantage immediately. Muskie was forced to lapse back into his non-candidate status immediately after the broadcast. An attempt to raise funds to pay for the program failed. Thus, in contrast to our own experience, Muskie's failure had shown that if his support was broad, it was unenthusiastic. We were beginning to appreciate the depths of commitment of McGovern supporters.

Although we felt that Muskie had now moved close to locking up the nomination, we continued with our planning for the announcement, which was scheduled for early January. In December, McGovern spoke in Texas, delivering a speech drafted by Dick Goodwin. To the surprise of those attending the dinner in honor of Ralph Yarborough, McGovern's appeal for political recognition of the new South stole the show, even outshining Humphrey, who had just been elected to the Senate. (Muskie was not present.)

While McGovern discerned the formula for attracting support from the progressive wing of the Democratic Party from the outset of his 1970 campaigning, the key to fund raising came later. Indeed, just on the eve of McGovern's announcement when it looked like we were out of money, McGovern's friend Henry Kimelman, who was the campaign's finance chairman, saved the day by rounding up about $60,000 from his own friends.

The break came when Morris Dees, an Alabama lawyer, who had once heard McGovern speak in 1969, contacted McGovern in late 1970 and said he would like to join the campaign. Still in his early thirties, Dees had made himself a millionaire in the direct mail businesss. He knew how to sell books and other products by mail and had had the encouraging experience of a successful million-dollar fund drive for congressional candidates conducted in 1970 over McGovern's signature that showed liberals would pay by mail. Now he wanted to try selling a candidate for President.

Dees's direct mail expertise facilitated McGovern's desire to announce his candidacy in a letter to all those people who had expressed an interest in his political activities or whose names had been collected at the places where he had spoken in 1970.

Working with Tom Collins, a New York ad agency man who had teamed up with him on commercial mailing ventures, Dees drafted a seven-page letter based on McGovern's own speeches. Almost all of us thought the letter was too long, but Dees argued it would be far more effective than a short letter with a brochure enclosed. That was too impersonal. And in his own work, he had found that long letters brought results. At the end of the text was an appeal for financial support. The letter was so long, however, that the edges of each page had to be shaved in order to keep the missive under one ounce and avoid higher postage.

The letter was mailed so as to arrive on the day McGovern announced. If all went well, Dees said, he could predict how much we would receive on each day after the mailing. The letters went to some 240,000 names which had been collected by the Senate and campaign offices over the years.

The mailing worked. It brought in enough revenue to pay for itself and for the campaign operations. In addition, it brought in sufficient funds to pay for additional mailings. Dees devised scheme after scheme for extracting money from liberal voters by mail. The most important of Dees's schemes was to get the kind of person who contributed $10 to such a drive to commit himself to that same contribution every month. Soon we had an assured income of $50,000 a month.

Our income was far below what Muskie would reach. But it would close off a key source of funding for other liberal candidates. The small contributors could keep McGovern afloat until the big money could accept him as a possible winner.

With the hope of adequate financing and growing optimism about his ability to reach progressive Democrats, McGovern formally launched his campaign. Soon after the mid-January announcement, the newborn campaign had two opportunities to prove itself. The meeting of the California Democratic State Committee in Sacramento at the end of the month would provide head-on encounters with Muskie and Bayh. Each of them had more than a dozen staffers to work the delegates. Only three of us from the staff made up the entire McGovern delegation. But McGovern was able to draw almost as much visible support from the delegates, most of whom were Kennedy backers, as did Muskie, and he scored well before the press. He topped off his

California appearance by making a major foreign policy address on China at the University of the Pacific in Stockton. We succeeded in syphoning off some of Muskie's travelling press corps to cover that speech, which forecast much of what Nixon would do a year later. But, at the time, it seemed to be a bold address and it was well reported.

From then on, McGovern would move into key states to meet with progressive leadership in the Party. In January, we gained the support of Dorman Commons and Bill Norris in California. They had been the managers of the successful campaign of Wilson Riles for the post of Commissioner of Public Instruction, an elective statewide office. In February, the leaders of the McCarthy forces in New Hampshire said they would work for McGovern. And so it went in state after state, although there were some disappointments. We had hoped for the support of Governor Pat Lucey of Wisconsin, but the best we could do was to obtain his assurance of neutrality.

We focused on those states where nationally recognized primaries were held and where McGovern had some chance of winning or of making a good showing. New Hampshire was first, coming in March 1972, and Joe Grandmaison, who had been active in the Johnson primary campaign four years earlier, agreed to take charge of our campaign. Wisconsin was also a natural, given its progressive tradition and its proximity to South Dakota. Nebraska was added to the list because it was a farm state bordering South Dakota, and McGovern had a solid farm record. Gene Pokorny, a young political organizer who had been a 1968 McCarthy delegate, was asked to manage Wisconsin and Nebraska. Oregon had gone for McCarthy in 1968 on the basis of his good organization in that state, and it was a natural for us. Blaine Whipple, the Democratic National Committeeman, was an important addition to the campaign. And we had to concentrate on California with its winner-take-all primary. Its strong support for Kennedy in 1968 indicated that we might be able to win there. Other states were studied for possible inclusion on the key list. West Virginia was kept under consideration, because McGovern recalled John F. Kennedy's important victory there in 1960. But most of us, including our volunteers in the state, thought he should not make a major race there.

McGovern's travels in 1971 were concentrated in these states, although a number of stops were also made in New York and in Florida, whose primary would come right after New Hampshire's. In most places, we would try to organize public gatherings. Often, as in New Hampshire, we might have a reception for 20 people in a supporter's home. In Wisconsin, we would have a couple of hundred people attending a reception in the local hotel. And everywhere, McGovern spoke to cheering university crowds. McGovern went to many small towns never before visited by a Presidential candidate, and wherever he went, McGovern workers would get the names and addresses of every person who came to one of these meetings, and they each received a follow-up letter. Many of them agreed to work in the campaign.

In this way, we built up an organization. In some places, where McGovern did not even travel, organizations would grow up spontaneously. I remember one day in 1972 learning that we were doing well in the local caucuses in Nevada. Our national organization was only dimly aware that there was anybody out there working for us.

The McGovern organization was not a national organization. In many states, our campaign existed only on paper. But in those states where we would have to win and where the national press was centering its attention, we were building solid organizations.

In fact, the only poll McGovern won was conducted among county chairmen, who thought that McGovern's grass roots organization was superior to those of the other candidates. But the polls did not measure the real depth of commitment. They could not gauge the fact that at midnight on any night, a group of volunteers would be busy preparing mailings in our Manchester, New Hampshire, headquarters while the Muskie headquarters there had already shut down six hours earlier.

Among our campaign stops in 1971, McGovern's first visit to New Hampshire in February stood out. Joe Grandmaison, still working as a volunteer, made sure he would meet the top Democrats, make a major speech kicking off the campaign, and begin his tour of the campuses. McGovern's arrival in the state was greeted by an editorial blast from the right-wing Manchester *Union Leader*. In one of its usual front-page editorials, the paper accused McGovern of being responsible for the deaths of thousands of Americans in Vietnam.

We were due to walk down Elm Street in Manchester on Friday, February 26. We expected to meet a combination of apathy and hostility. If the reception would be hostile anyway, McGovern said, why not go directly to the offices of *Union Leader*. So we went.

It was a brilliant show for the media accompanying us. McGovern walked into enemy territory. William Loeb, the publisher, was out of town. McGovern asked if he could walk through the plant and shake hands. The reception was anything but hostile. The pressmen were astonished that the candidate had enough guts to visit them. The national media was impressed and the national coverage was favorable. (It was a sharp contrast with a visit one year later by Ed Muskie to the *Union Leader*—the famous "crying incident.") We were off to a good start.

In August, we added a new element to the strategy of people and money. Although McGovern was an extremely effective campaigner, his schedule was designed mostly in response to invitations he had received, and often invitations from supporters in key states would conflict. Then, Steve Robbins, a lawyer who had worked in several earlier state and local campaigns, joined the McGovern headquarters and gave us what we had never had before—a coherent scheduling strategy. He also began assembling an outstanding group of young advance men and women to make sure the schedule was executed with precision.

Robbins wanted to exploit the major media markets while the work of building the McGovern organization went on. He perfected the so-called "visual" event. The candidate must *do* something rather than merely *say* something, and he must do it early enough in the day to make the evening television news where most people find out what's going on. If the candidate was pictured moving through a factory shaking hands with workers, Robbins believed that workers and their families watching the evening news would pick up the impression that McGovern really cared about workers and their problems. Another day, he would visit a hospital and ask the patients and administrators about their problems. Result: People would see that McGovern was concerned about health care. A by-product of this approach was a real education for the candidate and the people with him.

This new scheduling operation would bring some relief to McGovern who had been highly critical of the amateurism he had been forced to endure. (On one schedule, a meeting with George Moscone, a leading California State Senator, was listed as a session with Willie Mosconi, a pocket billiards champion.) But, even with Robbins, McGovern would continue to complain, sometimes with great anger, about the arduous pace of the campaign.

Here, from my notes, is a sample of what life was like on the campaign trail:

October 6, 1971

I climbed out of bed at 6:15 A.M. at the Parker House in Boston. Glad I didn't have to get up any earlier to pack, but fortunately we would be back at the Parker House that night. We stayed here because Joe Grandmaison, our New England coordinator, likes the Dunfey family, who manage the place, even though they support Muskie. Figure that out.

Dressed and awake, I make sure the Senator is up at 6:45. We can't afford to get off to a late start, as we usually do, because we have a plane to catch in mid-morning. While McGovern is shaving, I check downstairs with Jim Connell, the advance man, to make sure the cars are at the front door, in proper order and aimed in the right direction. Then back upstairs to get the Senator and the two bags we will carry with us all day. One of them the Senator and I call "the heavy bag" as a kind of in-joke. It weighs a good 50 pounds and contains all of his speech files, pending correspondence, notes, newspaper clippings, Bartlett's *Quotations* and his shaving gear and television make-up. I regard it as my personal body-building program.

On the way down in the elevator, I thrust at him a couple of 3 x 5 cards with notes on the people who will be at the first event—what in Robbins's lingo is an "eddy board number," i.e. a meeting with the Editorial Board of the *Boston Globe*.

(Robbins developed his own vocabulary for the schedule

which kept the rest of us amused. A meeting with retired workers was a "geriatric number," while a campus appearance was a
"kiddy number." No event put on the public schedule was a
"rally"; it was a "reception" in case only 10 people showed up.
No event was ever cancelled; it was "bagged.")

Jolly Joe Grandmaison piles in the car with us and tosses off
a couple of one-liners to loosen the candidate up. Then he chats
about the *Boston Globe* while we speed to make our 7:30 appointment in Dorchester. When McGovern, Jeff Gralnick (the
press secretary), and other local campaign people pile into the
breakfast meeting, I stay outside so as not to add to the crowd
and to give myself some time to eat breakfast and check the
day's schedule. Nobody is in the office yet in Washington. At
8:30 I check with the Senate office and leave word that I would
like to know what will be happening on the floor of the Senate
that day. Then I start worrying that McGovern will stay beyond 9 A.M. when his meeting is due to end. After sending a
few notes in to the meeting, I manage to break it up at about
9:10. Fortunately, unknown to the candidate, there is about 10
minutes "pad" in the travel time allowed so we are in good
shape.

McGovern reports that the interview went well and the
Globe people seem as favorable as any editors he has met. He
asks me, as he will several times that day, if the bags are in
the car. They are.

Joe fills him in on the Paul Benzaquin Show, a half-hour
television interview program that he will do next in downtown
Boston. By that time, I have seen the morning papers and mention that there is little chance that anything will arise in the
program based on the day's news. I suggest that the candidate
hit Phase I of Nixon's economic policy and the Vietnam war,
since Massachusetts is peace-oriented.

Just as I deliver McGovern to the studio, I get a message
about a call waiting for me. It is Sara Ehrman, the legislative
aide in the Senate office. She says that there will be a vote early
in the afternoon on ending the embargo on Rhodesian chrome.
The purpose of the embargo has been to show U.S. displeasure
with the rebellious and racist policies of the Southern Rhodesia

government. We agree that this will be an important vote, because blacks would take a vote against ending the embargo as a sign of McGovern's commitment to their cause. Sara doesn't know if the vote will be close but says she'll check right away. As usual I ask her to try to get a live pair (when a Senator present on the floor and voting the opposite of McGovern agrees to withhold his vote) and as usual she says she'll try. As we are leaving the studio, Sara calls back to say that the vote will come between 1 and 2 P.M. and that our side says it's going to be close. We agree that they're probably exaggerating the closeness of the vote, as they do 99 times out of 100. But it will be a touchy one to miss.

Out of the studio at 10 A.M. and into the car. I inform McGovern of the Rhodesian chrome problem and he is plainly worried about missing the vote. We are still debating whether we should miss the noon event in New York, McGovern's first mass fund raising effort where hundreds are expected, as we stand beside the American Airlines ticket counter. At the moment, the decision seems to be the most crucial one of the campaign. McGovern opts against a return to Washington and as we hurry toward the plane, I call Sara and ask her to inform Robbins who has been tearing his hair out at the prospect of our cancelling the fund-raiser in New York. When I get on the plane, I am a little worried about the news coverage, because Muskie, who is coming to New York later that same day, is staying in Washington to make the vote. But, in any case, we are on the way.

I give McGovern his heavy bag and he goes to work on the speeches for the day. Because of the pressure of campaigning and the four major speeches that he will have to give that day, we have no prepared texts. I review with McGovern a memo I've written based on a conversation with Abby Levine, one of the organizers of the luncheon. He would like to see the Senator stress the war, civil liberties, new priorities. In short, Levine wants a standard liberal speech, but delivered in as hard-hitting a manner as possible. Mankiewicz had prepared a good little story showing that the wealthy who condemn welfare themselves benefit from government hand-outs. McGovern likes it.

We talk about later meetings that day. I am convinced that McGovern can speak well extemporaneously, but he likes to have his speeches blocked out as much as possible. At the hearings of the New Democratic Coalition, a reform group in the Democratic Party which certainly should support McGovern on the basis of similarity of views, we agree that he will discuss the work of the McGovern Reform Commission. Later he will speak before the "rump" Liberal Party dinner composed of those progressives who have split away from the traditional Liberals. These are his supporters and he can be at ease with them, but he must be careful not to take any shots at the Liberal Party itself.

The Liberal Party dinner itself is the main reason for the trip to New York. John Lindsay, the darling of the Liberals who has not yet turned Democratic, and Ed Muskie, the front-runner, will also speak. McGovern will have had a much tougher day and it will be hard competing with them. I suggest that he throw in a surprise and, instead of speaking, announce that he will take questions from the floor. He's great at fielding questions and I believe they will stimulate him to reach heights which he might not achieve in a straight speech. McGovern is interested in the idea.

We land at La Guardia in New York at 11:20 and are met by Kevin Connell, the advance man and Jim's older brother. The New York City police has assigned a plainclothesman to McGovern but no car, so we put him in our follow-up car. Dick Wade, formerly at the University of Chicago but now teaching in New York and serving as campaign chairman, rides into Manhattan with McGovern and fills him in on the day's events and the political who's who. We arrive at the Americana, where it seems that almost all political meetings take place in New York, and McGovern decides to go up to his room to wash up. A local advance person tells Connell who tells me that everything is ready downstairs for the Senator. I tell McGovern.

After a few minutes, McGovern comes down in the elevator to a reception for those who have bought tables at the luncheon. Abby Levine and Eli Sagan, former Hughes supporters who came over to us when their man dropped out, shepherd McGovern around the room. Smiling and shaking hands, the Senator is told over and over what a fantastic turn-out there is at the lunch. I duck out of the room to check on the ballroom and find that it is indeed packed with more than 1,000 paying guests. Some of the national press corps that has come up from Washington to cover the Liberal Party dinner have dropped in on our luncheon. I also check on the security arrangements. We have no Secret Service agents yet and have never bothered to hire a bodyguard. How would McGovern get out in case of fire or a disturbance? Are there any people who look like they will disrupt the meetings? Are there any places where somebody unsavory may be hiding?

Then, back to the reception to check with Levine and Sagan. It's time to take McGovern into the ballroom. He enters to the wild cheering of the throng and proceeds to the dais, where he will actually try to eat some lunch while the program gets under way. He is due to stay until 2 P.M. which gives us an hour and a half. I complement myself on getting a full meal—the only one of the day—and I try calling the Senate office a few times to find out what happened on the chrome vote, but it has been delayed.

McGovern delivers just the speech that Levine asked for. He begins by telling the story about the chrome vote. The speech is such a success that it will later be widely reprinted.

After the lunch, we go back upstairs to a room opposite McGovern's for a meeting with a group of businessmen who had attended the lunch and each of whom could contribute more than $10,000. By now, McGovern is showing signs of fatigue. They are particularly agitated about McGovern's statement, made last August, that he wants to impose an excess profits tax on business so long as the wage-price freeze is in effect. He tells them this is what we have done in the past under such circumstances, but is unable to answer some of their technical questions about how it might work, because we have made no detailed proposal. I jump in to say that we would probably tax only those profits derived specifically as a result of the freeze. The meeting ends amicably, but major contributions from this group will not come until many months later.

Now, says Dick Wade, just stop in for a minute to talk with

some basketball players who are trying to organize professional athletes to bargain for their rights. But, I protest, that meeting was supposed to be cancelled. The Senator has to have some rest. Just a few minutes, says Wade, and McGovern dutifully goes into another room to say hello to the players and their business representative. A picture is taken and then we go back into McGovern's room for a "secret" session with Robert Morgenthau who has been the U.S. Attorney in New York and a worthwhile supporter if we can get him.

Wade wants to talk with McGovern and has a few more people waiting in the hall, but I urge him to let the Senator rest. He departs at last, and McGovern and I chat briefly about the Liberal Party speech. He thinks he'll do the question and answer bit. I leave him.

I get on the phone in the adjoining room and complain to Robbins about the basketball players. We were "mouse-trapped" by Wade, he says. What about knocking something off the schedule later today? We can't bag a meeting with ex-Peace Corps volunteers since there will be a large crowd. A planned cocktail party sponsored by Al Blumenthal, a leading West Side Democrat, can't be cancelled because people are paying. No, we won't get any of the money. Yes, the rumor is right, they will pay even more to meet Muskie another time and we'll just have to suffer the implicit slight. (And months later, we will have to attend another cocktail party of another West Side Democratic faction to balance off the supposed favoritism shown to Blumenthal.) Oh, incidentally, the chrome vote went to the other side by a big margin.

Meanwhile, McGovern has snuck out of the hotel to buy himself a pair of shoes at a fancy shop. (The shoes won't be delivered for months.)

At about 4:30 P.M. McGovern is ready to hit the trail again. Shaved and in a fresh suit, he looks like he's just starting the day. In the car on the way over to the NDC hearings, he scans the list of those who will interrogate him at the hearings. Wade stresses the importance of locking up the New York NDC, if we really want to get a corner on the "left."

About 15 minutes later, we arrive at the headquarters of Local

1199 of the Drug and Hospital Workers Union where the NDC is meeting. McGovern goes into an office to wait and I am inundated by people who want to tell me how well Muskie just did, or what McGovern should say, or how the mood of the meeting is. At last, they are ready and McGovern goes in. I notice that, for such a liberal organization, they have only one black on the panel of about a dozen people. McGovern hits party reform, the war and the need to change things, and takes a few standard liberal questions from the panel. It's not tough except the press is watching everything he says.

Then we adjourn to a meeting across the hall. Here McGovern talks privately with the NDC Executive Board. This is about as much power as these people have exercised, deciding who to endorse for the Democratic nomination, and they savor the moment. Because I am afraid what reports might come out of the meeting, I keep my small tape-recorder running. (I record all of McGovern's speeches, in case he wants a transcript, but also for protection.) They are mostly steamed up by McGovern's accepting support from Matt Troy, their arch-enemy in Queens. McGovern calmly explains that he needs that support but promises that Troy won't cut the NDC out of the McGovern operation in his borough. The meeting lasts for more than an hour, too long for me since the ceiling has sprung a leak just about where I am sitting.

At about 6:15, only fifteen minutes late, we pile into the car and head for the Hotel Riverside Plaza, a relic of an earlier era. There McGovern plunges right into a meeting with several hundred returned Peace Corps volunteers. By now the batteries are running down a bit (his and mine) but he goes into a few remarks to be followed by questions and answers. I find the pay phone and check in with Robbins. Our remaining problem for the day is making sure we catch the 10:30 shuttle from Newark to Boston, the last flight out that day. McGovern meets with Massachusetts political leaders for breakfast the next day. It looks good, although Robbins relays word from the advance man that there's a big crowd at the next stop.

Back in what used to be the Riverside Plaza's ballroom, McGovern is grinding down. I edge toward the front of the crowd and get the impression that he might have caught sight of me. To make sure, I get word to the chairman that there's only time for one more question. Fortunately, he is one of these people who has the nerve to tell that to the audience. Many chairmen are afraid to cut off the questions.

Once again into the car at about 7 P.M. on our way to a plush private townhouse where the Blumenthal reception is taking place. The gracious hostess spirits McGovern away upstairs where he can wash up and I trudge along with the heavy bag. Then he goes down and plunges into the crowd, while I get rid of the bag and begin to plot how I will extricate him on time. A call to Robbins tells me that the crowd will be ready and waiting when we get to the next stop. I also put in a call to John Holum to talk about what's happening in the Senate and some work the Senator wants done on a speech.

As I leave the phone, I hear McGovern speaking. I snag a drink, say hello to the few people I know and wonder why the Senator is giving a talk when he was just supposed to "mingle around," as he would say. Of course, it was the simple "sand-bagging" operation—once he was introduced, what could he do? But it does get us out fairly quickly (except for the slow progress I make in cutting a path through the crowd). The crowd now knows that he has a couple more stops. They tell him how great he was and we climb back into the car. More cards on whom he will meet and we pull up in front of the Pyrenees Restaurant on West 51st where the "rump" liberals are meeting.

Eldon Clingan, the minority leader of the City Council and a supporter, meets us at the door and takes McGovern around table-hopping. Nice, friendly atmosphere. I grab a hard roll from an empty place to consume in lieu of dinner. McGovern sits down, and it looks like they're going to eat before he speaks. *They* don't care about the other Liberal Party dinner. I find Clingan's assistant and get word through that time is tight. McGovern is introduced as the greatest thing since sliced bread, thanks them for their support, talks about better times ahead and sits down. Time pressure is building so I tell him we have to go. We go. However far behind schedule we may get, Mc-Govern never misses the last plane out of town.

We're in the home stretch now. On the way to the Americana, to the same ballroom where we were that morning, I tell McGovern that Muskie and Lindsay had a little tête-à-tête at the Plaza in late afternoon. But Lindsay couldn't manage to meet McGovern that same day. He shrugs it off. Wade tells him that the proceedings tonight at the Americana are going to be broadcast live on a local radio station. But he doesn't tell the Senator that nobody will listen. McGovern is silent.

We hit the Americana ballroom at 9 P.M.—right on time. McGovern is going to have to sit through a couple of other speakers, but everybody has a strictly allotted time to speak and I don't worry. I find Matty Troy, the Queens Democratic leader, and tell him that McGovern is going to take questions. Could he make sure a few are planted so that the Senator isn't left with his face hanging out and to make sure we hit the right issues, such as the war and the Middle East. He says he'll take care of it.

All of a sudden I realize that Simeon Golar, a New York official active in the civil rights and housing areas, is delivering a full-dress speech and a damn good one at that. While I appreciate the prose, I worry about the time. There's nothing I can do now, because McGovern is next anyway, so I retire to the sidelines, where I can watch the reaction of the national press and find another dinner roll. McGovern is introduced and begins to speak. It's a standard speech but I ask myself whatever happened to the questions and answers. Finally, about halfway through his time slot, McGovern says he'll take some questions.

A woman asks about the war and then, to my surprise, Troy's chauffeur and assistant, gets up and *reads* a question. Our entire attempt at making the question period look spontaneous is blown. Even the Sunday *Times* will note this gaffe. McGovern takes another question, takes his seat, gets up, and takes leave of the chairman.

It is now 10 P.M. and we are 15 minutes late. We have to make a plane out of Newark in a half-hour. As we move toward the exit, trying not to attract attention, Ed Muskie who has just been introduced, lofts a barb at us: "Good night, George." Exeunt, definitely not laughing—at least, not us. I'm making bets with Connell about whether we'll make the plane. I'm a pessimist.

We do the Americana to Newark run at 90 miles an hour, when we get enough clear space to really open up. Out of the car, grab the bags, say good-bye and thanks, run for the plane.

Yes, Miss, a vodka tonic for the Senator and a Jack Daniels for me. McGovern is teed off. He thinks the Liberal Party dinner was a bomb. Though I don't like to say so, I'm forced to admit it. I ask him why he gave part of a speech. He says it was because he owed it to the live radio audience. Fortunately it was too late for the television news. But it turns out later that Muskie delivered a solid speech on the responsibilities of liberals (written by Bob Shrum, who did Lindsay's speech for the dinner last year and will do McGovern's next year). McGovern notes that Golar's speech will probably turn out to be the best of the bunch. McGovern is not in a good mood, although it was a successful day for the most part. I take the rap for the Liberal Party dinner, but he never criticizes me.

Arrival at Logan airport. Grab the bags. Cheery driver asks how it went in New York. Well I bombed, says the Senator. I think it was a pretty good day, says me. And so to the Parker House, pulling in at about 12:10 A.M.—almost exactly 17 hours after the campaign day began. So we stop in the bar to have a drink with former North Carolina governor Terry Sanford, who has filled in for McGovern at a campaign stop in New Hampshire. (Later, he'll seek the nomination for himself.)

Exhaustion grips me. I remind the Senator that he can sleep until 8 in the morning since the first event is in the Hotel at 8:30. I set my alarm for 7:15. Last thing I remember is one of the Boston staff saying: Gee, you don't even look tired.

(*End of Day*)

This hectic pace seemed to be helpful. We gained good local media exposure. In addition, we were building up credit with groups whose help we would need during the primaries. If Mc-

Govern had not come to New York, for example, we could not have recruited volunteers for the campaign from among the Peace Corps veterans.

By the beginning of 1972, the McGovern campaign was in high gear. We entered the early primary season, where all of the strategy and campaigning would be tested. McGovern would have to produce surprisingly good results to remain in the running in the later primaries—Nebraska, Oregon, California, and New York. And if he were to have a real chance at the nomination, he would have to win. New Hampshire provided the best chance for a surprise showing; Wisconsin could be the scene of McGovern's first victory. But Jimmy the Greek still saw McGovern as only a 50 to 1 shot.

On a crisp, winter day—January 4, amidst the proverbial winter snows, George McGovern filed his candidacy for the Democratic Presidential nomination in the New Hampshire state capital at Concord. At the last minute while the TV cameras waited, we discovered that we did not have the $500 filing fee in cash and Joe Grandmaison ran to a bank across the street to cash his own check. When he got back, he had to shoo away former Massachusetts governor Endicott Peabody, who was running in the Vice Presidential primary, when he tried to horn in on McGovern's media coverage. Then, we were on the way.

McGovern planned to spend about 28 days in New Hampshire out of the 62 that remained until the primary. We were uncertain of Muskie's plans, although he retained enough flexibility to match us day for day. McGovern would also go to Arizona and Iowa, where the non-primary delegate selection process would begin later in January. In addition, he would file his delegate slates in Illinois, which held the third primary, and spend some time in Florida, which would come second, just one week after the New Hampshire primary.

For our first trip into Illinois, we boarded a small charter plane in Chicago late in the evening of January 11 heading for Springfield, the state capital. The plane was full and McGovern and I sat together in the rear. He asked me to go over the lists of delegate candidates that would be filed the next day. By a flickering cigarette lighter I found that 13 of the lists had too many men and one had too many women if we followed a general rule that at least 40 percent of a congressional district slate must go to the minority group by sex. Only three slates met this test. McGovern decided that, despite the protests of his state coordinator, he would refuse to file the slates that he considered to be out of compliance with the McGovern Commission guidelines. This step would let Democrats everywhere know that McGovern was serious about the enforcement of the reforms and would probably mount challenges if others did not adhere to the same standard. It wouldn't hurt with the women's lib movement either.

Just as we were beginning to move the primary campaign ahead, we suffered a cruel, and I thought mortal, blow. We were in St. Petersburg Beach in Florida on Friday afternoon, January 21, when I got a call from Ted Van Dyk in Washington. The new Gallup Poll would be out Sunday. After a year of campaigning, we had reached five percent support among Democrats. But the new data would show that McGovern had fallen to three percent. The campaign looked like it was a disaster. It fell to me to tell McGovern. He took the news somberly but well.

The polls had taken a national sample, which was not relevant to winning primaries. For example, neither they nor the national press looked at how many votes we could pull out of each Wisconsin congressional district and how many each of our competitors might gain. But Gene Pokorny, constantly travelling the state, had a solid estimate.

Yet we had hoped by the beginning of 1972 to have moved from the four and five percent we had been getting throughout the preceding year into double figures. Even McGovern's around-the-world trip to Vietnam had not brought him the press attention we had hoped for.

As a result of our failure to move up in the polls, even in comparison with Eugene McCarthy who was not actually campaigning, a strategy began to impose itself on us. The only thing that could save our campaign would be a breakthrough. Since we could not count on our opponents making a mistake and, after the Vietnam trip, we could not devise any major new moves on our own, the only possible opportunity seemed to lie in scoring a surprise in New Hampshire.

Out of our low standing in the polls came the decision to take the primary states one at a time. That meant concentrating the candidate's time in each primary state in succession and pouring virtually all of our resources into one state after another. Hart even redeployed our volunteers from other states into New Hampshire. National staff personnel left their desks in Washington and moved into the cities and towns of New Hampshire.

Muskie, on the other hand, chose to spread his resources over many states. As the frontrunner, he obviously felt that he had to run a national campaign. And he decided to run against Nixon rather than his competitors in the Democratic primaries.

At the same time, we decided to treat Muskie as our sole competitor. This was substantially true in New Hampshire, and it gave the campaign a sharper focus throughout the country. Thanks to a suggestion from former Assistant Attorney General John Douglas, we challenged Muskie to debate and to make public the sources of his campaign financing. McGovern published his own contributors' list and eventually Muskie agreed both to a debate and to disclosure. His capitulation would be more important to legitimizing our contest with him than the substance of the debate or the disclosure. Muskie had been trying to project the same kind of open image to his campaign as McGovern so in the end he would be forced to accede to our demands.

If all this worked, if we were able to come close to Muskie in New Hampshire, we knew that we would pick up support in other states. We were pleased when Scoop Jackson and John Lindsay decided to stay out of New Hampshire. They thought that Muskie would eliminate us there and chose to concentrate on Florida.

Our strategy was to do well in New Hampshire and then survive the Florida and Illinois primaries which came in the two succeeding weeks. Unless the groundswell of support after New Hampshire was considerable, we could not expect to do well in those states. Ted Van Dyk, the former Humphrey aide who had joined the campaign in 1971, had been monitoring Florida and saw little to encourage us anyway. At best we might win in two of the 12 congressional districts, but we might very well drop them all. Wallace was solidly ahead, he reported, with Muskie and Humphrey vying for second. We would be battling Jackson for fourth with Lindsay bringing up the rear.

In Wisconsin, we would go all out to win. If all of this succeeded, Mankiewicz argued that we would have all but eliminated Muskie, leaving Humphrey as our principal competitor for the nomination. We could then defeat Muskie in Massachusetts on the basis of the peace vote. We could beat Humphrey in Nebraska or Oregon or California because he was a known quantity, disliked by a large segment of the Democratic electorate in those states, while McGovern was a new face.

All of this was decided without a formal staff meeting. The January poll results had thrown it all into sharp focus. There really was no alternative strategy for the primaries.

While we concentrated our resources on the primary states, Rick Stearns, who had directed campaign research since mid-1970, was given the assignment of corralling delegates in the non-primary states where we might win support in caucuses or state conventions. We worried first about Arizona, which would be the first state to select delegates. Iowa, which came next, was also given all the help we could spare, because it was a neighbor of South Dakota, and we could not afford to do badly in the Senator's home area. In such states, the commitment of our supporters was a valuable element in winning delegates, because we could count on "packing" local caucuses (by getting out more of our supporters than those of any other candidate). Sheer willingness to get out and work would pay off in these states.

Although we were sure that Lindsay would falter in his hand-picked primary test in Florida, the press credited him with more strength. On January 29, the Arizona caucuses were held. McGovern had made one brief visit to the state and had spent very little money there. Lindsay had been there for several days and was spending about $80,000. In the end Lindsay won six delegates and McGovern five. Muskie was the winner. But the press played Lindsay's victory as the beginning of a major drive for the Presidency. McGovern was more angry with the press reaction than discouraged by the outcome. A week earlier, an event of greater significance than Lindsay's Arizona showing had taken place in Worcester, Massachusetts.

The state's liberal Democrats, most of whom had supported McCarthy in 1968, had agreed to hold a statewide convention. If one of the candidates achieved more than 60 percent of the votes at the convention, he would get the support of that wing of the Party. McCarthy came to campaign and other candidates sent representatives. Former Senator Ernest Gruening of Alaska represented McGovern. The South Dakotan was the clear winner, easily topping the required majority.

This victory was the first sign that our effort to "coopt the left" was working. The same day that Lindsay won six Arizona delegates, McGovern won the endorsement of the liberal New Democratic Coalition in Lindsay's home state. Frank Mankiewicz had begun moving from state to state to meet with reform Democratic leaders and, before we were finished, McGovern had won the endorsement of the Reformers in several key states, including Pennsylvania, Florida, and California.

On the campaign trail, Robbins used the schedule to turn necessity into virtue. In early 1972, we had no money to rent our own plane and too small a press corps to merit one in any case. Each time we went to New Hampshire, we would have to fly to Boston and then continue from there by car or small plane. Robbins scheduled McGovern for a "visual" each time we passed through Boston. Television from that city blanketed New Hampshire and, no less important, we were building familiarity with the Massachusetts electorate where McGovern would also face a primary. Meanwhile, Muskie, with his own plane, would overfly Boston and go directly to his first stop in New Hampshire. He caught on to what we were doing, but too late.

These "visuals" were imaginative and successful. On Monday, January 31, for example McGovern and I had breakfast with Mrs. Mary Houton in Dorchester. A member of the housekeeping staff of Boston City Hospital, she was struggling to keep up with her property tax payments to avoid losing her home. Together with McGovern she sat in her living room and told her story to the nation's press. It was a smashing success.

Into February, we continued our intensive campaign in New Hampshire. We would be at a plant gate at 6:30 A.M. to greet the incoming workers and continue through plant tours, high school talks, drop-ins at local lunch counters, and ending with a talk to a local reception late at night. Grandmaison concentrated McGovern's activities in the smaller cities and towns where McCarthy had done well in 1968. We were even facing unusual problems among the young voters, some of whom were registering Republican in order to vote for California Congressman Pete McCloskey who was challenging Nixon. But Grandmaison felt we could count on winning about 25 percent of the vote. One evening, Grandmaison and Hart were called upon to defend their conduct of the campaign. McGovern argued that he would have won 25 percent without even campaigning. Grandmaison was crushed. While he maintained that all we could do was minimize our losses among the conservative Democrats of Manchester, McGovern repeatedly insisted that he wanted to campaign there more because most of the Democrats in the state were there. Grandmaison was deeply depressed.

Finally more Manchester stops began appearing in our schedule. Friday, February 18 was to be devoted entirely to the city. The first major stop of the day was the J.F. McElwain shoe factory on Silver Street. We were totally unprepared for the reaction. The workers were enthusiastic. Some had seen Charles Guggenheim's first spots on local television. They knew McGovern and they liked him. For the first time in any plant, a clear majority said they would vote for him. McGovern and I looked at each other in happy disbelief. The next stop was a Roman Catholic high school. Here again the enthusiasm was high. In late afternoon, McGovern visited some of the Franco-Canadian clubs and, in the largest, was once again warmly received. We knew that Manchester would be good to us.

That night the Manchester City Democratic Committee had scheduled a debate among the Presidential candidates. Only Muskie refused to attend because he was afraid we would pack the hall. We did.

The McGovern campaign had turned the corner. The Senator was becoming the candidate of working people as well as of the liberal, peace community.

The next day we were back in Washington, but Ed Muskie was in New Hampshire. He mounted a platform that snowy

Saturday afternoon in front of the Manchester *Union Leader*. He had come to protest their publication of a letter charging that he had denigrated French Canadians. (The letter turned out to have been the work of Republican saboteurs.) But Muskie got carried away and criticized the paper's reprinting of a *Newsweek* story offensive to his wife. He choked up and, whether it was tears or snow, his cheeks were damp. This was the famous "crying incident." The press pounced. If Muskie could not stand this pressure, could he be President?

Muskie was now on the defensive. He reluctantly agreed to a televised debate with the other candidates and he planned to step up his own campaigning in New Hampshire.

McGovern was now climbing rapidly. Our telephone canvassing, conducted in secret so that even our own campaign workers would not know it was under way, showed us gaining daily. Miles Rubin, a California businessman, was now making sure we had the money we needed and he supervised the phone canvass.

On primary day, March 7, McGovern scored impressively. He won some 37 percent of the vote against Muskie's 46. Clearly the man from Maine had failed to protect his own flank. We had proved him to be vulnerable. But at our headquarters in Manchester's new Howard Johnson's, George and Eleanor McGovern did not think we had won. To them, winning was getting more votes than the other guy. But, as I led them through their wildly cheering supporters into the celebration as I would do after many other primaries, they must have known that we had achieved a major victory.

First, we had delivered a telling blow to Muskie. The frontrunner was not invincible. Muskie had seemed to regard McGovern as an annoying but minor nuisance. After all, everybody else who mattered had chosen to concede New Hampshire to the man from Maine. Muskie had thought that he was the candidate of the center, able to appeal to the broad mass of working people and the more realistic progressives who would recognize that McGovern had no chance.

Instead McGovern had just about split the Manchester vote evenly with Muskie. Oddly, in the Salem area, where young professionals were expected to vote for McGovern, they went to

Muskie. They probably believed that McGovern was the better candidate but that he was not a viable candidate because he could not win in working class areas. They, at least, had bought the Muskie line.

Although the press and Muskie himself were not sure, we knew that Muskie had shown sufficient weaknesses to insure his loss of the nomination. Not only would the "crying incident" plague him, but we had demonstrated that depth of commitment did matter in primaries. Our statewide organization had performed brilliantly. Our workers had carefully identified McGovern voters and got them out to the polls. In one Nashua ward, we had located 800 supporters and we received 800 votes. That showed both the thoroughness of the canvassing effort, carried out by students who came to New Hampshire each weekend, and a good get-out-the-vote operation. Voter after voter had told McGovern how impressed they were by the commitment of our young canvassers. Working people no longer seemed to mind long-haired students.

Powerful blows had also been dealt to Lindsay and Jackson who had chosen not to run in New Hampshire. McGovern did more good for himself in Florida by running well in New Hampshire than he could ever have done by intensive campaigning in the South. He had made himself a credible candidate. Meanwhile Lindsay was still struggling to establish his candidacy. Jackson might have done well in New Hampshire, especially if the *Union Leader* had painted both McGovern and Muskie as hopeless liberals, as it almost certainly would have done. Instead he let McGovern gain as a serious contender while he concentrated all of his effort on Florida, where he would make the same kind of gamble we had made in New Hampshire.

We went directly from New Hampshire to Florida where the primary would take place one week later. We understood that we had little chance there, but hoped to get some rest. In addition, if McGovern were to be a national candidate, he would have to be willing to campaign in primaries in all parts of the country.

Our tactics here were simple. We would campaign every day in the Miami and Tampa media markets. This meant flying back and forth across the state in a rickety Martin 404. On the last flight, the plane lost one of its engines.

On Saturday, March 11, we altered our plans to stop in West Palm Beach. Here McGovern would meet Ethel Kennedy who was catching a flight north. Their meeting would carry the implication of her endorsement, the first tangible indication of support from the Kennedy family. But when an inexperienced radio reporter asked Mrs. Kennedy why no one in her family and contributed any money to the McGovern campaign, she was obviously upset. The meeting ended abruptly. McGovern left furious, but we had accomplished our purpose, to judge from the pictures in the papers the next day.

Sunday saw the only debate of the Florida primary. McGovern met Lindsay on a local television interview program. All of our staff was concerned about the confrontation, which, however, we had sought after the New York mayor had demanded a debate with Wallace. Lindsay was forced to accept. McGovern was widely considered to be lacking in charisma, the mystical quality that was Lindsay's long suit. There was little difference between them on the issues. But McGovern generated a feeling of self-confidence growing out of our victory in New Hampshire. Lindsay, laboring under the frustrations of the Florida campaign, did no better than our man. Our success made us overly optimistic about the outlook for the primary.

As the votes were tallied on election night, we knew that we had lost. McGovern asked his aides for suggestions on a concession statement, but we were sadly lacking in originality. Wallace had won about 42 percent of the votes. Humphrey was a distant second with 18 percent, followed by Jackson (13 percent), and then Muskie (9 percent). Lindsay was fifth with 7 percent; McGovern held 6 percent. McGovern retired to the bedroom to prepare his statement. Before he went to the ballroom, we watched Muskie's concession. The Maine Senator talked as if a major catastrophe had befallen the world. And he as much as charged the Wallace supporters with being bigots.

McGovern's remarks were brief. He placed the Florida primary in the perspective of our campaign. But he cautioned against considering the Wallace voters as racists. He knew that many of them were disillusioned with their government. Despite his remarks, McGovern chose not to telephone Wallace to congratulate him. He would regret this failure later, because it implicitly

denied to the Alabama Governor the same recognition that Mc-
Govern had extended to Wallace's supporters.

Lindsay was eliminated in the Florida primary, although he
did not acknowledge defeat until Wisconsin. He had used most of
his resources and every publicity technique imaginable to maxi-
mize his attraction for the voters. Perhaps many of them, ex-New
Yorkers, rejected him because of his record at home. But more
important, even the weak McGovern organization in Florida was
superior to Lindsay's techniques. This was probably what saved
McGovern from the kind of adverse press coverage that his
showing deserved.

The fact remained that McGovern had come in sixth. He had
been perceived as a liberal in a state where there are only a few
pockets of support for liberal Democrats. He had failed miserably
among blacks, who voted overwhelmingly for the candidate
whose record on their behalf they knew best—Hubert Humphrey.
Even where we had a good get-out-the-vote operation like
Daytona Beach, Humphrey walked away with the black vote.

Next on the agenda was Illinois where, if anything, the outlook
was even less favorable. In order to avoid a fruitless contest with
the Daley organization in Chicago, we had filed delegate slates
only in the downstate area. In addition, Mankiewicz and Hart
had decided to keep McGovern out of the preferential primary
which was not binding on the delegates. Gene McCarthy had
decided to make his all-out bid in this primary, where only
Muskie was entered. He hoped to topple Muskie the same way
McGovern had done in New Hampshire. Our campaign managers
were afraid of splitting the liberal vote with him and finishing
third.

While the McCarthy campaign in the preferential primary and
the McGovern bid for delegates should have been complemen-
tary, they were not. For one thing, McCarthy was running a few
delegates against us in the most liberal districts. And there were
undoubtedly Democrats who, disliking McCarthy, would vote
for Muskie in the preferential and McGovern in the delegate race.

McCarthy seemed to think that McGovern and he should play
the game by a different set of rules. In January, our local supporters in Madison, Wisconsin, had put out an anti-McCarthy sheet,

urging his supporters to abandon him for McGovern. The sheet contained no misstatements or distortions, but it was sharply critical of the Minnesotan for his performance in the years after 1968. McCarthy phoned McGovern in his office during February to deliver a severe tongue-lashing for this broadside. Then, during the Illinois primary, communicating through people who were major financial backers of both campaigns, he again bitterly protested that McGovern's managers in the state had advised our partisans not to vote for him in the preferential primary. Apparently he thought we would allow him to enhance his standing with the electorate by a good showing in the primary and perhaps by winning a few delegates.

For these reasons, McGovern had turned down a proposal by McCarthy which had been transmitted to us by one of his backers during the New Hampshire primary. McCarthy offered to endorse McGovern there if McGovern would return the favor in the preferential contest in Illinois.

We saw the McCarthy offer as a no-win proposition. McGovern was likely to do well on his own in New Hampshire. But if we accepted his endorsement, McCarthy would claim part of the credit for our success. In Illinois, on the other hand, a McGovern endorsement in the preferential primary without McCarthy's withdrawal from the few conflicting delegate races, would insure the defeat of our delegates in those districts. In addition, despite the results of the Worcester caucus, McCarthy refused to pull out in Massachusetts, where he had no chance, but where he would undoubtedly drain votes away from McGovern rather than Muskie.

Our campaign in Illinois was a disaster. The much publicized McGovern organization was non-existent. We were able to win only 14 delegates as compared with some 59 for Muskie and about 100 for the regular uncommitted slates around the state. McCarthy was soundly beaten in the primary, ending his brief campaign, but he managed to drain enough votes away from McGovern in the delegate contests that he denied us 12 delegate slots. McGovern never expressed a bitter word about McCarthy.

Finally, we had reached what we regarded as the big show—

the Wisconsin primary. Here was the primary that we knew we could win. The surprise New Hampshire showing and the weak performances of Muskie, Lindsay, and McCarthy had paved the way. We had originally seen the contest as between Muskie and McGovern. When Lindsay had entered the race, Gene Pokorny, the state coordinator, worried about the New Yorker's drawing off some of our sorely needed support. Humphrey, surging ahead like McGovern, was even more likely to worry Muskie in the same way.

Pokorny had created a superb organization around the state. In every city and town there was a McGovern committee which was active in canvassing. As in New Hampshire, we had an accurate appraisal of our strength around the state and the ability to get our people to the polls.

Muskie, who a year earlier had been expected to sweep the state, was on the ropes. Even the Illinois victory had not helped him. He had run there against little opposition and had come in second to the uncommitted regular slates. Although his campaigners stressed his ethnic identification in hopes of carrying the fourth congressional district with its Polish-American population, we had begun to see in New Hampshire that mere ethnic identification would have little meaning to blue collar voters.

As we moved into Wisconsin two weeks before the primary, Humphrey seemed to be the greatest threat. In the two congressional districts in the western part of the state he would be strong, because they bordered on Minnesota and, in a large area, the *Minneapolis Tribune* was their dominant newspaper. In addition, Humphrey was well known in the state and could expect support in much the same way as Muskie in New Hampshire. But, unlike in New Hampshire, we felt that we had to make a breakthrough to victory.

Lindsay seemed to be less of a threat as the campaign moved toward its conclusion. His personality had failed to attract the grassroots support for which we had worked over the preceding year. His Florida campaign had drained away most of his resources. He was at a distinct disadvantage against McGovern who was a Midwesterner and who enjoyed growing financial support thanks to the strong New Hampshire showing.

The impact of Wallace was imponderable. He had virtually no organization and had not begun to campaign in the state until after the Florida primary. Obviously he would have a strong appeal in the blue collar areas of Milwaukee. One rally he hastily organized there was a great success. We felt that he had started so late that he could not catch up. In addition, he was not likely to run strongly upstate in the farm areas.

McGovern kicked off the final stage of the Wisconsin campaign with a speech designed to carry the Florida message to the potential Wallace voters. We wanted them to know that we did not consider them racists but as people who were "turned off" by the system and that McGovern intended to respond to their needs. (This analysis would give him a considerable advantage over Muskie in Wisconsin. The Mainer and Wallace would be vying for the same electorate in south Milwaukee. By his statement, Muskie had alienated many of those voters. McGovern, not Wallace, would gain from this.) But probably more effective than this oratory was our blitz campaign of the bowling alleys. We had discovered in New Hampshire both that the candidate could meet a large number of people in a short time there and that the response was surprisingly favorable. People were surprised that a candidate would drop in on them on bowling night. Word spread like wildfire and these stops turned into a triumphal tour.

But McGovern also kept up a heavy schedule on the campuses around the state. He was drawing larger crowds than the other candidates (Wallace did not venture onto a campus), and we knew that these would be the campaign workers and voters who could make the difference.

We were now travelling "in style." Muskie might have his turbo-jet "The Josephine." And Humphrey might have the freshly painted but dowdy "HHH." But we had the "Basler Bomber," a chartered Martin 404 that always seemed on the verge of disintegration. Usually packed to capacity, the pride of the Basler Airlines fleet carried a jovial staff and press corps around the state. These may have been the happiest days of the campaign, because we were still the fighting underdog, but the smell of victory was in the air.

And we had some good breaks. On Saturday, April 1, just four days before the primary, McGovern held a press conference to announce the formation of "Athletes for McGovern." But he fumbled question after question about the reserve clause or other technical points. The day was saved when I got word from Washington that Wisconsin Senator Proxmire had announced that he had voted by absentee ballot for McGovern. Proxmire does not back losers.

On the day before the primary, Bill Dougherty, the South Dakota Lieutenant Governor who was travelling with us as McGovern's political adviser, arranged for the candidate to meet Governor Pat Lucey at the Madison airport. Lucey told the press that, while he was endorsing nobody, he predicted that McGovern would win.

But the "non-endorsement" of greatest value came from Senator Gaylord Nelson, McGovern's closest friend in the Senate. In March, Nelson told McGovern that he planned to introduce a tax reform bill designed to give property tax relief to Wisconsin. He urged McGovern to become a co-sponsor and to campaign in the primary on the "Nelson-McGovern" bill. Every day during the final two weeks of the campaign, McGovern spoke of this bill, capitalizing on voter discontent with rising property taxes and on Nelson's popularity. It was a week before Humphrey caught on to what we were doing, although he himself also co-sponsored the bill. Muskie never seemed to figure out the ploy.

On April 4, we reaped the rewards of all of our labors since 1970. The McGovern family and I left the Milwaukee Inn, where we had been staying, to await the returns at the Pfister Hotel where the victory celebration would take place. As we stepped into the elevator on our arrival there, a hotel man told McGovern: "The television is projecting you as the winner." That was the first news of the first McGovern victory. It was hard to believe.

The next day, McGovern left to fly to the West Coast for two fund raisers while the rest of us returned to Washington. Muskie would fly out of Milwaukee with a planeload of press. McGovern was still accompanied by the solitary reporter of The New York Times. But as he boarded the plane, McGovern turned to me and said "Well, that's phase one." It was not a memorable phrase, but it was delivered with rare emotion. To both of us it meant that the obscure and neglected candidacy had emerged into the front rank. We were serious and nobody could now deny it. We had fooled the pundits. Now, we had a clear shot at the nomination.

Just as I had felt after New Hampshire that McGovern was sure to stay in the contest all the way to the end, I felt after Wisconsin, where he captured 30 percent of the vote, that McGovern would win the nomination. With 10 percent Muskie had certainly been eliminated. He had finished fourth in Wisconsin, even in the Polish district of Milwaukee. His contributions were drying up just as ours gushed in. Lindsay (7 percent), finishing sixth behind Jackson (8 percent), had accepted the obvious and had withdrawn gracefully.

I believed that over the long haul we could beat Humphrey. He had come in third in Wisconsin with 21 percent of the vote and had carried two congressional districts by small margins. But I could not see the voters of California, with their strong liberal attitude, or Oregon, where we had campaigned hard, choosing Humphrey over McGovern. Wallace could not win the nomination if for no other reason than that he had not filed delegates in California, New York, Pennsylvania, and Ohio. (Some staff member noted that if Wallace had had Rick Stearns, he might have been able to get the nomination.) But Wallace had done well in Wisconsin, finishing a surprising second with more than 22 percent of the vote. Although we had beaten him in the Polish and other ethnic areas, we had not been able to take away his hard-core support. He could no longer be ignored by the Democratic Party.

The campaign had shown that we had developed and executed a simple but sound strategy. If a candidate could draw on truly committed supporters, he could put together a strong organization. In primaries, where the turnout is bound to be relatively low, an organization can make a great deal of difference. In addition, each primary feeds on those preceding it. Our success in Wisconsin was due, in large measure, to our surprise showing in New Hampshire. To our successful formula of organization, issues, Charles Guggenheim's media, and direct mail fund raising, we could now add momentum.

McGovern had reason for deep satisfaction as the first phase of his primary campaign ended. He had devised the strategy that had brought him victory. Convinced that Party reform would open the door to participation by many thousands of committed workers, McGovern set out to attract them to his cause. It was a calculated risk, because the media pundits and the traditional politicians said it could not be done. McGovern had demonstrated that not only was the liberal wing of the Democratic Party larger than many had expected, but it could mold itself into a powerful force if given the opportunity and the candidate.

He had benefited from some lucky breaks. He spent little time building his campaign staff. Yet many of those who were attracted to his campaign were the best young political technocrats available. They had learned the lessons of the 1968 McCarthy and Kennedy campaigns. They knew that the only virtues were hard work and a good mind, that they would not win simply because they were right on the issues.

McGovern was content to see them operate independently and effectively in state after state. His workers demonstrated remarkable self-discipline.

Everything was working out just as we had planned. There seemed to be an inevitability about success. After Wisconsin, there was nothing for McGovern and his staff to do but congratulate ourselves and keep on going.

3

THE CONTROVERSY
OVER $1,000

"His strength comes more from his program than from his personality."—*Life*, March 31, 1972.

From the beginning, McGovern was the issue-oriented candidate. His strategy for victory in the primaries depended on winning the support of millions of Americans who opposed U.S. involvement in Vietnam and who supported a wide variety of liberal causes ranging from women's rights to protection of wild rivers. He told these people that his candidacy was the best hope for the achievement of their goals and sought to enlist the effort they might have contributed to their own causes to his cause.

The Vietnam war was the main issue around which we could build support among the millions of progressive political activists. Demonstration after demonstration, march after march had indicated there was an army out there waiting for a leader. George McGovern intended to be that leader.

But McGovern and his staff believed that we would have to reach many of these activists by taking positions on many of the issues which most interested them. In part for this reason and in part because he wanted to demonstrate his complete commitment to change in most areas of American policy, McGovern sought to develop a comprehensive series of proposals on a broad range of subjects. Many of these proposals would be bold and imaginative in order to prove that McGovern's legislative creativity was not limited to the Vietnam war. By speaking out forthrightly on a wide variety of issues, McGovern could strike a clear contrast with Senator Edmund Muskie, the Democratic frontrunner, who cultivated caution as a way of broadening his support.

McGovern relied heavily on his staff and advisers for opinions on issues. Occasionally he would ask John Holum, his long-time legislative assistant, or me to have a proposal prepared on a specific topic. More often, the Senator would expect his staff to bring legislative or policy proposals to his attention. We understood the need to strengthen his credentials as a Presidential hopeful by getting him into a wider range of issues. And we, too, wanted to tap the support of the liberal constituency with its many pet causes.

McGovern was bored with the details of most issues. At the outset of the campaign, he was little schooled in such major policy areas as the military budget or the national economy. For the details, he relied absolutely on the advice of his aides. They were required to guarantee him that his proposals were technically sound and consistent with what he had said earlier. He would ask for a brief step-by-step explanation of the logic behind the proposal, and if he found it convincing, he would usually adopt the proposal. Often he would give the reasoning behind a proposal greater weight in his ultimate decision than the political gains or risks inherent in it. He would be more concerned about the substance of the proposal itself than about the groups that might favor or oppose it. Only when some of the details of a proposal came under close scrutiny by the press or by the parties directly affected would McGovern question Holum or me on the specifics. He expected us to have foreseen and dealt with such problems.

The Senator's basic conceptual tools were a progressive idealism and his practical South Dakota realism. If McGovern could couch an issue in terms of a "good" and a "bad" alternative, he had no problem in adopting and advocating his own position. To a great extent, his success in extending the food stamp program grew out of his ability to convince Senators that it was a "mother-hood issue"—one which was impossible to oppose. But as Robert Anson, his biographer, noted late in the campaign, McGovern's conceptual tools were often inadequate when he was forced to choose between two alternatives where the ultimate decision depended more on a political than a substantive evaluation.

Of all the major issues of national policy, George McGovern knew least about the economy. It was also the sector in which I was to play a major role. Prior to joining McGovern, I had written about economic policy for the layman and, once on his staff, I sought to act as an intermediary between McGovern and the circle of economic advisers that his candidacy would attract.

McGovern's instincts led him toward a traditionally liberal economic policy with considerable emphasis placed on the interests of the small farmers and small businessmen. Here the imprint of South Dakota was clear. His principal economic advisers before the campaign were Bob Eisner, an old friend at Northwestern who best understood McGovern's mind, and Ken Galbraith at Harvard. When I joined McGovern in 1970, I discovered that Ed Kuh at M.I.T. had been trying to lend a hand, but had found no staff member who was interested in economics.

In June 1971, Kuh and I organized a formal session where McGovern could meet with economists willing to work for him. We spent an entire afternoon and evening at a supporter's East Side townhouse in New York ranging over economic policy. That discussion would set the tone of McGovern's economic policy for the entire campaign. The economists who participated were Kuh, Jim Tobin and Robert Triffin of Yale, Les Thurow of M.I.T., Bill Branson of Princeton (who had been induced to leave the Muskie operation because he saw that McGovern would not only listen but speak out), and Eisner. Galbraith had written McGovern that he could not work in a group and preferred to channel his comments directly to the candidate.

Tobin convinced us that unemployment was a major concern and that our proposals should concentrate on that aspect of the economy, even more than on inflation. Although McGovern accepted this approach, he worried about inflation and raised the prospect of permanent controls, such as Galbraith had proposed to him many times. In fact, McGovern had almost announced the Galbraith proposals in his January 1971 statement and had only relented when I pointed out that no thorough consideration had been given them. In general, the group agreed with the notion of controls on major sectors rather than across the board, but only in time of need.

Thurow made the case for tax reform. In particular McGovern was agreeable to his suggestions on increasing taxes on inheritances. Thurow suggested that the traditional loophole-closing techniques had been proven ineffective for each time some loopholes were closed, others were opened. McGovern agreed that a minimum tax on high incomes would avoid this problem. That afternoon, we talked about what would be desirable from an economic and equity point of view, not what would be politically possible. Only when McGovern talked about farm policy did he make it clear to the economists that his practical experience would take priority over their economic formulations.

This discussion was to have an early pay-off. On August 13, McGovern delivered a major address to the Texas AFL–CIO where he laid out detailed proposals for creating more employment. The heart of his program was an immediate $10 billion increase in Federal spending for the express purpose of creating jobs—an idea suggested by Branson. This deficit spending could reduce unemployment by more than one point to about 4.5 percent in a year and return to the Treasury about half of the initial outlay in those 12 months. It was the first major alternative proposal to Administration inaction.

Then, on Sunday evening August 15, Gary Hart called me to ask if I were aware that the President would speak on the economy that evening. As a result of that call, I tuned in to the announcement of Phase I of Nixon's New Economic Policy. While he had at last acted to stem inflation through an ill-conceived wage-price freeze, the rest of his proposal was a hand-out to big business. He proposed a job development tax credit which was in reality a tax break to industry for already planned new investment. He cut the excise tax on automobiles, but did nothing to

give prospective purchasers more cash. In fact, in proposals supposedly designed to increase employment, he said he would cut
the Federal work force by 5 percent. He pulled a backdoor de-
valuation of the dollar by ending its convertibility to other cur-
rencies, and he imposed an illegal 10 percent tax on imports.

I immediately called McGovern who was vacationing in the
Virgin Islands. He had not heard the speech and I reviewed it
for him. I suggested that a strongly critical reply was called for.
He agreed, I believe, because he understood the implications of
the announcement as a result of our June discussion. He dictated
some tough language (calling the policy "economic madness,"
which later he thought was going a bit too far), and I phoned
the statement to the wire services.

To my surprise, the following morning I discovered that Mc-
Govern had been the only public figure to attack the proposal.
Most others were so relieved that Nixon had taken any action at
all that they were not prepared to criticize it. Only Senator Proxmire had indicated some of the same complaints, and I used
that bit of information to reassure the Senator when he called,
somewhat concerned, from the Virgin Islands. By the end of the
week, his instant criticism to the President's announcement had
made him a hero, particularly of organized labor. The AFL–CIO
leadership, the UAW, and others soon saw that there was little
for their members in Nixon's package.

Our initial success with a response in the economic policy area
encouraged McGovern. He asked me to invite a group of economic and financial journalists to lunch at the Capitol. This
meeting would enable him to comment further on Nixon's policies and to demonstrate his familiarity with economic issues. I
felt that he did well in the exchange and demonstrated that he
was no longer a one-issue candidate. But Richard Strout of the
New Republic, not usually on the economics beat, worried that
McGovern was abandoning the Vietnam war as an issue. Despite
the Senator's protest that people did not know his views on the
economy as well as his position on the war and that he did not
intend to abandon the war, an AP reporter wrote that McGovern
was dropping the war to concentrate on the economy.

In the ensuing days, the storm broke among McGovern's supporters. McGovern was forced to spend much of his time explaining that the economy and the war were linked.

But all of the furor about the allegation that he was dropping the war as an issue did not diminish McGovern's growing interest in economic policy. Ed Kuh, who was now the head of the formally constituted Economic Advisory Group, and I put together a package of proposals as an alternative for Nixon's Phase II. It included the $10 billion fiscal stimulus, inflation insurance bonds for those on fixed incomes, exemption of low wage occupations from wage controls, selective rather than general application of the controls to prices and wages, an excess profits tax for windfall profits, ending the new tax loopholes, and increasing farm income supports. These were solid suggestions many of which were later adopted by the administration. Unfortunately, McGovern never got excited about them, and he failed to claim credit for proposing them.

In discussions with the staff about new initiatives we would take, McGovern asked for proposals on tax reform. We set a target of early January for the announcement of his suggestions in this area. I laid before McGovern a variety of proposals ranging from loophole closing to the Thurow idea on a minimum tax to the closing of all tax loopholes and the consequent lowering of tax rates (the Pechman-Okner plan). The last idea appealed to McGovern the most, but, at a discussion in November 1971, I noted that it would be the most politically unpopular. Mankiewicz, who joined in the session with the Senator, agreed. McGovern then decided to go ahead with Thurow's proposals.

In the interest of saving time, I undertook to write the proposal using a draft prepared by Kuh and Thurow and remaining in constant telephone contact with them. The program that emerged called for a payment of taxes at least three-quarters of the statutory rate (the rate published on the tax returns) for all persons with incomes above $50,000 a year. In this way, we would not have to suggest closing a series of individual loopholes. Unfortunately, the proposal was a bit too complex for the press to grasp and they were often to write of it as though we wanted to take three-quarters of all a person received above $50,000.

A second aspect of the program called for returning corporate taxes to their 1960 effective rates. This meant closing loopholes, although Thurow had not been specific. Thurow had provided us with an estimate of the change in effective rates of corporate taxation from which we could derive an approximation of the new tax revenues to be raised. But the lack of specifics about the loopholes would later cause us trouble because Eileen Shanahan of *The New York Times* believed we could not raise the revenues we claimed unless we also went back to the 1960 formal tax rate of 52 percent instead of the current 48 percent. In fact, Thurow must have meant to include this measure, but because he hadn't and the calculations were murky, I denied Shanahan's inference.

Finally, we suggested that instead of taxes on estates of the deceased and on gifts, taxes should be levied on the recipients of such bequests just as on ordinary income. This tax should increase as the amount received increased over the lifetime of the recipient. We suggested that the tax might reach 100 percent—complete confiscation—when the receipts passed $500,000. McGovern was completely comfortable with this admittedly radical proposal, because we all shared the belief that most people had a strong bias against great concentrations of inherited wealth. The proposals would directly affect only a handful of people.

While work on these proposals was being completed, I also suggested that we should consider welfare reform or the principle of income redistribution. Leonard Greene, a New York businessman, had long been urging us to adopt his "Fair Share" proposal which provided a "demogrant" to every person. Under the demogrant idea, each person would receive a given sum of money from the government. For middle income people, part of the demogrant would be taxed back. For upper income people, the entire demogrant would be returned in taxes and the program itself would be financed by higher taxes on the wealthy. There would be no new Treasury expenditure; the money would be actually redistributed by the government from incomes (not the assets) of the wealthy to the poor and to low-income workers. The demogrant actually would act as a strong work incentive to the poor to seek jobs because they would not lose their full payment when they began to earn income.

I had been somewhat skeptical of the proposal at first but

found that it had a respectable history in economic thought. In fact, I discovered that Jim Tobin had written favorably of the idea and had outlined one way it might work in an article he published in 1968. I asked Kuh to have the Economic Advisory Group look at the idea. He reported back that those with whom he had talked, including Tobin, found the proposal attractive.

Intrigued by the principle and armed with this expression of support, I was willing to proceed further. In addition, our finance people kept up the pressure for the Senator to say something favorable about the Greene proposal, if our economists thought it sound, in hopes of a six-figure contribution from him. It was to be a vain hope, but regrettably it would help lead us into treacherous waters.

McGovern approved the proposals which I prepared for presentation at the University of Iowa in January. Then, in a year-end interview with the *Washington Post* on December 22, 1971, McGovern launched the income redistribution idea. The next day the *Post* wrote about McGovern's proposal for an annual Federal payment which "might involve a $4,000 grant to every family in the United States." McGovern himself was quoted as saying: "It's the only way I can figure to permit people to derive a minimum income, welfare assistance or whatever you want to call it without losing it when they go to work." The newspaper report concluded saying that McGovern would list alternative methods of operation for the program later.

In addition to the article in the *Post,* one or two other papers then carried articles on the proposal which they treated as highly innovative.

The fact that McGovern himself was the first person to discuss the income redistribution publicly and in some detail refutes some later charges that I had somehow slipped the proposal by him. I believe he was genuinely intrigued with the concept especially after the initially favorable press coverage. In due course, the tax and income redistribution proposals were issued in Iowa, but there was little more attention paid them in the press.

The tax reform proposals were effective, we discovered, and printed up a leaflet summarizing them. Widely circulated in New Hampshire, the leaflet had a positive but curious response.

I remember sitting one day in the Lafayette Club in Nashua with a group of workmen who opposed the idea of a confiscatory inheritance tax. Although none of them stood to be penalized by it, they argued that it was unfair to take away all that a man had received. McGovern was receiving similar reactions in the plants we visited and believed that all men nourished the hope of receiving a large inheritance or of winning a lottery. Because of this kind of response from average-income people, we altered the proposal to suggest a maximum rate of 77 percent. In addition, we tried to meet the concern of small businessmen who felt they could not leave a business intact to their children. We suggested a higher ceiling when inheritances included family-owned businesses.

As late as the beginning of April, when we published revised proposals, only the inheritance tax was changed. Public interest had not yet focused on the package mainly because McGovern was still given little chance at the nomination. The Senator stressed tax reform as a means of financing his new government programs, but he remained uncomfortable with the income redistribution concept as he had been since January. Despite my urging to stick to the statement of principle, he maintained it was easier to get the idea across by giving a concrete example. He chose to explain one of the proposed plans that would pay each person $1,000.

In drafting the original statement, I had been careful not to bind McGovern to anything other than the principle of the demogrant:

> There are a number of methods by which this proposal could be implemented. Some are discussed here. These methods require full examination by the best economic talent available, and the plan chosen must have the support of the President, if it is to have any chance of adoption. For those reasons, the present proposal is not designed for immediate legislative action. Instead it represents a pledge that, if elected, I would prepare a detailed plan and submit it to the Congress.

I argued throughout the spring that, if McGovern kept to this formulation, we need not get into specific proposals. But I had provided examples in the original proposal including suggested methods of financing them. This was the origin of most of our problems, because McGovern spoke more of these specifics, which were highly tentative, than of the basic idea. As a result, I became engaged in a process of finding the least onerous method of financing a relatively high cost proposal. Later in the summer, after Tobin and others had spent months working out detailed estimates I became aware of just how accurate McGovern had been when he had said that he could not give a cost estimate easily. The complexities of the proposal, as for any welfare reform plan, were overwhelming. We had simply been unprepared for McGovern's desire to talk about a specific plan rather than the principle of income redistribution.

Other aspects of the tax reform package began to cause us problems during the spring. Because the minimum tax on persons with incomes above $50,000 would reduce the benefits they might derive from the broad range of tax preferences, potential contributors and much of the Wall Street community were led to believe that McGovern proposed a complete closing of many of the most popular preferences such as the special capital gains treatment, exemption of interest on state and local bonds, and deductions for mortgage interest and property taxes. While the wealthy might not get the full benefit of all of these deductions, because their capital allowed them to get the benefit of so many more preferences than the average taxpayer, none of these loopholes would actually be closed. The average taxpayer would be unaffected.

Henry Kimelman, a close friend of McGovern's and our national finance chairman, wanted to clear the air of these misconceptions in hopes of reassuring potential contributors and the business community as a whole. He had a letter drafted to a New York broker who supported McGovern with a view to publishing the full text in the *Wall Street Journal.* I only learned of this plan after McGovern had cleared the text. I was concerned that we would seem to be backing down. But when Kimelman brought me the text the Senator had approved, I admitted that it was absolutely accurate. The text, with only minor changes to stress the need for congressional approval of such tax reform proposals, was then published.

Although the ad did not change our proposals in the slightest, the mere attempt to placate the wealthy had the effect of making it seem that McGovern was retreating or, just as bad, trying to have it both ways—tough tax reform which was too onerous for the wealthy. But, on one major point on which potential contributors had expressed concern—the inheritance tax proposals—McGovern did not yet yield. In fact, he would later say that he had no regret about the stringency of his proposal.

While McGovern had been increasingly questioned about his income redistribution and tax proposals as the spring wore on, the most serious attack against them came in California—almost at the end of the primary trail. On May 28, in the first televised debate between McGovern and Senator Hubert Humphrey, the Minnesotan lashed out at these proposals:

> When it comes to certain other aspects, such as in welfare legislation he calls a horrible mess, let me say that a $72 billion welfare proposal that Senator McGovern makes today is not only a horrible mess, it would be an unbelievable burden upon the taxpayer. And when you come to a tax program, that on the other hand the Senator says to the public—look, we've got to get the money from the rich—and on the other hand he'll run an ad in the Wall Street Journal that says, well, don't believe it, don't believe it. Here's a letter in the Wall Street Journal, right here, a letter to a brokerage firm, that says, now, don't worry, I'm not proposing, I have not suggested the elimination of tax exemption for bonds, I have not suggested the elimination of capital gains limitations. Now you can't have it both ways.

This attack came early in the program in answer to a question relating to Vietnam. Instead of replying to the charges, McGovern responded to the questions asked him about Vietnam. Thus, these charges remained on the table until after the midpoint break in the program.

After the station break, George Herman, the moderator, began by asking Humphrey where he got his $72 billion estimate for the cost of the McGovern welfare proposal. Humphrey cited a Senate Finance Committee study which evaluated the cost of a $6,500 minimum income plan proposed by the National Welfare Rights Organization. McGovern did not himself advocate this plan and indicated as much when he introduced the bill as a favor to NWRO. Humphrey knew all this, but it had not prevented him from earlier referring to it as "a $72 billion welfare proposal that Senator McGovern makes today."

Even if McGovern succeeded in neutralizing the Humphrey charge, CBS's David Schoumacher hit him for not having a price tag on his own proposal:

> But you're asking us to accept a program that you can't tell us how much it's going to cost?
>
> (Sen. McGovern replied) That's exactly right. There is no way to estimate the cost of this program. . . .

This admission was the crowning blow to our effort to get people thinking about new approaches to welfare and income supplements for the working poor. The fact remained, as it had since McGovern first proposed income redistribution in January, that there was no specific program and, as a result, we could not estimate its cost.

Earlier that week we had become aware that the question of the cost of a $1,000 demogrant would be raised on the first debate, and I suggested that we ask Ben Okner, a Washington economist who is an expert in calculating how such plans might work, to come to California to brief the press on the day before the program. Other members of the staff and McGovern himself agreed. As it turns out, I had made a bad mistake.

Okner was coming to California anyway, and I arranged to pick him up at San Francisco airport on Friday evening, May 26, and take him over to the McGovern plane in Oakland from where we would fly to Los Angeles. In that way, he would have a chance to talk with McGovern, and he and I could prepare the briefing for the following day. For some unexplained reason, Okner went directly to Los Angeles. When I learned this I raced to Oakland, only to learn that McGovern had given up waiting for us and had left seven minutes earlier. After another trip to San Francisco, a midnight flight to Los Angeles, and the trip into the hotel, I got to bed after 2:00 A.M. without having a chance to talk with Okner. We arranged to meet at 6:30 A.M. During a brief meeting over breakfast, I became aware that Okner did not have the kind of simple and hard information the newsmen, few of whom had any economics background, could digest. Okner did not have the answer to the key question: How much might a $1,000 plan cost?

We went ahead with the briefing which dragged on painfully for most of that Saturday morning. Precise estimates seemed to appear and then disappear in rapid succession as Okner struggled to give the press the answers they demanded. I tried to salvage what little I could. At the end of the session, we had proved our prior assertion beyond doubt—we did not know how much the plan would cost.

On Sunday morning, May 28, when the staff crowded into McGovern's hotel suite to discuss the proposal we easily convinced him that the best course to follow was to resist talking about any specific plan and to stress the need to replace the "current mess" with an entirely new and automatic system. The debate offered him the opportunity to say, if he felt it necessary, that he had never proposed a specific program and had been in error to use the $1,000 example as much as he did. But he felt that he had committed himself to the $1,000 and that he must persevere.

On the broadcast, Humphrey wanted to debate him on the income redistribtuion idea. Obviously he had asked some experts to study the implications of the suggestion. First, he claimed that McGovern really backed the NWRO proposal. Then, he managed to keep McGovern on the defensive as to how much the $1,000 plan would cost an individual taxpayer. He delivered a telling blow:

A secretary working in San Francisco, making $8,000—a single person—there are thousands, millions of single people in this country—would have an increase in his or her taxes, under Senator McGovern's welfare proposal of $567.

That simply is not true (said McGovern).

Well, it is true, (Humphrey replied) and a family that has $12,000 a year, a family of four, would have a $409 increase.

And that's not true (said McGovern).

Now the—the senator can say it's not true—he doesn't even know what the price tag to his bill is (added Humphrey).

(Then Schoumacher moved in.) Well, what figures—where did you get the figures? If he doesn't know what his program costs, how do you know what his program costs?

(Humphrey delivered the clincher.) May I say I know what the tax rate is, what his proposed tax rate is, because he has a surcharge tax rate. All I'm saying is if you take a thousand dollars per person, and there are 210 million people in this country, it's a $210 billion Treasury transaction.

Humphrey's individual cost estimates could have been right using an arbitrary surcharge of his own choosing. By our failure to determine such a tax rate, the field was open to him. But even more important, he went out of his way to leave the erroneous impression that the proposal would cost hundreds of billions of dollars. He protected himself by calling the entire operation a Treasury transaction because much of the transfer of funds would only take place on paper.

The newsmen began to press Humphrey on his own welfare proposals which were far less bold—expanding social security and the federal takeover of welfare funding.

I don't see anything in there that will essentially change the nature of the welfare system (said Schoumacher).

Yes, first of all you'll have work requirements (replied Humphrey). Senator McGovern's program is a share the wealth program but not share the work. There are no work requirements in his program at all . . . I just don't think it makes very much sense. I don't think the Congress would pass it; I don't think the American people will buy it.

Senator, you are champing at the bit to answer, (said Herman to McGovern), and we're champing at the bit to change the subject.

I just wanted to say the senator is making the same case against the bill that I made when I introduced it . . . (said

McGovern). Now the Senator talks about the present program being in a mess; I don't see anything in the proposals he has suggested here that's going to straighten it out. What I want to make clear is that even if we were to take the suggestion I've made of a minimum income supplement of a thousand dollars a person, that would mean for a family of four an income of $4,000. Now we've provided that you don't lose that when you go to work. There's no penalty for working. Under the present welfare system, if you get above a certain level, you are knocked off welfare and it's a discouragement to people to go to work. The program I have suggested here today and that I suggested repeatedly across the country would give the major benefit to working people.

McGovern had begun making the case for his idea, but it came after Humphrey had made his wild charges. Had McGovern at the outset said, "Hold off a minute. I've got a new idea and a good one and instead of throwing mud on it, we ought to look at it carefully" and then explained it, he might have been able to turn the proposal into more of an asset. We had no way of knowing what the public reaction would be to the income maintenance concept, because we had not used our opportunities to make the case for it. Instead, throughout the campaign we had been on the defensive—mostly because it was a new idea—and Humphrey had now succeeded in putting McGovern into the position of a desperate defender of his own proposal.

Early in the second debate on May 30, Robert Novak, a syndicated columnist hostile to McGovern, claimed that a congressional staff study showed that the McGovern income redistribution proposal would raise taxes just as Humphrey had charged during the first debate.

When McGovern countered that this must be the NWRO proposal, Novak told him it was the $1,000 proposal. McGovern's answer was, once again, that we could not estimate the cost. Perhaps this was an opportunity to explain the concept and explain why cost estimates were impossible.

My immediate reaction to Novak's question was to find out what study Novak was using. I looked frantically for Okner and eventually found him sitting calmly in the audience. He got on the phone to Washington and determined that one member of the Senate Finance Committee staff, probably working with the Humphrey campaign, had developed the cost figures and had made them available to people like Novak who were antagonistic to us. The figures were based on the worst possible assumptions about how the McGovern proposal would work. The basic calculations lacked the sophistication that would be required to derive realistic cost estimates.

The early discussion also focused on a statement by Humphrey on Monday that "When you start to have confiscatory taxation even against some of the big ones, you are not going to provide any jobs. That doesn't make you a liberal, that makes you a fool." Humphrey immediately apologized for inferring that McGovern was a fool and then proceeded to build the case that McGovern would have to overtax corporations or else raise taxes on average citizens in order to pay for his welfare and other proposals. Humphrey was clearly playing to his wealthy backers, many of whom were economic conservatives.

Then Humphrey moved in again on taxes after McGovern had given a strong and forthright defense of his inheritance tax proposals. In the face of that statement, Humphrey focused on other taxes. He claimed that McGovern would do away with the individual exemption, would not allow deductions of mortgage interest from taxes, and would not allow medical deductions. These were lies. During the break in the program, I hurried onto the set to remind McGovern that he had made no such proposals. Much later in the second half of the program, McGovern made a passing reference to the Humphrey charges and denied them. We would later find that these untruths, especially the one relating to mortgage interest, hurt us badly in suburbia.

Humphrey's repeated and savage attacks on McGovern's income redistribution and tax reform proposals made it inevitable that we would have to rework them. Where McGovern had only committed himself initially to the principle of income redistribution, he now had to come up with a specific welfare reform program. We had hoped to make the new proposals before the Democratic Convention in July, but the new proposals required such thorough study that we were not ready until late August. Mc-

Govern put me in charge of the tax-and-welfare salvage operation.

Adrian DeWind, a leading New York lawyer, undertook the task of reworking the tax proposals. He assembled a prestigious group of tax experts and organized weekly sessions to discuss progress toward a new tax package. No more expert a group, with practical knowledge of the realities of tax law and of politics, could have been assembled. At the same time, Dean Alvin Schorr of New York University put together a working group on welfare reform.

By July, McGovern had become vitally interested in the issues of tax and welfare reform and digested all of the working papers as they were sent to him. Frequently we would have lengthy discussion on the progress of the work and, for the first time, I felt that the candidate was enthusiastically involved in economic policy-making.

The proposals made by De Wind's group provided for the gradual closing of all major tax loopholes which determine what shall be considered taxable income. The theme of their proposals was a sentence Joe Duffey, the Yale professor and former Connecticut Senate candidate, had given me: "Money made by money should be taxed at the same rate as money made by men." In this vein, they suggested that capital gains should no longer be taxed at half the rate of wages and salaries, but should pay the full fare. In addition, such gains realized at the time of death are tax-free, so the experts suggested they be brought under the tax code. Other proposals were aimed at ending overly generous depreciation allowances given business. Like the oil depletion allowance, special breaks for real estate investors, and foreign profits of U.S. corporations. The total reform promised $22 billion in new revenues by 1975. And its effect was limited to the wealthy and to corporations because it covered only revenues not currently counted in taxable income and did not relate to the wide range of deductions presently allowed from taxable income.

Henry Kimelman was worried by these proposals, and because of his wealth and close friendship with the candidate, he seemed to think he had special authority in the campaign. He scorned the staff that McGovern had assembled on the grounds that, lacking in business experience, they could not run a political campaign. He claimed to speak on behalf of the wealthy contributors—"the fat cats"—and always argued for the most conservative policy option in the belief that such was their wish. He obviously believed that major contributors had a right to ask for special consideration in policy proposals, an idea somewhat antithetical to the McGovern philosophy. I had earlier shown a draft of the first speech incorporating the experts' proposals to a score of major campaign contributors. Kimelman was furious that I had not made my contacts through him. I found that they raised surprisingly few objections to the proposals and made some useful suggestions. Kimelman was undermined because he had warned us that their opposition to the proposal would cause campaign contributions, just recently flowing after the Eagleton affair, to dry up. He was particularly livid over the use of the word "loophole" to explain the special preferences in law for the benefit of the wealthy and the large corporations.

In contrast to Kimelman's representation of them, I found that the major contributors were exceptional. They were perhaps the most idealistic people involved in the campaign. Unlike many Republican contributors, they were not looking for appointments or preferential treatment. Instead they were deeply interested in ending the Vietnam adventure and were concerned about developing a new-priorities budget for the Federal government. They understood that McGovern meant what he said about tax reform. They were willing to accept his proposals either because they were confident that they would be administered fairly or, it must be admitted, because they gave them little chance of passage by Congress.

McGovern met in August with representatives of DeWind's group, including Joe Pechman, the renowned expert on Federal tax policy and Stanley Surrey, the former Assistant Treasury Secretary, and argued through each of the proposals. The debate focused on full taxation of capital gains, i.e., taxation at the same rate as ordinary income. If McGovern meant what he said about a tough tax reform, he would have to accept this proposal which could bring in as much as $12 billion in new revenues by 1975. Despite advice from some friends in Congress to softpedal this proposal, McGovern decided he would stick with his experts.

The McGovern tax reform proposals, made in an address to the New York Society of Securities Analysts in late August, became one of the high points of his campaign. The candidate was at home with his program, which received more coverage in the national media than any single proposal he had ever made. Whatever the outcome of the campaign, I took great satisfaction from the verdict of the press. *Time* wrote: "Even if he goes down to the crushing defeat now so widely predicted, he has crystallized questions about the equity of the tax system and the nation's spending priorities that will not fade away."

Revamping the welfare reform proposals was more difficult. Jim Tobin worked out the demogrant proposal in detail, but it conflicted with McGovern's wish not to have to raise the taxes of average-income people. We had to search for other alternatives. We carefully considered the idea of a tax credit which would lower the taxes of many working men and women. For the poor, who paid little or no taxes, the credit could be converted into cash. Heather Ross, an economist at the Urban Institute and a member of the Economic Advisory Group, suggested a negative income tax. All of these proposals, which maintained the concept inherent in the demogrant of an income supplement for low-income people which would also serve as an incentive for the poor to seek work, involved increasing taxes on the wealthy.

In contrast to these proposals, Alvin Schorr suggested what he called less costly interim measures—the expansion and improvement of social security, the extension of unemployment compensation, and a modest tax credit plan. The last element merely raised the same problems as the broader redistribution proposals and was put aside. Except for Wilbur Cohen, the former HEW Secretary who had joined our discussions, most of DeWind's group favored the negative income tax. DeWind felt it was important to maintain a semblance of the original concept.

Throughout these negotiations, I tried to maintain my neutrality while safeguarding McGovern's political interests. I am sure that advocates of each position felt I opposed them. When some of the group met with the Senator around the pool at Ethel

Kennedy's home in early August, I felt that he would adopt the negative income tax approach. After further consideration, however, he adopted the Schorr suggestion of extending social security to include the aged, blind, and disabled on welfare. In addition, thanks to the initiative of Nancy Amidei, a welfare specialist on his Nutrition Committee staff, he opted for a major public service jobs program which could take as many as one millon people (3.3 million including their families) off of welfare. Finally, he wanted to raise the annual minimum welfare payment at $4,000 in cash and food stamps, thus preserving a vestige of his $1,000 proposal.

In late August, Bob Shrum, who was assigned to write the tax and welfare speech, and I labored day and night on it, literally working around the clock. Shrum came up with an imaginative way to present the welfare package; he called it National Income Insurance, since the term welfare was held in such low repute and income redistribution no longer was applicable.

McGovern followed the course of successive drafts closely, and the proposals were not completed until August 28, the day before he was to deliver the speech. I arranged a lunch in the Senate Dining Room for McGovern with Art Okun, a former member of the President's Council of Economic Advisors, Joe Pechman, and Charles Schultze, former head of the Bureau of the Budget. They urged McGovern to add a pledge that his program would include income supplements. Playing devil's advocate, I said that such a proposal would open him to many of the problems we had had with the $1,000. But, to my pleasure, he was convinced by his three advisers. Then, that afternoon, Schorr called me to say he would have to withdraw from the enterprise if the offending concept were added. He called McGovern and got the impression that the Senator had agreed to omit the income supplements statement. McGovern told me that he would stick with the position adopted at noon. When Schorr remained insistent, I called McGovern again, reaching him this time in the Senate gym. I was uncertain of the exact content of his discussion with Schorr, but said that if the professor was misrepresenting McGovern's views, we should certainly reject his demands. The Senator then decided that he would go along with the arguments I had raised at lunch and avoid anything other than a commitment to study tax credits and tax reductions to assist low and moderate income persons. Although I was relieved that a final decision had been reached, I was disappointed at the disappearance of the last vestige of innovative thinking about welfare reform in the 1972 campaign. Thus, the $1,000 was interred.

Despite the tremendous problems caused by the income redistribution proposal and, to a lesser extent, the tax reform proposal, McGovern could take some satisfaction from his efforts.

For the first time in a presidential campaign, a candidate put forth a comprehensive tax reform proposal. In the past, candidates have been reluctant to move in this direction because they feared the loss of contributions from their major backers. But McGovern was convinced that he would draw sufficient financial support from small contributors to enjoy the freedom to advance these bold suggestions. As early as the first session of Congress after the election, there was a new wave of interest in the kinds of reforms he had proposed. As ways are found to increase the number of small contributors to political campaigns, the chances for the kind of tax equity that McGovern proposed will improve.

Despite his ultimate decision to move away from income redistribution, he had, for the first time, opened serious political consideration of the only workable alternative to the present welfare system. Unless the electorate continues to accept this cumbersome, costly, and often unworkable welfare operation indefinitely, McGovern will find that he has once again set the terms of the national debate. I would not be surprised if one day the President of the United States journeyed to McGovern's home for the ceremonial signing of the Income Redistribution Act of 1991 in the presence of the man who first made it possible to talk about the concept in the political arena.

A billboard we used during the New Hampshire primary best expressed what his proposals would mean: "McGovern . . . if you *really* want a change." The impulse for change was the greatest legacy of the program he proposed.

4

THE GREAT DEBATE

"This last month for McGovern has been the
most spectacular for any political figure in
American history."—Massachusetts Congressman Thomas O'Neill, April 1972.
"The honeymoon with George McGovern is
going to be over within a couple of weeks."—
Democratic National Committee official, May
1972.

On May 28, 1972, a sunny Sunday in Los Angeles, George Mc-
Govern walked into the CBS television studios there for the first
of his debates with Senator Hubert Humphrey, his chief competitor for the Democratic presidential nomination. He and several members of his staff who went to the studio that day enjoyed a feeling of optimism and anticipation. McGovern was a
winner and today he would provide the final proof.

Following his primary victory in Wisconsin, McGovern had
gone on to a stunning triumph in Massachusetts. On April 25,
he had won 52 percent of the vote, and all of the state's 102 member delegation would be bound to support him on the first ballot
at the Democratic Convention. That same day, finishing third,
close behind Governor Wallace, McGovern had captured 37 delegates in Pennsylvania. McGovern now had more delegates than
any other contender. And Muskie was all but eliminated.

The change in McGovern's fortunes was most obvious in the

nation's press. Editors had previously skimped on coverage of McGovern because he stood so low in the public opinion polls. Gallup and the other pollsters said that McGovern did not do well in their surveys and was, in fact, excluded from some of them because his recognition was so low. They attributed this to his relative lack of coverage in the media, especially television. It was a vicious circle.

A year earlier I had lobbied the press about this problem and finally *The New Republic* published its lead editorial on May 8, 1971, "Later George, Not Now":

> Senator George McGovern, like Vice President Agnew, is unhappy these days with the news media, but whereas Agnew doesn't like what he reads and sees, what bothers McGovern is what he doesn't see in the newspapers and on television. McGovern is the first announced candidate for the Democratic presidential nomination in 1972. He's a member of a major party. He's a two-term senator. Because he is a well-known officeholder seeking the nomination of his party for the highest political office, it would seem proper that he be included in the polls and sundry published lists of potential candidates. But often he is not. . . .
>
> Granted that anybody can *say* he's a candidate, and that the saying of it doesn't make his candidacy credible or confer upon him an equal claim to attention; news judgments *do* affect news coverage. Yet McGovern can't be dismissed as if he weren't there. He's the only serious, confessed candidate there is! . . .
>
> The polls also have been playing the nonrecognition game. . . . The reason McGovern was omitted [from test heats with Nixon] despite his being the only professed candidate, George Gallup, Jr., says, is that "it would be unrealistic at this point" to include him, because less than half the electorate has even a vague idea who he is. . . .
>
> Such polls help *make* facts, by publicizing and thus enhancing the prospects of some politicians and diminishing others. . . .
>
> An article in the *Times* and one Gallup poll hardly constitute a conspiracy, and there isn't one against McGovern. Fairness is another matter. As California's new Democratic Senator John Tunney noted before a meeting of newspaper editors in New York a few days ago, non-candidate Muskie has been getting far more publicity than candidate McGovern. Members of Mc-

Govern's staff, disturbed by what they consider the sparse coverage of their campaign, have confronted newspaper editors and have been told in so many words that they don't think McGovern's chances of getting the nomination are good, and that the news coverage is influenced by what they, the editors, gauge the candidate's chances to be. The prophecy becomes self-fulfilling. Scant newspaper coverage does nothing to ameliorate a candidate's "familiarity" problem. Unless the cycle is broken somewhere, the editors and pollsters exercise an influence over the outcome they ought not to have. "On a number of positions," says one McGovern partisan, "McGovern has been first and Muskie has been about a week later. And the Muskie statement has gotten the coverage."

The *New Republic* then documented six important stories, which I had cited to them, where *The New York Times* had given McGovern no coverage at all. Then it noted that, if we attempted to purchase television time, we were turned down on the grounds that it was "too early" for political broadcasts. "Who is it who determines when a campaign opens?" the magazine asked. "Is it the candidate, the networks, Gallup, *The New York Times?*"

The national columnists, when they deigned to mention McGovern, were rough on him. In May 1971, Joseph Alsop wrote: "Take that amiable and virtuous shallow-pate, Senator George McGovern of South Dakota. He wants to cut the defense budget by one half or more." Evans and Novak, who made no bones about their opposition to McGovern, tried to harpoon the campaign every time they wrote about it.

The combination of sagging polls, brush-offs by editors, and the disdain of the national columnists discouraged but did not deter us. During the period I had served as press secretary, I had begun to establish a network of contacts with key local newsmen in the primary states. From my own experience with the Washington press corps, I realized that the national media would pay little attention to McGovern. But I soon learned that the local media was better respected than the national press and would have a far greater impact of the electorate.

In New Hampshire, for example, few people read *The New*

York Times and almost nobody reads the *Washington Post.* The leading paper is the *Manchester Union Leader,* not generally rated high among the nation's quality newspapers. Famous for William Loeb's blistering front-page editorials, its position, as the old saw has it, is somewhere to the right of Genghis Khan. On McGovern's first trip into the state after his announcement, Loeb wrote: "We consider Senator McGovern to be personally responsible for the deaths of American boys [in Vietnam]." Despite such attacks, we always kept our good humor in dealing with the *Union Leader* and our lines of communication were open. In part because we did not spurn Loeb and attack the newspaper, we got reasonably fair coverage in their news columns as compared with Muskie who often sounded like he was running against Loeb instead of McGovern.

On the local scene, reporters had a better grasp of political reality than the occasional visitor from the outside. It was not simply a matter of reporters taking our word for our claims about organizational strength. Instead, sharp reporters on the scene could dig into what was taking place and compare it with earlier campaigns. As a result, Jim McCulla of the *Milwaukee Journal* was the first to perceive that McGovern's growing organization in Wisconsin could give him a primary victory there. To his credit, Ken Roeslein of the *Milwaukee Sentinel* did not refrain from coming to a similar conclusion even after his competitor had the jump on him. Both were far ahead of the national press. By the same token, in New Hampshire, Bill Kovach of *The New York Times* Boston bureau properly evaluated our strength long before the Washington pundits. Although he knew New England less well than the *Boston Globe* writers, he had a good deal of political reporting experience and was free of the *Globe's* feelings of local loyalty to Muskie.

In short, the lack of full and fair attention from the national media turned out to be an advantage. It encouraged us to pay more attention to the local press. And it made our early successes seem that much more significant. As *Newsweek* wrote in May: "[McGovern] himself complained that he was unfairly ignored by the press until last month, but his past failure to make a splash now lends his candidacy an unusual freshness in view of the fact that he has been in the field for almost sixteen months; McGovern is both the tortoise and the hare of this election year."

When the press discovered McGovern was a serious contender, our campaign could do no wrong. Many of us who had labored anonymously for so many months found our pictures in the national press. The era of good feelings was to last until the Democratic Convention in July. With the exception of such persistent critics as Evans and Novak, our initial successes would blind many newsmen to our shortcomings until they had become all too apparent. And all the press adulation finally gave us a bad case of "victory fever"—the feeling that you can't make any mistakes.

In early April, soon after the Wisconsin victory and feeling the momentum engendered by the press, the campaign leadership decided to enter the Ohio primary which came just a week after Massachusetts. It would be a head-to-head test with Humphrey and would give McGovern a chance to measure the extent of his support among working men and women. Pat Caddell, our pollster, told us that Humphrey's support was "soft." Then, McGovern's impressive showing with workers in Massachusetts further encouraged us.

Humphrey had spent some time in Ohio as he shuttled between Pennsylvania and Indiana, whose primary also fell on May 2. McGovern, who had wisely opted out of Indiana to conserve resources and avoid what would be at best a very difficult race, would arrive in Ohio the day after the Massachusetts contest. On primary night itself, we had gone to Boston's Logan Airport to see off about 85 campaign workers who were shipped directly from their precincts in Massachusetts to reassignments in Ohio.

In the Buckeye state, Humphrey had pretty well locked up the leadership of organized labor. Frank King, the state chief of the AFL–CIO, was nominally neutral, but passed the word on behalf of the Minnesotan. Jack Gilligan, the governor, was on the sidelines because he had backed Muskie, who was no longer contesting primaries. Now he had to sit back and watch McGovern and Humphrey battle for the Muskie votes.

Scoop Jackson was also a problem: Ohio represented his last ditch effort in a campaign that would not produce for him a single delegate outside of his home state. But he fought a dirty campaign aimed entirely at McGovern. He distorted the South Dakotan's position on amnesty, military spending, and marijuana. He even charged wildly that McGovern wanted to legalize homosexual practices. He added the old canard that McGovern had supported Henry Wallace in 1948, which McGovern had never denied. Such a campaign could hurt McGovern, but it would not benefit Jackson. The chief beneficiary would be Humphrey. At the time I tended to dismiss the possibility that Humphrey would back such tactics, but his later attacks led me to believe that there could have been collusion, at least among the supporters of the two candidates. (The same explanation might well apply to Senator Vance Hartke's fringe candidacy in New Hampshire. Hartke later endorsed Humphrey, which Jackson, with ambitions of his own for 1976, did not.)

Our greatest error, probably costing us the primary, was a press conference on Saturday afternoon, April 29, with Congressman John Conyers of Detroit. Conyers and other black leaders announced their support in Cleveland for the McGovern candidacy. Louis Stokes, Cleveland's black Congressman, had opposed the press conference, because he did not want another black leader getting national publicity from his turf. But Conyers had insisted on it. We were put in the position of alienating Conyers and the others or of offending Stokes, who was uncommitted, but leaning toward Humphrey. We went for Conyers because his endorsement was expected to mean solid support. (Unfortunately, we later learned that Conyers was also supporting Chisholm.) The only positive result of the press conference was to ridicule the Jackson slanders. When asked about them, McGovern said: "Why doesn't he talk about what I did when I was ten years old? I confess to having stolen a—a watermelon." The blacks were completely broken up by this rare and pointed display of McGovern wit.

But Stokes was angry. He refused to meet with McGovern or take his calls. And on primary day, he delivered his 21st congressional district to Humphrey. Our Ohio staff believed that he would have remained neutral if the press conference had not taken place.

Coupled with voting irregularities, due to the incredible incompetence of the Cuyahoga County Board of Elections, the Stokes votes were enough to defeat McGovern in Ohio. Although Dick Sklar, our able Ohio coordinator, was able to get a court order requiring the Election Board to keep open and in some cases to provide for new voting the following week, it was clear that Stokes had denied us a chance for the at-large delegates which went to the candidate with the greatest plurality. Humphrey finished with 41.5 percent to McGovern's 39.3 percent. Muskie, who had not compaigned, came in ahead of Jackson.

Actually, the Ohio primary was a victory for McGovern. We had just about evenly split the vote with Humphrey in a state that was acknowledged to have a representative Democratic electorate. Many Democratic voters are working men and women —the so-called backbone of the Party—and McGovern had demonstrated convincingly that he could capture their vote as well as the more traditional candidate could.

Just one week later, May 9, we faced the Nebraska primary. Here was one race where Humphrey could trip us up badly. We had let Nebraska slide because of our concentration on Wisconsin. When our workers returned there after the Wisconsin primary on April 4, they discovered a full-fledged Humphrey operation. The Minnesotan had originally said that he planned to stay out of Nebraska, but now he thought he might embarrass McGovern in his own home area.

When Humphrey arrived in Nebraska, his campaign took on a new tone. Borrowing from the kind of attacks Jackson had made, the Minnesotan bore in on amnesty and abortion. Most of the Democratic vote in Omaha was Catholic and Humphrey thought he could score well on the charge that McGovern favored "abortion on demand." His forces placed a large ad in the local Catholic newspaper leaving us no time to respond.

McGovern counterattacked. Charles Guggenheim and his crew flew into Omaha and on the Saturday morning before the primary we taped a discussion between McGovern and a handful

May 12, 1970. National telecast on behalf of McGovern-Hatfield Amendment. L.-r.: Sen. Frank Church (D.-Idaho), Sen. Charles Goodell (R.-N.Y.), McGovern, Sen. Mark O. Hatfield (R.-Ore.), and Sen. Harold Hughes (D.-Iowa).

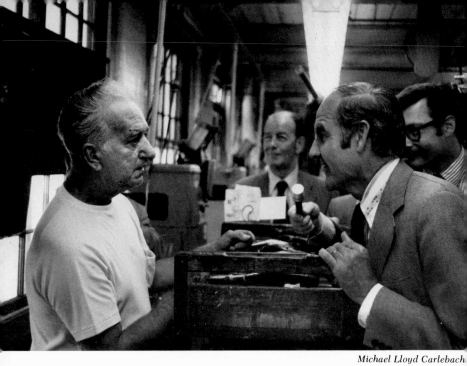

At J. F. McElwain shoe factory, Manchester, N.H. In center is Sen. Thomas McIntyre (D.–N.H.).

Joe Grandmaison kidding with the candidate.

Michael Lloyd Carlebach

McGovern writes his concession statement in Miami on March 14 after losing Florida primary.

Warren Beatty and his sister Shirley MacLaine (with campaign worker). They were hard-working campaigners.

Michael Lloyd Carlebach

Frank Mankiewicz (l.) and Pierre Salinger in "situation room" on Wisconsin primary night.

Michael Lloyd Carlebach

McGovern acknowledges cheers on his Wisconsin primary victory.

Michael Lloyd Carlebach

Michael Lloyd Carlebach

Campaigning with Kathleen Kennedy in Harrisburg, Pa. Center in doorway is Ted Van Dyk. Bill Dougherty stands behind Kathleen.

Stuart Bratesman

Disastrous Cleveland press conference with Detroit Congressman John Conyers, April 29, 1972.

Whistle-stopping Nebraska on May 6, 1972, with former Gov. Frank Morrison.

Stuart Bratesman

Meet the Press, NBC News

May 30, 1972. The second "debate" with Humphrey. On panel (second from left) is Robert Novak.

L.–r.: Kirby Jones, Henry Kimelman, Gary Hart, and Frank Mankiewicz after third California debate.

Stuart Bratesman

Michael Lloyd Carleback

After late night meeting with Democratic governors in Houston, McGovern faces the press with Gov. Pat Lucey (Wis.), left, and Gov. Marvin Mandel (Md.).

June 6, 1972. Flanked by his family (left) and key California supporters, McGovern acknowledges cheers on four primary victories on a single day.

Stuart Bratesman

June 29, 1972. Meeting with "Establishment" leaders at McGovern home. Among those attending were Stewart Udall, Paul Warnke, Sen. Frank Church, Gen. James Gavin.

July 10, 1972. McGovern watches Democratic chairman Larry O'Brien as convention opens.

Michael Lloyd Carlebach

In "situation room" at Doral. L.–r.: Frank Mankiewicz, Jean Westwood, the author, Rick Stearns.

Gene Pokorny in McGovern command trailer behind the Miami Beach Convention Hall.

Stuart Bratesman

McGovern meets with National Welfare Rights Organization. Although he did not back $6,500 demand, this picture hurt him.

"Showdown at the OK Doral," July 12, 1972. McGovern got these demonstrators to disperse.

Sen. Thomas Eagleton meets press soon after he was chosen as McGovern's running mate.

McGovern and Eagleton at meeting where R. Sargent Shriver was chosen to replace the Missourian.

McGovern with (l.–r.) Fred Dutton, Dick Dougherty, Frank Mankiewicz.

Michael Lloyd Carlebach

Grim-faced encounter in August 1972 with Gary Hart (left) and Frank Mankiewicz.

Michael Lloyd Carlebach

Michael Lloyd Carlebach

Anti-McGovern demonstrators brand candidate as "radical" on his arrival in California in September 1972.

Sen. Edward Kennedy with McGovern in candidate's cabin aboard the *Dakota Queen II.*

Michael Lloyd Carlebach

McGovern and Shriver receive tumultuous greeting in Texas in August 1972.
On left is Texas governor Preston Smith.

Michael Lloyd Carlebach

November 8, 1972. The lobby of McGovern-Shriver national headquarters in Washington. "What Happened Last Night?"

of Nebraska voters. One of them was a Roman Catholic nun who asked about abortion. McGovern denied supporting abortion on demand and barred any Federal action on the subject if he were President. Guggenheim got the program on the air immediately and replayed it. The impact was solid.

On Saturday, we went across the state on a previously planned whistle-stop tour. McGovern spoke from the rear platform of the train at stops all across the state. Local pols were shuffled on and off the train at each stop. It was the most fun we had had campaigning in a long time. But most important, former Governor Frank Morrison and his equally popular wife accompanied us throughout the day. Morrison would get up on the platform and in his rough, frontier voice boom out: "George McGovern is no radical. If George were a radical, do you think I'd be up here with him?"

McGovern won with 41 percent to Humphrey's 35 percent. Effective campaigning and an excellent grassroots operation did the trick. We carried every town through which the train had passed while losing communities more than 20 miles away from the track. In this conservative state, Wallace, who had not campaigned, won 13 percent.

We felt that we had beaten the mudslinging with our counter-campaign. We believed that having shown Humphrey that he could not win with smears, he would drop them. Instead, his attacks and those made by Jackson in Ohio encouraged Senate Minority Leader Hugh Scott to launch his charges that McGovern favored the three A's—abortion, amnesty, and acid.

These were clearly peripheral issues to the campaign but the Republicans, following Humphrey's lead, tried to create the impression that they were key issues for McGovern and that McGovern's position was out of step with the majority of the American people.

As McGovern travelled in the pre-primary days, he had occasionally been asked about abortion. Our presumption was that a "liberal" stand would hurt us with Roman Catholics, but it would help us with the women's rights people. McGovern decided to state his own position without advocating it as public policy. He said that he thought abortion was a matter between the woman and her doctor and any other person she wished to consult. Ethel Kennedy had spoken strongly with McGovern on the issue and as a result of their conversations he avoided advocating any steps to put his own views into Federal law.

By the time of the Nebraska primary, McGovern had shifted the emphasis in stating his position. He said that he did not favor any Federal action to implement his personal views or indeed on the matter of abortion reform at all. This was no change from his previous position, although it was designed to allay the concerns of those who opposed abortion reform without worrying too much about the women's rights movement.

But McGovern gave the impression that he had changed his position on abortion by refusing to state his personal view. I spoke to him about describing both his personal position and his attitude toward public policy, but he was adamant, obviously believing that Catholic voters would not make the distinction. Unfortunately the course he followed led people to believe that he personally favored abortion on demand, although he was backing away from saying so.

Ironically, we all may have misread the voters. On the day before the Nebraska primary, a poll showed that almost two-thirds of those surveyed in this most conservative state favored abortion reform.

On amnesty, McGovern believed that historically it had not been dishonorable to flee your country to avoid military service in a war you thought wrong. Millions had fled from Europe to America for just that reason. He believed that once the war was ended, those who had gone to jail or to foreign exile should be allowed to come home. He preferred a case-by-case approach for deserters.

As we flew to Hawaii on the return from our Vietnam trip in September 1971, McGovern dwelt more and more on the issue. He believed strongly that amnesty should be granted and that he should make it part of his program. He knew there was a great deal of interest in the issue on the campuses. The only question in his mind was the right time to announce his position. Holum and I counselled delay until we reached the mainland and could properly publicize and explain his position. But, when asked about amnesty by a student at the University of Hawaii, McGovern made his position public.

The promise of amnesty became a part of every campus speech that fall and never failed to draw wild applause. That issue, more than any other, stirred the enthusiasm of the campus activists. Muskie avoided taking as strong a position, thus opening the way for McGovern to sweep the support of those activist students who would work long hours for the candidate of their choice. Looking back, McGovern would say that it would have been much easier in the fall if he had not spoken of amnesty in the spring, but that he recognized that the nomination might not have come if he had remained silent on the issue.

We knew that only about 20 percent of the electorate shared McGovern's view. Eleanor McGovern urged publicly and privately that he make his amnesty pledge conditional on performance of alternative service. But he did not believe that alternate service should be required of those who had already suffered in jail or abroad. In addition, we were all concerned about the appearance of backing down on the issue.

We hoped that the public would admire McGovern for his courage in taking an unpopular position particularly on an issue that affected so few of them directly. But because McGovern was labelled a radical for the $1,000 and abortion and marijuana and military cutbacks, the amnesty issue could never emerge as that one courageous statement of principle.

Nixon, reading the same public opinion polls, would abruptly change his position on amnesty. In January 1972 he had said he was prepared to be "very liberal" about amnesty once the war was ended. In the fall he would say he would "never, never" grant amnesty. The President and his campaign surrogates used the issue with working men and women to show that McGovern was more concerned with a few longhairs than he was with their sons who served patriotically. McGovern's response that amnesty was well precedented in American history could not change any minds.

Acid, the term that Scott loosely used to describe the legalization of marijuana, would also cause us as much trouble. Very

few people were willing to admit they favored legalization whatever their own personal practices. So, to support legalization
was unpopular and symbolic of the kind of permissiveness that
Nixon claimed was the cause of many of our country's troubles.

McGovern, whose own daughter had been arrested on the
charge of marijuana possession, never favored legalization. He
would disappoint campus audiences with his position in favor
of the removal of jail sentences for the possession or use of small
quantities.

In February 1972, McGovern had issued proposals for dealing
with the drug problem in the United States. Deep in a lengthy
document that Holum had prepared was a section on marijuana.
It was hardly a plea for popular use of the substance:

> Yet many experts who were once convinced that marijuana
> was a harmless substance have become less sure as it has been
> more widely used. As research continues, no more can be said
> than that it is vastly less dangerous than was once supposed—
> hardly a positive recommendation.
>
> Continuing investigations on the overall effects of marijuana
> leave unsettled the related but separate question whether society
> can or should attempt to completely prohibit its use. The most
> relevant historical precedent—prohibition of alcohol, a substance
> which, unlike marijuana, is often physically addictive and which
> is used by as many as 80 million Americans, at enormous eco-
> nomic and human cost—produced an obvious, abject failure.
> That experience, along with limitations on enforcement personnel
> and the grave costs involved in imposing severe sentences and
> prison terms on usually law-abiding young people and young
> adults, suggests a more promising route might be to regulate
> marijuana along the same lines as alcohol, while continuing and
> expanding educational programs aimed at discouraging its use.

Neither our press release nor McGovern's statement at his
press conference at a Boston rehabilitation center nor the reporters' questions there had touched on this section or on the
legalization of marijuana. Had the newsmen asked, they would
have received McGovern's usual answer.

When we reached New Hampshire, we had been startled to
see quotes from that section of the position paper in the news-

papers with the claim that McGovern favored legalization. The radio news was even more categorical. When I tracked down the source of the story I discovered that a UPI reporter had lifted that section out of the story and written a long article on marijuana. Then UPI radio news had cut that story to about three sentences saying that McGovern favored legalization.

I quickly drafted a restatement of McGovern's actual position, and we managed to stop the story within about 12 hours. But during that time, it had appeared in many afternoon newspapers and had been widely broadcast on the air. Our disclaimer appeared to many as an attempt to back down when McGovern saw the negative reaction to his original statement.

If McGovern had wanted to announce a new position on marijuana, he would certainly have made a major point of it and would not have tried to sneak his announcement into a major campaign document. But the press, especially the outlying wire service reporters, were not always sharp, and the political opposition could not be expected to take a charitable view of our problems.

McGovern's strong finish in Ohio and his victory in Nebraska led us to underrate the importance of Humphrey's smears. We felt sure that, once having been defeated after having raised his charges, he would not do so again. While he refrained from renewing these charges, the Scott statement, supported by what Humphrey had already said, lingered to do McGovern much damage.

Easy primary victories in Oregon and Rhode Island further dulled our senses to the problems that McGovern's positions and, more important, the distortions of them would cause us. Weak showings in Michigan and Maryland were dismissed as signs of unusual conditions favorable to Wallace by both McGovern and the national press. We focused our attention on the June 6 California primary.

When ABC's Sunday discussion program "Issues and Answers" asked us if Senator McGovern would be willing to appear jointly with Senator Humphrey on a one-hour broadcast just prior to the California primary, McGovern and his staff jumped at the opportunity. We were completely confident that McGovern was at his best in a confrontation situation and when he was answering questions rather than making a speech. In addition, he was the frontrunner and was not likely to endanger his lead by participation in a debate where he would, at worst, hold his own. Finally, ever since the New Hampshire primary, McGovern had been urging debates, although admittedly less frequently as his fortunes improved. Obviously he would have to show as much enthusiasm for debating when he was ahead as he had when he was behind. By meeting Humphrey, McGovern would be in a better position to demand debates with Nixon in the fall.

Once we had agreed to a joint appearance on ABC, the other networks' Sunday interview programs came through with similar invitations, and we agreed to all three. They were all to take place within the 10 days preceeding the California primary.

When we arrived at the CBS studios for the first debate, our confidence was bolstered when we noticed that McGovern had come into the studios with a far larger press corps than Humphrey and was clearly the focus of media attention. The panel of George Herman and Dave Schoumacher (who had been covering McGovern for CBS) and David Broder of the *Washington Post* took their places, and the debate was on the air.

Herman's "teaser" question at the beginning of the program—why either man thought he could beat Nixon—gave no hint of what was to follow immediately. Herman's next question went to Humphrey—was the California primary "crucial" to his campaign? This was a question designed to put Humphrey on the defensive, because he had said that the whole race would be determined there, and now he was trailing.

After a brief denial that the California primary would necessarily determine the Democratic nominee, Humphrey launched into a blistering attack on McGovern:

> And I believe that Senator McGovern, while having a very catchy phrase, where he says right from the start with McGovern, or McGovern right from the start—that there are many times that you will find that it was not right from the start, but wrong from the start. We were both wrong on Vietnam. Senator McGovern is wrong on Israel. Senator has been wrong on unemploy-

ment compensation. Senator McGovern has been wrong on labor law, and on the three great issues here in California, on his massive, unrealistic, and I think rather outside welfare program, he's wrong. In taxation, he's contradictory and inconsistent, he's wrong. And on defense cuts, I believe they cut into the muscle in the very fiber of our national security.

Within minutes of the opening of the broadcast, Humphrey had disclosed the nature of his campaign. He had chosen to make McGovern the issue and to attempt to put the frontrunner on the defensive.

We were rocked a bit by this attack, but remained confident that McGovern would come back strong. We knew he had the ammunition.

On Vietnam, McGovern had first spoken out against the war in 1963, had voted against military appropriations after 1969 to demonstrate his opposition and had sponsored in the Senate the principal anti-war legislation in 1970 and 1971. Humphrey, in contrast, had enthusiastically supported the Johnson policy, had never voted against military appropriations even after he returned to the Senate in 1971 and had been somewhat reluctant to offer his support for the original McGovern-Hatfield End-the-War proposal in 1970.

Humphrey's charge that McGovern was wrong on Israel was based on the rumor spread by Humphrey's people about McGovern's unwillingness to provide the kind of military aid that Israel had requested. When McGovern had voted against all military appropriations as a protest against the Vietnam war, some aid to Israel had gone by the board. Despite McGovern's explanations on this point, Humphrey implicitly argued that the need for aid to Israel was great enough to outweigh any symbolic vote against aid to Vietnam. In addition, Humphrey would later argue that McGovern's alternative defense budget would weaken the American military presence in the Mediterranean, thus lessening our possible support for Israel in time of crisis.

Israel was one issue where Humphrey would score in California. Although McGovern had taken the standard liberal Democratic positions in support of Israel, many Jewish voters questioned his sincerity. Why?

McGovern had supported all pro-Israel positions over the years and, in 1970, he began to give closer consideration to the problem of peace in the Middle East. With the increasing presence of Soviet forces in the Arab countries, McGovern sought to make proposals for government policy that would take the heat out of the situation and insure Israel's survival.

At the same time, McGovern was concerned that his opposition to American military participation in the Vietnam war would be construed as opposition to military aid to Israel. He viewed the countries quite differently, especially because Israel did not ask for U.S. troops. In May 1970, he became a member of the first group of Senators asking the President to sell jet aircraft to Israel. All seven of the original group were "doves" on Vietnam who reaffirmed their support for Israel.

In pursuit of his longer-run objective of making proposals for restoring peace in the Middle East, McGovern asked me to draft a speech for delivery in the Senate. The draft called for direct negotiations among the parties in the Middle East, the end of the state of war, the acceptance of responsibility by the Arab government for acts of aggression committed from bases in their own territories, and an international guarantee of any agreement reached by the nations of the Middle East. Basing himself on the lessons we had learned from the haggling over Viet Cong participation in the Paris peace talks, McGovern added a point asking that the Palestinian refugees also participate in the Middle East talks. None of these proposals would arouse opposition from Jewish leaders.

But the draft also included a suggestion that an escrow account be established to compensate Arab refugees who could never return to Israel. The Jewish State had itself accepted the principle of compensation. But McGovern would be criticized for paying that much attention to the needs of the refugees.

In addition, the speech again urged the sale of jet aircraft, but added: "The United States should express clearly its wish that the aircraft sold to Israel should not be used for such incursions to extend the area of combat." This statement brought on the storm, because the Israelis considered their air force an extension of their artillery and thought it necessary to extend their front line of defense by sending their planes out on missions over Arab territory.

The McGovern proposal merely expressed a wish and did not relate to the limited incursions that the Israelis frequently made. But he recalled the deep penetrations to the Cairo area in early 1970 where innocent civilians had been killed. Those raids had been the pretext for Soviet involvement in the Middle East. We felt that such attacks could set off the powder keg, particularly if Soviet installations in the rear were brought under fire.

Thus, McGovern had strayed from orthodoxy and had opened himself to criticism.

In March 1971, McGovern and I attended an informal dinner in Washington with a group of newsmen who had been Nieman Fellows at Harvard. The questions got around to the Middle East. McGovern said that among the possible solutions for the status of Jerusalem was internationalization. He did not endorse it or exclude other possibilities. In addition, he was asked whether or not he agreed with the policy of "insubstantial modifications" in Israel's boundaries. This was the language of the Rogers Plan and referred to the pre-1967 boundaries. McGovern misunderstood and, thinking the reference concerned the post-1967 boundaries, said in general he favored that policy. He stressed his support, above all, for direct negotiations. Later in the discussion he realized the possibility of error in what he had said earlier and clarified his statement. But the damage was done.

The New York Times reporter who had asked some of the questions on the Middle East left the late evening meeting and immediately filed a story indicating McGovern's support for the Rogers Plan and for considering internationalization of Jerusalem. It was a good story because here was a liberal Democrat straying from the reservation. The next day we were in New York and prepared a clarification for *The Times* which we had hand-delivered. We searched the paper the next day, but found no mention of our new statement. At a lunch with *The Times*'s editors later that month, McGovern brought up the case. Several of the editors said that they had never seen the clarification and that they doubted it had been received. They promised to keep an eye out for the next McGovern statement on the Middle East.

Yet at the end of March, when McGovern spoke at the Harmonie Club in New York in an effort to lay his position on Israel out in detail, *The Times* buried the report of the speech in a story dealing with McGovern's day in the city. In the end, the original story in *The Times* was to do far more damage to the McGovern candidacy than its later endorsement was to help it.

In short, McGovern was as sound on Israel as any Democratic candidate had ever been. But he had made the mistake of actually thinking about the situation in the Middle East rather than simply making the ritual statements of support.

Humphrey saw these few deviations from orthodoxy as an opening where he could hope to undermine McGovern's standing with an important portion of the Democratic electorate. He tried to say that McGovern's defense budget would weaken our ability to aid Israel, an assertion that was factually untrue. He even found a pro-Arab advertisement signed by Rick Stearns, a senior campaign official, in 1967 and charged that McGovern was surrounded by aides unsympathetic to Israel. Stearns had nothing to do with policy, being responsible for delegate selection in the non-primary states, and had changed his views in the intervening years. But in the heat of the campaign that was difficult to explain.

Humphrey's charge that McGovern was unsympathetic to unemployment compensation came directly from the propaganda mills of the AFL–CIO. Several years earlier, McGovern had in fact voted against a single amendment relating to unemployment compensation on the ground that the states could not comply with it in time to prevent their losing Federal funds. While he supported the amendment, he opposed even a brief interruption in Federal funding for unemployment compensation. He had voted with a clear majority of the Senate on this matter.

Humphrey's question of McGovern's position on labor law related to his refusal in 1965 to vote in favor of ending debate on the repeal of the right-to-work provision of the Taft-Hartley Act. This rule, which prohibits the "closed shop" where only union members can obtain employment, also existed in South Dakota law. McGovern was unwilling to jeopardize his position at home when he knew that even if he voted to end the anti-labor filibuster, his vote would make no difference in the final outcome in the Senate. At the time, he had obtained the agreement of the AFL–CIO to his vote, and in 1971 George Meany had told him that he did not hold him responsible for the failure to cut off debate. Yet, in the primaries, Al Barkan, Meany's political lieutenant, had been spreading the story of McGovern's disloyalty, and the Senator had made a public admission of error several times.

Humphrey's allusion to McGovern's welfare proposal was merely a start of the attack he was going to make on what McGovern had said about public assistance in the past. He also hinted at the effort he would make to confuse McGovern's tax proposals with his welfare ideas. And on national defense, it seemed that Humphrey was planning to continue the attacks he had been making in California on the alternative defense budget on the grounds that it would eliminate jobs.

McGovern immediately responded:

> Could I comment on the Senator's analysis since my record was very heavily involved in this opening statement. I find it almost impossible to believe that the Senator from Minnesota would attack my record on Vietnam. . . . Let me just cite one quote, and I'm not going to belabor the record, but as late as October 1967, several years after I had referred to Vietnam as the worst moral and political disaster in our history, Senator Humphrey was saying Vietnam is our greatest adventure and a wonderful one it is. Now this is not a record that encourages me to believe that the Senator's experience during that period as Vice President is one that commends him to take us out of Vietnam, and to prevent future catastrophes of that kind.
>
> As to my position on Israel, I see no essential difference between the views that I've held and the view that Senator Humphrey holds.

In his answer, McGovern betrayed his surprise with Humphreys' sharp attack. It was indeed "impossible to believe" that his old friend and fellow Senate Democrat would strike out so hard and so inaccurately. McGovern's use of the phrase "the Senator from Minnesota" indicated that he would be reluctant to give up the courtesies of Senate debate for the rough-and-tumble Humphrey wanted. Although he had resorted to the same kind of defense on Israel that Humphrey was using on Vietnam, McGovern clearly could seize the advantage by pressing the Vietnam issue.

As a result, the program moved onto the subject of Vietnam first. Humphrey was apparently trying to weaken McGovern's credentials with the large peace constituency in California by demonstrating that there was not much difference in the positions of the two candidates. But McGovern's record was so well known to these voters that it was clear to us that Humphrey would be wasting his time taking this tack. Humphrey probably recognized this, because he turned Broder's follow-up question into another broadside:

> Now the fact is that Senator McGovern wasn't right from the start any more than I was. We both voted the same way in the United States Senate—that's where we start—and the fact is that all during his Senate career, he voted for the appropriations for the war in Vietnam. There is no doubt that he spoke out against it, but he voted for it, and that's the record.

The Minnesotan tried to move off onto welfare and tax reform, but was forestalled by Broder. At the same time, Humphrey was laying a debater's trap for McGovern. After a little more skirmishing, the frontrunner responded to the Vietnam charge:

> When a Senator speaks out against Vietnam, as I did, all during the 1960's, but is confronted with a situation where he has to vote for the military budget of the United States, in which Vietnam appropriations are included, he does not have the option of saying, I'm against the Vietnam portion, so I'm going to vote no on that, and vote yes on the rest of the defense budget. You have the choice of either saying, I'm against the entire defense budget of the United States and I vote for zero appropriations, or you get up and speak against the war, you try to change policy, then you do as I did on the floor of the United States Senate and explain that your vote for the defense budget is not entitled to be interpreted as a vote for the Vietnam War.

But McGovern had failed to cover himself for those occasions on which he had voted against the entire military aid appropriation, and Humphrey moved in:

That didn't bother Senator McGovern when it came on the vote to aid Israel. He voted against the foreign aid appropriation because he didn't like what was in it about Laos, yet he had voted earlier to put some money in for Israel, but on the end he votes no. He just can't have it both ways.

In his earlier answer to Broder, Humphrey had also repeated his shots at McGovern's labor voting record. Then he began hammering away at two themes that were to do a great deal of damage. He blasted what he called McGovern's "$72 billion welfare proposal" and he criticized the ad in the *Wall Street Journal* which had seemed to weaken McGovern's tax reform proposals. McGovern, ignoring this attack for the moment, continued to respond to questions on Vietnam.

Aside from the points that Humphrey scored by using a number of half-truths and distortions, he was subtly planting a doubt about McGovern. He repeated the point: "You can't have it both ways." This argument could lead the way to the conclusion that McGovern changed his mind on the issues.

The program then turned to a discussion of reductions in military spending, when Schoumacher delivered a telling blow to Humphrey that we also had been prepared to raise. He noted that, while Humphrey criticized McGovern's proposed military budget of $55–58 billion, he had suggested in 1970 that: "We can cut the Pentagon budget to as low as $50 billion a year and still have real security for the United States."

Humphrey nimbly countered that his reductions would have cut clearly wasteful programs including the Vietnam war and then took advantage of the detailed McGovern budget to list the specific cuts that we would make. He made it seem that, because he had been vague he could cut more fat, while McGovern's detailed list proved that he would cut muscle.

The Minnesotan's most telling argument was that McGovern proposed unilateral disarmament. He adopted the Nixon line in total: "You cannot—you cannot negotiate with the Russians from a position of weakness. If we haven't learned that, we've learned nothing." By implication, McGovern was naive.

McGovern had been determined to pump some real meaning into the tired expression "setting new national priorities." To him, that meant shifting resources out of the bloated military budget and into civilian operations. Most politicians would have left their commitment at a pledge to bring about such a shift, but McGovern wanted to show that he meant what he said.

John Holum had begun, as early as June 1971, to prepare an alternative defense budget. He had no trouble convincing Mc-Govern, who had supported legislation to cut the military budget every year since he had come to the Senate, to accept the principle of a "zero-base" budget—in short, starting from scratch. Holum worked through the rest of the year, drawing on the help of experts who had been associated with the Defense Department but who had later become critical of its steadily increasing budget.

The most important feature of the budget Holum produced was the detailed analysis of the military potential and intentions of America's adversaries and of the U.S. defense posture. He argued that traditionally military budgeting had been based simply on what had gone before without any new look at how the situation in the world had changed over the past quarter century. This was his line of reasoning:

> Our defense posture has been built upon conservative planning assumptions—on preparing for "greater than expected threats." The alternative posture accepts that premise in part. It starts by assuming that the major communist powers, China and the Soviet Union, will remain actively hostile to U.S. interests, and that there is a real risk of confrontation if one or the other can expect military advantage as a result.
>
> Hence the proposed budget retains more nuclear weapons than necessary for deterrence, as insurance and as a hedge against possible build-ups on the other side. General purpose forces are maintained against dangers which are both slight and exceedingly remote, given the expected military balance and political out-look. Intensive research and development efforts are proposed, to maintain the clear U.S. lead in military technology.
>
> But conservative planning can be pushed too far.

Only by making such a fresh appraisal could a true "zero-base" budget be constructed. And Holum was faithful to his principle; the cuts he proposed reflected the assumptions about the world that he had adopted.

McGovern seemed to underestimate the importance of this new appraisal of the world. He had never argued against his opponents on the grounds that they were living in the past. And when Defense Secretary Melvin Laird had charged that McGovern proposed a "white flag" budget and asked what he would do if the other side stepped up its preparations for war, McGovern had answered that we would have to do the same rather than countering that his budget made allowance for such an eventuality. Instead of advocating a new look at our defense posture, he placed far greater emphasis on his pledge to cut the tremendous waste in the military budget.

When Holum put a price tag on the new budget, he estimated it would come in at some $32.5 billion less than the Nixon budget in 1975. Obviously it was impossible to predict the scope of the Nixon budget or changes in the intervening period which would require us to adjust our own budget. By attaching a disputable figure to anticipated savings, we drew attention away from the sizeable savings that certainly could be realized and the desirability of a completely new look at the budget. Instead, the debate came to focus on such specific points as the $32.5 billion or the six carrier task forces we had proposed in lieu of 15 or the sharp reduction in manned bombers.

McGovern accepted the Holum budget and stuck with it throughout the campaign even though he was not entirely comfortable with the $32.5 billion figure. By September, he would talk of a $10 billion cut over the next three fiscal years, which sounded less drastic. Despite his restiveness with having to defend the proposed cuts in detail, McGovern knew that he could not back off from them in the slightest, because of the charges against him of wavering, notably on the welfare reform proposal. So he stuck to his guns.

Even before the California debates, Humphrey was scoring points on the most obvious weakness in our new priorities proposal. We had laid such heavy emphasis on cutting the military budget that we caused many defense industry workers legitimate concern about their jobs if McGovern were elected. Humphrey cultivated these worries, especially in Orange County and San Diego.

Holum quickly ground out a paper to accompany the budget which demonstrated that a shift of resources from the military to the civilian sector would actually create more jobs. Using material prepared by some of our economic advisers, Holum demonstrated that the transfer of $32 billion over four years would protect almost 5 million jobs phased out in the military sector and add 1.5 million more. In addition, he stressed McGovern's proposals to step up government funding of research and development and for a Federal spending increase designed to boost employment.

But the fatal weakness in our response to the threat of job losses was McGovern's half-hearted espousal of economic conversion. Ever since 1963, when he had first proposed reduced military spending, McGovern had also sponsored legislation for assisting workers and industries to convert to civilian production. At its best, however, the conversion bills provided for a period of unemployment compensation rather than employment. We found that people wanted to work and, even if they agreed about the need to shift away from defense spending, they preferred their current jobs to the vague prospect of new ones.

In the brief periods when I campaigned on behalf of McGovern in Ohio during the fall, I would discover that only if we pledged that no job would be ended until another one was already available in the civilian sector could we sell our proposal. In the latter days of the campaign, McGovern would adopt this approach.

Another problem inherent in our proposal was the effect of a quarter century of the Cold War. To judge from the reactions we met, American voters wanted to be sure that the national defense was far more than adequate to meet any possible attack. Voters told us that they were willing to accept waste and excessive overkill capacity rather than run the risk of having too little.

The only effective argument that I would find against this ingrained belief was to show that military waste implied a decision not to do many of the other things that people want from their government. Holum stressed the approach "where does the money come from?" in drafting speeches for McGovern. The answer had to be the military budget. I preferred to emphasize the choice: "You can't have better schools and health care and more money for law enforcement, if you don't reduce the military budget. *You* make the choice." McGovern always seemed to believe that he could convince voters that waste should be ended by showing them the extent of the waste; only rarely did he tell them that there was a direct relationship between their discontent with government's inability to respond to their needs and the military budget.

In view of Humphrey's criticism of the McGovern budget, the panel tried to test to see if Humphrey regarded himself as a cold warrior, but McGovern only lightly touched the point that even after his proposed reductions, we could still negotiate from a position of strength.

Humphrey dodged the issue by challenging the McGovern cuts on the grounds that the United States would be weaker in the Mediterranean and unable to aid Israel. McGovern responded with a solid defense of his own proposals, but failed to note that they involved no reduction whatever in the Sixth Fleet in the Mediterranean.

The battlefield was already pockmarked by the salvoes that Humphrey had launched, but the worst was yet to come in the second half of the broadcast.

Although I noticed that members of Humphrey's staff appeared to be quite satisfied with their man's performance, Mankiewicz, press secretary Kirby Jones, and other members of our staff did not appear in the least worried. My own feelings, based on Caddell's poll findings, was that viewers were probably more interested in style than substance. On that score, McGovern was coming over a reconciling force, while Humphrey seemed to be the strident stereotype of a politician.

The second half of the broadcast opened with a discussion of McGovern's income redistribution proposal. He was unable to state how much a $1,000 demogrant would cost, but Humphrey jumped in with his own estimates, designed to make the concept look outlandishly expensive. Although the Minnesotan was unable to come forward with any proposal that might end the welfare mess, he succeeded in putting McGovern on the defensive.

In the light of his scorching attack on McGovern's welfare reform ideas, Schoumacher asked:

> Senator Humphrey, will you still be able to support Senator McGovern if he gets the nomination?

> Over Mr. Nixon? (replied Humphrey) Of course I will. In the meantime I'll talk to Senator McGovern and get him off some of these kicks that he's on, on the welfare program.

We had no idea how badly we had been hurt when the program ended. McGovern had given solid answers in defense of his proposals, but he had not answered the fundamental charges that were implicit in the Humphrey attack—that he was a radical and that he was unsure of what he actually was proposing.

I continued to believe that Humphrey could not win in California using his aggressive approach, because the people did not want candidates who came across as politicians, making wild charges against their opponents. Obviously, there was some merit in this belief as we learned from the immediate favorable reaction to the broadcast. Caddell's polls would show us holding firm right after the first debate. But Humphrey had planted serious doubts in people's minds about McGovern. Merely by taking a positive approach and not counterattacking, we were not going to be able to erase those doubts. Most important, we did not share them because we had become overconfident.

Two days later we went into the second joint appearance, this time a special broadcast of NBC's "Meet the Press." Larry Spivak was firm that the candidates would not be allowed to cross-examine each other and that they would have to be responsive to the panel which included Robert Novak, the syndicated columnist who was openly antagonistic to the McGovern candidacy, Haynes Johnson of the *Washington Post*, Richard Bergholz of the *Los Angeles Times*, and NBC's Tom Pettit. Humphrey claimed that this format muted his attack, but obviously he had decided to use a less strident tone.

Novak moved in immediately on the welfare proposal. The discussion quickly moved to tax reform and Humphrey played loose with the facts of McGovern's proposals. Once again, the Minnesotan had seized the advantage.

Now Johnson chimed in to ask how McGovern could promise to keep air bases open at the same time as he proposed to reduce the number of manned bombers. Clearly, we had no specific idea about which bases would have to be closed and avoided admitting that any particular one would have to be shut down.

For a few minutes the newsmen were able to probe the positions of both candidates. Johnson bore in to ask McGovern about aid to people laid off because of defense cuts, and Pettit asked about a McGovern promise to provide special tax breaks, if necessary, to American Motors. Novak explored the weaknesses in Humphrey's Vietnam stance.

Then Novak zeroed in on McGovern again saying that his spending proposals would reach $100 or $160 billion. Obviously he was using the Humphrey cost estimates of our programs. And Novak brought up the *Wall Street Journal* ad again. McGovern's answers were strong: probably because of his dislike of his questioner.

As the program ended, Bergholz summed up for McGovern the obvious meaning of the first two debates:

> Senator, this campaign, rapidly coming to a conclusion here, has been in large part an attempt by Senator Humphrey and his supporters to portray you as a man who is perhaps too liberal, too extreme, too radical—whatever term—to entrust to the Presidency.

The third debate was an anti-climax. In the intervening period, Shirley Chisholm had obtained a court order allowing her to appear on ABC's "Issues and Answers." Los Angeles Mayor Sam Yorty (who would that same day drop out of the race in favor of Humphrey) and a representative of Governor Wallace thus also appeared. There was little chance for a confrontation. In fact, the broadcast was so boring that I went to the lunchroom for about 20 minutes.

The only new element which emerged in that third debate was a shift in emphasis in Humphrey's position on Vietnam. In the second broadcast, he tried to give the impression that his present position was essentially the same as McGovern's. Novak reminded Humphrey: "Your contention is that there is no real difference

between you and Senator McGovern." Obviously Humphrey did
not want to concede to McGovern any advantage with the peace
constituency. But on the following Sunday, Humphrey was more
attuned to the Wallace and Yorty position and backed off. He
said: "I cannot agree with Senator McGovern" when asked about
a Vietnam settlement. Most of the exchanges, however, were re-
runs of the earier debates.

Humphrey clearly felt he was gaining as a result of the debates. He challenged McGovern to a fourth encounter on Monday evening, the television time to be purchased by the two
candidates. Although McGovern agreed in principle, we did
not go ahead with the debate. Immediately after the third broadcast, McGovern and the staff met in his dressing room and decided to reject the offer. Having already participated in three
such meetings, McGovern would suffer little criticism for avoiding a fourth.

McGovern and Humphrey had participated in the second most
important national debates in American history after the Ken-
nedy-Nixon debates of 1960. Although the formats were not
strictly those of debates, they offered the opportunity for a direct
confrontation of views in the presence of impartial moderators.

If the impact of the debates in California was unclear, the national effect was obvious. Humphrey had been able to cast Mc-
Govern in an unfavorable light:

—he made "foolish" or radical proposals;

—he changed his mind about what he was proposing;

—he was not a true friend of Israel (the mere assertion of
   this by Humphrey, a long-time ally of the Jewish State, was
   impossible to overcome);

—he favored a wildly costly welfare plan (the $1,000) that
   would raise the taxes of average people;

—he was willing to negotiate with the Communists from a
   position of military weakness;

—he wanted to raise taxes on the rich by too great an amount;

—he would take away tax deductions for mortgage interest
   and medical expenses; and

—he was a big spender.

For many people across the country, the debates were their

introduction to George McGovern. Humphrey had made sure that the man who had risen meteorically on the national political scene made a very bad showing in his first major national appearance. It was no wonder that Humphrey was asked by the panelists whether he could support McGovern if the South Dakotan got the nomination. He had spent almost all his time attacking McGovern and had said little to criticize Nixon.

Hubert Humphrey's defense for his savage attacks was that McGovern had to be able to withstand such charges in the primaries, because he would certainly face them in the general election campaign. To a certain extent, Humphrey was right. But to a far greater degree, he provided the Republicans with all the ammunition needed to destroy McGovern. Humphrey had made charges which stuck, so the Republicans needed merely to make them bipartisan issues. It seemed to be of no importance to either Humphrey or the Republicans that most of these charges were totally false. And it did not concern Humphrey that he was providing the Republicans with ammunition bearing his own seal of approval.

One of the main elements in the fall campaign was to be a series of television spots sponsored by Democrats for Nixon and directed against McGovern. Of John Connally, who headed that wing of the Republican campaign, Humphrey had said during the last debate: "I might suggest that a man of the firmness and strength and the quality of a former cabinet officer, John Connally is the man [to go to Hanoi to negotiate peace]." One Connally spot would show McGovern continually changing his mind. The unspoken punchline was: "After all, Hubert Humphrey said so." The second would allege that he wanted to cut into the defense muscle of the country. "After all, Hubert Humphrey said so." The third would claim that, under a McGovern bill—the NWRO bill, he would put 46 percent of the nation on welfare. "After all, Hubert Humphrey said so."

The combined effect of the original Humphrey charges and their repetition by the so-called Democrats for Nixon was to be devastating. And at no time during the fall campaign would Humphrey withdraw his original charges. Small wonder that some of his principal backers decided to support Nixon. They and many other Americans may have believed that McGovern was a radical and possibly dangerous man. "After all, Hubert Humphrey said so."

Some of our people argued that Humphrey was seen as a tired politician around the country and that people would discount his charges on that basis. But Humphrey had been fighting for his political life when he had spoken out in California. If he reneged later, he might be acting simply as a Democratic politician, his original charges more to be believed than his endorsement of McGovern.

McGovern had chosen in California to remain above the fray and to refrain from a direct countercharge that Humphrey was lying because he would do anything to win. His reluctance to counterpunch stemmed from his belief that the people did not want politicians trading charges; they wanted a new leadership that looked to a better future. In addition, he remained attached to his old personal friend, his next-door neighbor for 10 years in Washington, and refused to hit back. He could slam Republicans hard; he found it difficult, even in his own defense, to rough up "old Hubert" who was both a friend and a fellow Democrat.

The debates undoubtedly influenced the outcome of the primary. McGovern carried every part of the state except the Jewish community in Los Angeles. There the Humphrey charges had hit home. And elsewhere around the state many people who did not particularly like Humphrey felt that McGovern had been ineffectual in his own defense. It was a case of McGovern losing strength as more voters became familiar with him. Still, as a relatively unknown candidate, he was preferable to Humphrey, the known quantity.

But the final debate followed by McGovern's obvious desire to patch things up with the Establishment (in the form of the Democratic Governors) also had an impact on the results. Some McGovern supporters turned to Shirley Chisholm whom they saw on the last debate as an uncompromising liberal. Since they felt McGovern would win anyway, they wanted to let him know that they expected greater "purity" than he had displayed. These were mostly white liberals, because, for the first time McGovern carried the black community as well as the Mexican-Americans.

McGovern attributed the largest part of the slippage to his having left the state on the eve of the primary. Our campaign workers reported that many volunteers did not work on primary day and many of our supporters did not bother to vote because they felt that if McGovern could be off-hand enough to leave the state, he certainly wasn't depending on their help. In short, this was a case study of the aftereffects of victory fever.

Finally, our campaign in California had lost some of the warmth and feeling of personal contact that had characterized our earlier efforts. In New Hampshire, a young man or woman had come to the door and spent as much as two hours talking about George McGovern. In California, a professional telephone canvasser, who sounded a bit mechanical, would call and run down questions from a checklist. The voters could sense the difference.

Yet, no one could dispute that the bandwagon was now rolling at full speed. McGovern won not only California, but also New Jersey, New Mexico, and South Dakota. There seemed nothing that could prevent him from getting the nomination. After California, he led not only in delegates but also in popular vote. All that was left for his opponents was to attempt to block him from a first-ballot nomination in hopes that his supporters would become frustrated and turn to another candidate. Humphrey, Muskie, Jackson, and Wallace underestimated the commitment of the McGovern supporters and overestimated their own potential appeal to our people if they defected. In fact, the alternatives they proposed to a McGovern nomination were either chaos (with McGovern the ultimate winner) or the nomination of Ted Kennedy.

We moved into the New York primary campaign in hopes that Humphrey and Muskie would yield to the inevitable and withdraw so as to improve the chances for post-Convention unity. Muskie let it be known in the wake of the California primary that he was re-evaluating his own position. Since Muskie's decision at the end of April not to run in primaries, McGovern had made sufficient progress to preclude any chance that there could be a deadlock at the Convention which would result in Muskie's nomination. In fact, the longer Muskie held on, the less likely it would be that McGovern supporters could be reconciled to him. Some backers of the Maine Senator wanted to jump to Mc-Govern. In the Illinois delegation, many Muskie delegates were close to breaking with their candidate.

In this atmosphere, McGovern and Muskie met privately in a small office off the Senate floor during the afternoon of June 8. Muskie laid out some of his concerns about McGovern's positions. McGovern found the comments reasonable and, in many cases, not in conflict with what he had been saying as opposed to what Humphrey and others had said about his positions. But he gave Muskie the impression that he wanted the Maine Senator's support so badly that he was willing to give way easily on the issues. In his anxiety to get a commitment from Muskie to withdraw, he may indeed have been too willing to make concessions. But, more important, he had to struggle against the misconceptions resulting from the debates. At the end of their discussion, McGovern came away with the definite impression that Muskie would withdraw the next day, perhaps even in his favor. Muskie, on the other hand, had come to the meeting inclined to withdraw, but his discussion with McGovern made him doubtful once again.

The next day Muskie spoke before the National Press Club. He told the members that he would remain in the race. During the long night, those advisers who felt he should not throw the nomination to McGovern had prevailed. McGovern got word of the speech while sitting in the manager's tiny office at Dubrow's Restaurant in New York just after a campaign stop. When I reported to him on the Muskie press conference, he was deeply disappointed and somewhat bitter. Victory had just been snatched from his hands. Muskie had the nerve to say that he would begin travelling across the country in hopes of lining up additional delegate support.

That day ended on a sour note. Flying from New York to Oklahoma for the Democratic State Convention, our plane was forced down in Pittsburgh due to a bomb scare. When the plane's stairway failed to operate properly, we slid down the emergency chutes to the ground. Some newsmen were injured, one seriously. It had been a terrible day.

Hubert Humphrey was no more cooperative than Muskie. Although he was not running in New York, he hoped for the election of the uncommitted Regular delegates who would be likely to support him. He kept up his drumfire of misstatement about McGovern's positions. Finally, McGovern's anger overcame his friendship for Humphrey. He told the press bitterly: "I am afraid that my old friend has forgotten that there is such a thing as wanting too much to be elected." McGovern swept New York.

Despite his impressive series of primary victories after Wisconsin, McGovern had begun to run into serious difficulties. Humphrey's attacks on his proposals made McGovern appear to be a radical. But McGovern did not want to run as a radical because he felt himself to be a progressive committed only to essential and needed change.

McGovern's problems were compounded by his own supporters. The drafting of the Democratic Platform, which began after the New York primary, did little to dispel the radical image, thanks to the efforts of McGovern delegates.

After each state delegation to the National Convention had been chosen, the delegates named their representatives to sit on the Platform Committee or the Credentials Committee or the Rules Committee. McGovern delegates remembered the platform fight of 1968 where the McCarthy and Kennedy forces brought forward a minority plank opposing the continued massive military involvement in Vietnam only to be defeated on the floor of the Convention. The confrontation on the streets of Chicago had been repeated in the Convention Hall, they believed, over what McGovern himself insisted on calling "the war plank."

The McGovern delegates were determined that, in 1972, they would prevail in the platform decisions. Given the great symbolic importance they and the news media had attached to the 1968 platform fight, they believed that a victory on the Platform Committee and then on the floor of the Convention would be the clearest demonstration that the old ways had been swept aside by reform in the Democratic Party.

These delegates were, in many cases, committed to liberal causes and had used the McGovern candidacy as a way of furthering their own programs. McGovern had gained their support, thus denying it to other liberal candidates, and in return they hoped to shape his platform.

Because McGovern delegates were at least as issue-oriented as they were candidate-oriented, they fought hard in their states to gain appointment to the Platform Committee. The party pros gave way relatively easily, and the McGovern forces found themselves able to dominate the work of the Committee. In this effort, their majority was insured by the full cooperation of the Muskie delegates. As a result, they could command a clear majority.

The party pros and labor leaders—men like Daley in Illinois or Frank King in Ohio—recognized that, without a President in the White House whose policies must be defended as in the 1968, the platform battles would be of little significance. They concentrated their efforts on the Credentials Committee and let the McGovernites move into Platform Committee slots.

McGovern himself recognized that, except to the delegates themselves, the platform would be of minor importance in the campaign. But when he saw that I had been quoted in *The New York Times* as saying that the platform would be forgotten a week after its adoption, he cautioned me against showing such cynicism about the interests of our own people.

The Muskie leadership supported us to demonstrate their support for the likely nominee even before Muskie himself withdrew. In addition, those who served on the Platform Committee were probably the most issue-oriented of the Muskie crew and hence the most likely to agree with the positions of the McGovern delegates.

Early in the spring Ted Van Dyk asked McGovern directly for the responsibility of representing our interests before the Platform Committee. He put the question to McGovern as we flew across Pennsylvania on the day before the primary in that state. Both because the platform held so little interest for him and because the platform debate seemed so far off, McGovern was glad that Van Dyk was willing to relieve him of further concern about it.

Van Dyk's action turned out to be wise; he was able to prepare for the Platform Committee well in advance and to keep matters in hand. (I could only wonder later whether a word to Hart at that time would have encouraged him to think about assigning similar responsibility to somebody for the Credentials Committee. If he had, perhaps some of the problems we were to face could have been avoided.)

Van Dyk's apparent intention was to come up with a platform couched as much as possible in the generalities that were acceptable to all Democratic leaders. By not insisting on specific points, he felt that our forces could gain the good will of the others and demonstrate that we were not "crazies."

At the same time, he had to be careful to preserve clear McGovern positions where an overly general statement might lead people to believe that the Senator was backing down. He worked closely with the early drafters of the platform planks and then with the Drafting Subcommittee itself. Even when the full Committee insisted on playing a more direct role in the drafting and a number of task forces were established, Van Dyk managed to maintain his influence over the shape of the draft. As the platform draft was readied for submission to the Committee, McGovern assigned me to work with Van Dyk in insuring that the result would not cause him any problems in the fall.

Our principal adversaries in the Platform Committee were the Wallace delegates, mostly from Alabama and Florida, and the Jackson people from Washington. We had little opposition from the Humphrey delegates who, we soon learned, would concentrate their efforts on the Credentials Committee.

The greatest surprise was the ease with which we could work with the Wallace leaders, Fred Folsum and Pierre Pelham. This may have been due to McGovern's promise that if they lacked the necessary 10 percent of the Committee members to submit a minority plank, he would ask his own delegates to assure them the necessary votes. After the shooting in Maryland, I had proposed this gesture to him in hopes of gaining Wallace support. It had occurred to me, immediately after the Wallace shooting, that this man, who had the support of millions of Democrats, might be denied the representation intended by the McGovern reforms.

We were actually able to come to terms with the Wallace people on almost all of the plank on law and order. On other matters, we agreed to disagree quite civilly, although we were given the clear impression that the people with whom we dealt were more tractable than the Governor or whoever was acting in his behalf at the hospital where he lay paralyzed.

It was a sign of the change in the Wallace position in the Democratic Party when Annie Gunter, an Alabama official, twice heaped praise on Newark Mayor Ken Gibson, a black who was chairing the meeting, and finally pinned a Wallace button on him. Gibson told the Committee that he wasn't worried about the gesture, because the people back home understood him. This brought the house down.

The Jackson people concentrated on a tougher plank for military support for Israel. They claimed that the McGovern cutbacks in the military budget might reduce our forces in the Mediterranean. Even the Jewish representatives felt that the basic draft was tough enough, and the Jackson move was defeated.

The most difficult struggle came with our own supporters over the abortion issue. Many of the delegates were militants in the women's rights movement, and they badly wanted some token recognition that abortion reform was necessary. Shirley Mac-Laine, the movie star who was a California delegate, took on the job of mediating between Van Dyk and me and the women. Out in the Mayflower Hotel lobby during the day, I talked with some of the Committee members, and we negotiated a compromise text: "In matters relating to human reproduction, each person has a right to privacy. Freedom of choice and individual conscience should be fully respected consistent with relevant Supreme Court decisions." But some of the women, who watched somewhat suspiciously from the distance, obviously did not like the idea of negotiating with a male staff member. They felt they could not gain their objective with any compromise on wording.

One militant delegate put forth an unequivocal abortion reform plank. To counter this proposal, MacLaine offered a plank which said that the issue should be kept out of partisan controversy. She and her allies determined to vote against the more militant plank, and it went down to defeat. She assumed that the militants would, however, support her position. And on a voice vote at 2:00 A.M. it looked like her plank would pass. Then, a roll call was requested and the MacLaine amendment went down to defeat. Obviously, those who would vote in favor of it if they remained anonymous, would not do so if their votes became a matter of public record. The net result was what MacLaine had hoped to achieve—the removal of abortion from partisan controversy, at least so far as the Democratic platform was concerned. There was simply no abortion plank.

As Ken Gibson brought the proceedings to a close the next day, the entire committee was suffused with a feeling of cooperation and friendship. Here, we felt, was the Democratic Party reuniting and demonstrating a willingness to work together in the fall. We were quickly to learn that the "era of good feelings" was due more to the personal relationships among Committee members and the relative unimportance of the platform than to any more fundamental understanding on issues among the various factions.

The platform came to the floor of the Convention in Miami Beach on Tuesday, July 11. The session began shortly after 7:00 P.M. and did not end until almost 6:00 the following morning. Larry O'Brien told us it was the longest session in political history. None of us realized how much harm it would do the McGovern cause.

The national audience that viewed the platform session in prime time saw the only appearance of Governor Wallace before the Convention. He came to ask for the adoption of a series of minority planks that his people had submitted. These planks included a call for the death penalty, for prayer in the public schools, and for complete opposition to busing. There was no doubt that these planks would be voted down. In fact, each was shouted down with unrestrained enthusiasm by the McGovern delegates. Their feelings were so high, that McGovern floor managers had earlier urged them not to boo Wallace. The votes did us great harm. We had repeatedly made efforts to gain Wallace's support and to appeal directly to his supporters and then we made a national display of our opposition to those positions he deemed the most important. There was no possible way to avoid this situation.

Despite our concern that the real debate of the evening would focus on a moderate anti-busing plank, our efforts were devoted entirely to taming the enthusiasms of our own people. A plank on tax reform, reportedly prepared by supporters of Senator Fred Harris as a way of promoting him either for Vice President or some other position, was defeated by voice vote on a very close call by Yvonne Brathwaite, the California congressional candidate who was presiding.

On gay rights, a young woman from the Ohio delegation rose to oppose the minority plank and launched into a most distasteful attack on homosexuals. But, however offensive her remarks might be to some McGovern delegates, we knew that the plank must be defeated.

A minority plank on abortion, the same one I had worked out in the lobby of the Mayflower, was presented. If anyone bothered to read the text, they could see that it was not even an abortion reform plank. But it had acquired great symbolic meaning and it, too, had to be defeated.

On the Middle East, we asked to have a McGovern speaker on the tough Jackson plank. I quickly recruited Bob Abrams, the Bronx Borough President, and he made the Jackson people furious by using our time to support their minority plank. By stealing their show, we had removed a potential new problem with the McGovern position on Israel. The Jackson plank was adopted.

In all, there were 19 platform votes that evening and we won them all including one on Indian rights where we sat back and allowed a minority plank to be shouted in. That "free vote" was a pressure valve for delegates who were unhappy about voting against their own favorite issues for the good of the cause.

Much was made of the McGovern organization and its ability to wring the votes it needed from the delegates. In fact, its operations were far removed from the power politics of the past. Where a delegation chairman could once require support for the party line by threatening delegates with the loss of public jobs, the best we could do was to try to convince, cajole, and badger delegates to accept our view, reminding them that some of the more radical minority planks would make it harder for McGovern to defeat Nixon. This common sense always prevailed although we had the toughest time with the big McGovern delegations from New York, Massachusetts, and California. Sometimes Van Dyk and I were worried, as when some Wallace women delegates voted for the abortion plank. We thought we were the victims of a sabotage effort, although it later turned out that those women sincerely favored abortion reform.

The entire McGovern floor operation—regional desk people in the candidate's trailer behind Convention Hall, and regional whips spotted on the floor supplemented by Van Dyk's own whips—was devoted to defeating our supporters. McGovern's sole telephone call to us was to admonish us to do just that. (He had seen some McGovern delegates on television promising to oppose the candidate on abortion.) We understood that our most zealous partisans were alienating many average Americans. Clearly we would have to pay a price for our effort to put a rein on our own people by reducing their enthusiasm for McGovern after the Convention. Some of the delegates never forgave us for abandoning absolute "purity" on all issues. That was a risk we had to take in order to clear the decks for the best possible race against the President. But for those who watched through the night on television, there was the spectacle of the Democratic Party haggling over abortion or gay rights or sweeping tax reform. They saw only a passing reference to Vietnam or to jobs or to inflation. Of course, these issues were mentioned, but because they were not controversial, they attracted less attention than the more radical issues on which votes were held.

Later, this session was to be used by the party pros and the Meany wing of the labor movement to show how a radical fringe had dominated the proceedings of the Convention. For those who knew what was happening, the platform session was a great success. Solid liberal delegates from the Midwest, deeply rooted in the Democratic Party, had joined with the more conservative Democrats to defeat all of the unwanted planks. Yet few followed the Convention closely and, as a result, they came away with a new reason for believing that George McGovern had given the country a Democratic Party more dominated by radicalism than realism.

5

THE REGULARS

"I think I've got the skill and the common sense to quiet the fears of those people and bring them on board at some point."—George McGovern, April 28, 1972

The man who had built the South Dakota Democratic Party and who had a good voting record on labor issues thought of himself as a Party Regular and a friend of organized labor. In 1972 he might be the candidate of the disgruntled 1968 McCarthy and Kennedy forces, but he looked back with pride on his immediate demonstration of support for Hubert Humphrey, just after the Minnesotan won the Democratic nomination. In 1968, he had fought briefly and lost and had then rallied around the Party standard. In 1972, he expected others would do the same.

Party leaders and organized labor had been cool to McGovern ever since he assumed the chairmanship of the Democratic Reform Commission. They viewed his work, however well-intentioned, as designed to weaken their hold on the Party mechanism. McGovern was held personally responsible.

In practice, the McGovern Commission reforms gave the Regulars and labor leadership little comfort. McGovern partisans were determined to rectify the injustices of 1968, when, as McCarthy or Kennedy supporters, the Regulars had shut the doors on them. Victory for them meant replacing the traditional power brokers, not sharing control with them. McGovern was often unaware that in some states guerilla warfare was taking place between his supporters and those who he hoped would soon endorse his candidacy.

Almost a year before McGovern won the Democratic nomination, there had been reason to hope for support from George Meany and the top leadership of the AFL–CIO, the most powerful labor group in Party affairs across the country.

In August 1971, McGovern had promptly criticized President Nixon's announcement of his New Economic Policy. A few days later, organized labor rallied to the position that McGovern, alone among possible Democratic candidates, had taken. Meany was surprised and pleased by the South Dakotan's instinctive pro-labor stance. Meany agreed to meet McGovern that same week at the Washington AFL–CIO headquarters. McGovern hoped he could bury the hatchet with the labor chief.

I accompanied McGovern to the meeting although the session itself was limited to the two men. Immediately afterward, McGovern told me he had begun the discussion with an apology for his vote on right-to-work in 1965. Meany had dismissed the matter, noting that McGovern's vote had not made any difference.

But Meany told the Senator that he was still nettled about a personal attack by McGovern in 1963. When the Kennedy administration had made a grain sale to the Soviet Union benefiting McGovern's South Dakota wheat farmers, the deal had almost been stymied by Maritime Union insistence that at least half of the grain be shipped in U.S. flag vessels. McGovern had held Meany personally responsible, when, in fact, Meany knew nothing of the matter. It appeared that the White House, on its own, had offered to impose such a requirement, if not an even more stringent one. McGovern, who learned all of this for the first time in his talk with Meany, apologized.

The other matter that had been a source of friction between the two men was the Vietnam war. Meany and the overwhelming majority of his executive board had supported the Johnson-Nixon policy that McGovern had so vigorously opposed. But Meany dismissed the differences between them on the grounds that the war would have dwindled in importance by the next year.

McGovern left the meeting greatly encouraged about his relations with organized labor. He thought that Nixon's August 15 statement had opened the door to better relations with Meany. My only reservation was that, as with the war, Meany had been reminded that McGovern made up his own mind without "checking" with organized labor.

Later that month we were in Denver, where Herrick Roth, the head of the state AFL–CIO, told McGovern that Meany had asked that a taped broadcast he, Meany, had made before the August 15 announcement be held up and reviewed. In addition to updating the broadcast, Meany wanted to make sure there were no negative references to McGovern.

Next, in his Labor Day statement, Meany listed McGovern as one of the four Democrats who would be acceptable to him as the Presidential nominee. Then, McGovern received an invitation to address the biennial AFL–CIO National Convention in Miami on November 19. The other candidates were also invited as was the President.

McGovern and I arrived in Miami late the preceding evening. He talked that night and again early the following morning with Senator Mansfield concerning important votes coming up that day in the Senate. We decided that McGovern could give his speech and, because we had a chartered jet, make it back to Washington in time for the scheduled votes, which were important ones for the AFL–CIO. By a quirk of scheduling, none of the other candidates would be able to attend the Convention, because they would have to stay in Washington for the votes.

President Nixon spoke to the Convention at 10:30 and got a coldly polite reception to his plea for support for his wage-price freeze. Then McGovern spoke, delivering a solid pro-labor speech that had Meany roaring his approval. Here was a solid achievement, particularly on national television, or so I thought.

But Al Barkan, Meany's lieutenant for political matters, was raging that McGovern had not gone back to Washington without giving his speech so as not to gain an advantage on the other Democratic hopefuls. Barkan felt that the Party reforms endorsed by McGovern would reduce AFL–CIO influence, and he detested McGovern because of it. He was, therefore, irate that McGovern should be allowed to gain an advantage at the expense of other candidates. In addition, we did not fare well on television that evening. The union was made to seem impolite and disloyal to the President, and McGovern was tarred with the same brush.

Yet we felt that a corner had been turned with Meany. Even if we did not have his wholehearted support, he was almost certain not to veto McGovern.

By early 1972, however, our gains with the AFL–CIO were disintegrating. Barkan, still angered by the ongoing Party reform, travelled the country smearing McGovern by spreading the story of his right-to-work vote in 1965. Although he failed to get labor leadership to take a serious interest in the delegate selection process, he managed to stimulate anti-McGovern sentiment among many middle-level labor leaders. At Barkan's urging, Meany himself was blunt enough to say that he thought little of McGovern and that among those with acceptable labor records, McGovern would be his last choice for Nixon's challenger. At the AFL–CIO Executive Board meeting in Miami in February, McGovern was unwanted and unwelcome. Even our few friends of the Committee, notably the Meatcutters, were afraid to challenge Meany. They still hoped he would support McGovern if he won the nomination.

Throughout the primaries, McGovern had made little effort to cultivate Party leaders. Because most of them had lined up with Muskie and because Party reform had reduced their role in the delegate selection process, he felt that he would be wasting valuable time and effort in courting them. However, as the California primary campaign drew to a close and with the nomination within his grasp, McGovern made his first major effort to break through to the Regulars.

Bill Dougherty, McGovern's personal political adviser, who was at the Democratic Governors' Conference in Houston together with Wisconsin's Pat Lucey, urged McGovern to extend a planned trip to Albuquerque to include a stop at the meeting. The Governors were hostile to McGovern. Only three thought McGovern could carry their states, and many believed the false charges that had been circulated by Humphrey and Jackson. In addition, the southern leaders were especially concerned about McGovern's pledge to reduce military spending, since the fruits of congressional seniority—in the form of military installations—were concentrated in their part of the country. McGovern agreed to Dougherty's suggestion.

Late Monday evening, on the eve of the California primary, McGovern was closeted with about 20 of the Democratic governors. He had few allies—Lucey, Dick Kneip of South Dakota, Jim Exon of Nebraska, and surprisingly, Wendell Anderson of Humphrey's home state of Minnesota and Ken Curtis of Muskie's home state of Maine. Jimmy Carter of Georgia had cast himself in the role of the chief critic of McGovern. He had told reporters that McGovern's nomination would hurt the Party's candidates across the south. Kentucky's Wendell Ford and North Carolina's Robert Scott were implacable in their opposition. They and others pressed McGovern on all of his positions and the Senator acquitted himself well, although he gave his inquisitors little satisfaction on matters of substance. He was in the difficult position of wanting to heal the breach with them while recognizing that too much conciliation would be seen as weakness.

Preston Smith, the host state governor, had spent only a few minutes at the meeting, so McGovern was accompanied to the 1 A.M. press conference by Maryland's Marvin Mandel, who was chairman of the Democratic Governors. Mandel indicated to the press that McGovern had made a good impression, although he was careful to avoid outright praise. But it was clear from both Mandel and McGovern that no minds had been changed by the meeting. The next morning, after attending a prayer breakfast, McGovern flew back to Los Angeles.

Many of these governors would become leaders of the "Anybody But McGovern" movement at the Convention in Miami Beach the next month. Although they had shown McGovern the courtesy of attending the meeting, they were too deeply alienated by his positions or, more often, by the activities of his supporters in their states to allow for any reconciliation. Because he had gone so far without their help, they also felt that he might well ignore them in the future.

The New York primary, which followed California by two weeks, illustrated the problems that existed between McGovern's supporters and the Regulars.

New York was a certain victory for us. The only real contests were in Buffalo, where we faced Muskie slates in the most Polish districts in the country, and in Albany, where we would have to defeat the entrenched O'Connell organization. In some places, we seemed to be running against ourselves. In Brooklyn, for example, full McGovern slates were running, but Meade Esposito, the county leader, had endorsed McGovern and pledged that his delegates, running on a separate slate, would vote for the South Dakotan. Esposito would have preferred us to ease off our campaign in his borough.

A somewhat different situation existed in the Bronx. There, Bob Abrams, the Borough President and a leader of the Reform Democrats, had been an early McGovern supporter. Later, Pat Cunningham, the Bronx Democratic leader and chief of the Regulars, had also endorsed McGovern. Their delegate slates opposed each other with Abrams asking for McGovern's endorsement of his own delegates, while Cunningham preferred neutrality. But, like Esposito, he told McGovern that he understood our need to campaign for our own delegates.

Dick Wade, the history professor and old McGovern friend who served as one of our state chairmen, and Joe Grandmaison, the New Hampshire man who was state coordinator, distrusted Esposito and Cunningham. They feared that if their delegates were sent to Miami Beach, they could not be counted on to stick with McGovern if there were any doubt of a first-ballot victory. They feared that McGovern was being seduced by the friendly sounds emanating from the Bronx and Brooklyn Regulars.

On June 12, McGovern arrived at Brooklyn Borough Hall to speak to a noonday crowd. I noticed that Esposito and Sam Leone, the Borough President, were both absent. When I talked with one of Leone's aides, I discovered that they had not been consulted about the rally until the last minute.

My own feeling was that we should not chase after the Regulars, but when they stepped forward to support McGovern, whatever their motives, we should accept that support. McGovern could not lose by demonstrating that he had wide support, although he might lose if he seemed to be running after the Establishment. The New York campaign organization obviously thought such a distinction was not possible.

When McGovern learned of the situation from me, he contacted Leone. Pete Hamill, the New York columnist, and Shirley MacLaine were both great partisans of Esposito, and they urged that McGovern patch things up. The net result was a private lunch at McGovern's room in the Biltmore with Esposito, Leone, Eugene Gold, the Brooklyn District Attorney, and Cunningham. I sat in on the meeting with McGovern. He made no concessions to them, and in fact stressed that he would have to support his own committed delegates. The others merely asked McGovern to make sure they were consulted about stops in their boroughs.

This meeting infuriated Wade and Grandmaison. They feared that even such consultations would open the way to sabotage by the Regulars. They were almost as distressed that McGovern had met in Buffalo with Joe Crangle, the Democratic State Chairman, who was remaining neutral during the primary.

This split between Reformer and Regular in New York, a fact of political life in the state, was to plague the McGovern campaign even after the primary in which McGovern delegates won in all but the Albany area. At-large delegates remained to be selected, with McGovern forces entitled to almost all of them. Esposito and Cunningham hoped for some representation in that group but were handled rudely by the McGovern leadership which continued to distrust their intentions in Miami. Unfortunately, their exclusion from participation in the campaign at this point would have a lasting effect in the fall and would indicate to Regulars in other parts of the country that the McGovernites wanted to go it alone.

While McGovern and the Regulars had ignored each other and sparred occasionally in the months of the primary campaigns, they finally clashed head-on in June 1972. The Regulars, aided by organized labor, settled in for last-ditch effort to block McGovern's nomination.

On the morning after the California primary victory, I had chatted briefly with the Senator in his room as the bags were packed and carted out. I told him that I had heard that morning on the radio that a challenge to the winner-take-all rule in that primary was being planned by representatives of some of the defeated candidates—notably Humphrey and Muskie. He dismissed the news lightly both because the Party rules were clear that the winner-take-all primary was acceptable and because Humphrey himself had said that he would abide by that principle. The California Supreme Court had ruled in favor of it. Ken Bode of the Center for Political Reform had dropped his own suit in Federal Court on the basis of a commitment by McGovern that he would back a change in Party rules for 1976 ending the winner-take-all system.

Despite Humphrey's own statement that he would accept the result of the California primary, his staff began work on a challenge. Stan Bregman, a Washington lawyer, and Mark Siegal, a young political scientist working in the Humphrey office on a grant and a student of the McGovern Commission reforms, took charge of preparing the challenge. Ironically, because of Siegal's interest in political reform, he had originally sought to work in the McGovern Senate office, at no cost, but had been turned down on the grounds that there was no space left in the office.

The challenge was not based on any failure to meet the one-man, one-vote principle which would have been the heart of a court suit, nor was it based on any alleged violation of the McGovern Commission guidelines that had been duly accepted by the Party. Instead it depended, in theory, on the supposed violation by the McGovern Commission of the directives given it by the 1968 Convention. The challengers claimed that the Commission had not dropped the winner-take-all primary as it had been instructed. In fact, the challenge was made because of a cold estimate by the ABM (Anybody But McGovern) movement of the number of votes they could muster. They knew they could beat us.

In the states, the Humphrey and uncommitted labor delegates had fought hard to insure themselves of maximum representation on the Credentials Committee. In Texas, where McGovern should have been entitled to two of the six seats, he had none. In Ohio, which Humphrey had won in a very close and dubious primary, McGovern could have expected two of the five seats. He got none. In Wisconsin, on the other hand, where McGovern won by a substantial margin over Humphrey, one of the three seats went to anti-McGovern forces in an attempt at reconciliation. Even in Massachusetts, where McGovern had swept the primary, a Chisholm representative occupied one of the delegation seats.

Immediately after the conclusion of my work at the Platform Committee session on Tuesday, June 27, with McGovern still away on his southern swing, I went to the Shoreham Hotel where the Credentials Committee was in session. To my surprise, I discovered that, unlike at the Platform Committee, our staff people had no clear delegate count of supporters and non-supporters. Indeed, they did not know who all of the Committee members were because some delegations were still straggling in. In fairness, Eli Segal, who had been our coordinator for the California primary, had belatedly been put in charge of the staff work on credentials and was trying mightily to catch up. But he entered the situation long after Committee members had been chosen and so was forced to play with a deck stacked against him.

McGovern, back on Thursday from the South, was constantly on the telephone, worried about the prospects of a challenge. Following up on staff members' contacts, he spoke directly with members of the Committee and with many of the political powers back home. At the same time, Humphrey had decided that he would go all-out to topple McGovern as did the national leadership of the AFL–CIO.

In the end, we simply didn't have the votes. The ten California delegates were not allowed to vote on a challenge affecting their own delegation. It might have been argued that the portion of the delegation not subject to challenge should have been allowed to vote (after all, McGovern would certainly get a major part of the delegation even if the winner-take-all were rejected), but the rules were clear. The Humphrey forces, the uncommitted, almost all Muskie delegates plus the Jackson and other non-McGovern delegations were able to provide the majority to sustain the challenge in committee.

I brought the news to McGovern who was then on the floor of the Senate. His reaction was cool, but tough. He asked if I thought that his initial reaction would be the best for the media. As a general rule, I felt that his own innate reactions were the best and most honest and told him so. But I added that he should not make it seem that he regarded the Credentials Committee action as a personal slap at him so much as a rejection of the will of the Democratic voters of California and of the efforts of many thousands of people who had worked on his campaign.

He first met with the writing press in a reception room just off the floor of the Senate and called the ruling an "incredible cynical, rotten political steal." I was surprised by his vehemence, particularly if he ever hoped for reconciliation with the Regulars. In the radio and television gallery on the third floor of the Senate wing, he repeated his statement. Unfortunately the main impression that he left was of personal injury. He also left no doubt that he would not support the nominee of the Party if the California Challenge were left standing by the Convention. This threat was an extension of his earlier comment that he would only support the nominee if the reform rules followed, but now it sounded more ominous.

The impact of the Senator's reaction was clearly negative. The press reported his indignation. Even though Humphrey had agreed to play by the rules and then had asked to have the rules changed after he lost, McGovern would have done better to make a rebuttal which showed statesmanship instead of petulance.

Before the Credentials Committee completed its work, it had to settle one major challenge. McGovern had decided not to run delegates against the Regular Party slates proposed by Mayor Daley in the city of Chicago. We felt that our delegates would have no chance against Daley's and that we would be obliged to stretch our limited finances to include the use of Chicago television if we contested the race there. But the Mayor put forward slates that violated the McGovern Commission guidelines on race, age, and sex. Alderman William Singer and Jesse Jackson, the leading anti-Daley black spokesman in Chicago, decided that they would bring a challenge to Daley's 59 delegates.

Through an intermediary, who called both Mankiewicz and me repeatedly during the week the Credentials Committee met, the Mayor let us know that unless McGovern ordered his supporters to oppose the challenge, he would neither assure his support at the Convention nor during the fall campaign. McGovern himself was caught between diametrically opposed pressures. He knew that he could not carry Illinois without Daley's help, yet he wanted compliance with the Guidelines and to support Jesse Jackson for whom he had developed strong bonds of affection in the past. His initial reaction was to remain neutral.

The obvious compromise, and the one that McGovern ultimately supported, was to seat both delegations, giving each delegate one-half vote. Mankiewicz, working through a Chicago congressman and Singer, passed the word to both sides. Both Daley (who in any case refused to accept Singer and Jackson on the delegation) and the challengers were reluctant to compromise.

Just as the voting began, yet another call came through to me from Daley's Michigan vacation home asking that McGovern move to postpone consideration of the challenge. Daley continued to believe that McGovern could oblige his delegates to bend to his will just as Daley himself could do. But McGovern never had such power over his delegates. We could not stop the roll call.

Even more important, the vote on the Chicago challenge came on the day after the California vote. The McGovern delegates, with all the original California committee members still empowered to vote, were determined to have their revenge. That night, the nation's television viewers were treated to the sight of pandemonium breaking loose in the Committee when the Daley delegation was unseated. Delegates danced in the aisles. But some of us around McGovern realized that not only Daley but also political pros across the country would draw the conclusion that the party had fallen into the hands of the "crazies." Perhaps that demonstration would harden their resolve to try to deny McGovern the California delegation at the Convention itself.

Both Daley and the unseated McGovern forces from California took the Credentials Committee decisions into Federal court. At first, the District Court judge refused to rule against the Credentials Committee in either case. On appeal, a three-judge panel ruled in favor of the McGovern California delegation on the grounds that it was legally elected and conformed with the Guidelines, and rejected the Daley suit because, although that delegation was legally elected, it was not in line with the Party rules. Naturally there was jubilation in the McGovern camp and warm praise for Washington lawyer Joe Rauh who had handled the California case. The last word went to the Supreme Court, which, wisely, we were forced to admit, refused to inject the judiciary into an internal dispute of the Democratic Party. So the challenges went to the floor of the Convention.

Rick Stearns, the inveterate delegate counter, assured us that we would have enough votes to reject the Committee's decision. But his calculation was only correct if we were to be granted a fair ruling on what constituted a majority for the purposes of the vote. That was far from an accomplished fact when we arrived in Miami Beach on Saturday, July 8.

The Humphrey forces argued that none of the California delegation should be allowed to vote on that state's challenge on the grounds that in the Credentials Committee an entire state delegation was barred from voting even if the challenge only affected a part of the delegation. In addition, the Humphrey people maintained that there was only one acceptable majority—the 1,509 delegates who represented one more than half of the total number of delegates from all states. Thus, they sought to deprive McGovern of even those California delegates that were not subject to challenge while pushing the required majority as high as possible. This formula might leave us 100 votes short of 1,509 unless we gained support from Muskie or committed delegates.

The McGovern camp stressed that the rules concerning which delegates could vote on the floor were clear. As opposed to the Credentials Committee, the Convention rules clearly permitted the unchallenged portion of the delegation to vote. As for the required majority, while we acknowledged that the rules were not explicit on this point, we argued that all that was necessary was one more than half the number of delegates eligible to vote on the challenge—probably 1,433, if the 151 challenged delegates were dropped from the grand total of 3,016.

Larry O'Brien, as Temporary Chairman of the Convention, would have to rule on these two points at issue. He also had to deal with the order in which the challenges would be considered, for, if the Daley challenge came first and was successful, the McGovern forces would be deprived of the 59 Chicago votes. He determined that California would continue to precede Chicago. This initial ruling angered the ABM leaders—Humphrey, Jackson, Wallace, and Mills (who wanted Kennedy in hopes of running for Vice President).

Late on Sunday, McGovern and Mankiewicz met with O'Brien to argue our case. No promise of future office was held out to O'Brien if his rulings were favorable. But it must have been clear to the Party Chairman that McGovern had by far the best shot at the nomination and that his future was probably most closely tied to McGovern.

On Monday, July 10, Muskie held a press conference. Hopes rose at the penthouse headquarters of the McGovern campaign in the Doral Hotel that the Maine Senator was at last ready to withdraw and to throw his support to us. Instead, he surprised us again by proposing a closed meeting under the chairmanship of O'Brien of the six remaining candidates to try to work out a compromise along lines he had in mind but did not disclose.

We immediately and unanimously opposed the idea of any such meeting being closed. We didn't like Muskie's trying to put McGovern in a bad light as the man obstructing a compromise. The Muskie compromise, it later turned out, was the simple expedient of seating both challenger and challenged and giving each delegate one-half vote. McGovern refused to participate in the meeting, and it never took place. There seemed to be no damage to our campaign because of this rejection. Nobody could expect McGovern to participate in an effort to reduce his own strength.

Meanwhile, O'Brien issued his ruling. The non-contested California delegates could, as the rules clearly indicated, vote on the challenge. This decision would turn Wallace against O'Brien.

The ABM people had forced O'Brien to look as if he were choosing sides. As for the required majority, if the vote exceeded 1,509 there would be no problem. The same would be true if it fell below the lower majority figure (1,433 in the case of California)—determined by counting only those eligible to vote on a particular challenge. Only if the results of the voting on a challenge fell into the "window" between the lower and the upper majority figures would the Chairman ask for a new vote by the Convention to determine which was the appropriate majority. And on that procedural vote, all delegates, even those challenged, would be eligible to vote. We thought we could win such a procedural vote, but we didn't want to find out the hard way.

As a result of this complex ruling, our objectives were simple. First, we must find 1,509 delegates who would support us on the California challenge. This task would be made easier by the inclusion of the Chicago anti-Daley delegates and of our own unchallenged California delegates. Second, we must prevent any challenge decided prior to the California vote from resulting in a majority falling into the "window." The precedent that could be set on such a challenge was obvious to Hart, Mankiewicz, and Stearns.

Earlier on Monday, McGovern had met with the Women's Caucus as he made his rounds of the delegation headquarters. The women were particularly interested in the South Carolina challenge which was based on there being an insufficient number of women on the regular 32-member delegation headed by Governor West. It was simply a matter of form for McGovern to pledge all our best efforts to win the challenge.

As the voting on the credentials challenges began on Monday night, McGovern, his secretary Pat Donovan, former California Governor Pat Brown, minorities aide Yancey Martin, and I plus a few others, watched on television from the Doral while Hart and Mankiewicz managed the action on the floor. Hart had wanted to direct the floor activities with the help of the young coordinators who had worked with him during the primaries. At first, McGovern had given him the impression that he might want somebody else to take charge of the floor activities, although he gave way to Hart without indicating who his choice might be. The Senator had insisted on the addition to the floor crew of a couple of Senate colleagues. In practice, they were not interested in serving as Hart's whips and his first task on Monday was hurriedly to make sure that all delegates were covered by people who would respond to his directives.

The South Carolina challenge came early and Hart and Mankiewicz soon recognized that votes would have to be held back in order to make sure that the challengers fell below the lower majority figure. This was delicate work, because the "window" on the South Carolina challenge was 16 votes. The difference between 1,509 and 1,493, the majority not including the South Carolina delegation. I could see that this plan had been put into action when Wisconsin and certain other McGovern delegations held back on the announcement of their votes. They seemed to be countering Ohio's reluctance to cast its votes. Hart guessed that the Ohio action, under the leadership of Frank King, the state AFL–CIO chairman, and a Humphrey delegate, might be an effort to hold out until the end and then cast just enough votes each way as to put the result in the "window."

McGovern was not aware of the maneuver until I pointed out that some of our delegates were holding back. Humphrey, we later learned, caught on to our tactic before any of his people. (In fact, the Ohio holdout was a function of internal jockeying in that delegation and not an attempt to force the key vote on what constituted a majority.) By the time that Senator Abe Ribicoff announced a sadly depleted Connecticut vote for the South Carolina challenge (we got only 7 of 51 delegates), McGovern was watching the proceedings with great relish. He enjoyed the grave speculation by CBS's Walter Cronkite about the newly discovered weakness of the McGovern forces on the floor. Then when the West delegation topped 1,509, we saw the victorious South Carolinians making broad claims about a victory that had actually been delivered to them on a silver platter.

No one will ever know if there were 1,509 delegates who supported the South Carolina challenge. But it was clear that our maneuver denied the challengers some delegates they might otherwise have had. When Mankiewicz and Hart were interviewed immediately following the vote they both professed that our forces had made the best effort possible on behalf of the women. When the networks finally figured out what had happened—with a little prompting from our own press staff—they revealed the tactic and related the disappoinment of the Women's Caucus. That story only made Mankiewicz and Hart look like they were trifling with the women's rights movement. At the Doral, it seemed that an honest statement of what had been done would have been preferable to a transparent effort to hide the maneuver. The net result must have been to build McGovern's image as a backroom politician, which we had, in fact, been trying to play down. All of the McGovern leadership, including the candidate, felt that his image as a non-politician was important if we were to gain the support of the Wallace discontented. But much of our effort in this direction was dissipated on the South Carolina challenge.

With South Carolina out of the way, McGovern knew that the California challenge was likely to succeed. The other candidates at last recognized that there was little point in resisting McGovern.

The presentation of the California challenge brought one of the high points of the Convention. Willie Brown, chairman of the California Assembly Ways and Means Committee and a co-chairman of the delegation, delivered an impassioned speech, ending with the plea: "Give me back my delegation." The wild applause indicated that Brown had been able to make the case to the Convention far better than our hand-picked debaters, who had already spoken. But he, like McGovern, put the challenge in personal terms, offensive to many.

The vote went easily and as we passed 1,509, we all knew that the nomination was sewed up. A restrained joy was shared by McGovern and those few aides around him, and we knew the same joy was shared in the trailer, parked in back of the Convention Hall.

One more major piece of business remained before the Convention that night—the Chicago challenge. But there was little drama left in this subplot. If there were to be any compromises,

Mayor Daley would have to make the first move. Jackson and Singer were confident they had the votes to turn back the Daley forces. The Mayor continued to insist on their removal from any compromise delegation. In order for the McGovern compromise—half-votes for each side—to be effected, it was necessary to waive the rules of the Convention. That motion, duly made on our behalf, required two-thirds approval. It received less than a simple majority and Mayor Daley was left out of the Convention for the first time in 16 years.

At last the McGovern organization was free to turn its attention to matters other than the credentials challenges. Every bit of talent and energy in the McGovern leadership had gone into the effort to insure the seating of the full California delegation. Reflecting back later, Gary Hart said that he felt such an all-out push was fully justified in order to assure success. McGovern obviously agreed.

But the cost of full attention to the California challenge was high. First, it meant a substantially greater outlay of money than would otherwise have been necessary had the other candidates conceded the nomination to McGovern before the Convention opened. Hundreds of thousands of dollars went into travel, mail, and telephoning in the weeks prior to the Convention. And a far more elaborate telephone system than that used by the Nixon campaign several weeks later had to be installed on the Convention floor.

But even more important, there was no time for planning our course of action after the Convention. McGovern had originally gone to his Cedar Point, Maryland, home in late June to work on the new campaign structure. With the New York primary behind us, he was to have a clear period to make the crucial personnel decisions that would determine the nature of the fall campaign and allow us to jump off to an early start. Instead he was preoccupied with the California challenge.

By the same token, no thought was given to the kind of campaign that we would run. What use would we make of the month of August? With the Democratic Convention so early in the summer, the nominee would have an added period to begin his campaign against the incumbent President. What sort of media effort would we make? Charles Guggenheim, who would obviously handle our television and radio as he had in the past, usually needed considerable production time, so he needed to know what we wanted as soon as possible. What role would our organization play and how would we handle our relations with the Party regulars and labor leaders who had been cool to the McGovern candidacy? What would be the relationship between the Democratic National Committee and our campaign? And finally, who would be the Vice Presidential choice?

There were no answers to any of these questions. McGovern and Hart believed that no answers would be needed unless the California delegation were seated, and they chose to take one thing at a time. They felt that such major decisions could not be delegated to others but would have to await the settlement of the challenge.

Most significantly, the California challenge struggle showed us that we were in a total war with all of the other candidates without any hope of a fair compromise and without being certain that we had the troops to beat them. They never offered to drop the challenge in return for their choice of McGovern's running mate. We had to accept their contention that any delegate who was not for McGovern was in the ABM movement, including the uncommitted delegates.

But it was also clear that unless all of the other delegates united around a single candidate, they offered no alternative to McGovern. In effect, we were fighting against the possibility of the nomination going to a new, compromise candidate who would appeal to McGovern delegates and many of the others. Clearly, the choice would point at Ted Kennedy, despite his sincere refusal to be considered.

The final result was to show that McGovern did not have the nomination well in hand without a victory on the challenge. After both Muskie and Humphrey had dropped out of the race, McGovern was still unable to collect as many as 1,800 delegate votes on the first ballot. In effect, that meant he had gained virtually all of the Muskie delegates and a few from Humphrey and other candidates. But most of the Humphrey delegates went to Senator Jackson who remained in the race until the end.

Here was a clear indication that the opposition to McGovern was deep-seated and that a large segment of the Party was not ready to rally around him even when he had the nomination locked up much less when there was even the slimmest chance of denying it to him. This made the decision to go all-out on the challenge correct.

But our victory on the challenge blinded us to the strength of the opposition to McGovern. We had been caught in a vicious circle. In order to get the nomination, we had to defeat the other candidates on the challenge. By winning them over decisively, we made it more unlikely that we could have their support after the Convention.

This state of affairs was the natural outgrowth of our own campaign against the traditional Party powers. We had campaigned against them in the naive belief that they would nonetheless rally around McGovern if he achieved the nomination. McGovern was convinced that they would react for the good of the Party just as he had done in 1968. He failed to notice the fatal difference: in 1968 there had been a split between Regulars and Reformers on the issues, while in 1972 the Reformers had made the Regulars themselves into the issue. The McGovern forces could not be so easily forgiven. The Regulars' reluctance to accept a McGovern nomination was buttressed by the statements of Hubert Humphrey, their recognized leader, that left the strong implication that George McGovern was a radical—the Goldwater of the Left.

As a result, the high price of fighting the California challenge had to be paid. The only major mistake from the viewpoint of our own organization was to ignore how thin our ranks were. With everyone involved in the challenge fight, no one planned ahead for the general election.

One major opportunity came to McGovern to deal with the concerns that the Regulars had voiced about his candidacy and to look beyond the Convention to the fall campaign. It arose by chance.

On Wednesday, July 12, in the early afternoon, groups of young demonstrators entered the lobby of the Doral. Soon several squads of riot police, armed with yard-long nightsticks and wearing helmets with plexiglass masks, cleared the demonstrators from the lobby. Then the youths were allowed to reenter the lobby after the hotel manager, reportedly at the urging of our staff, told the police he did not want them forcibly removed.

We could not determine the make-up of the group, and the rumors went as far as saying that the sit-in was dominated by extreme left-wing S.D.S. students who had no intention of being reasonable. The group had no leader and, in fact, seemed to reject any leadership. Eventually a young woman gained some minimal control of the group. She made it clear that the demonstrators were prepared to stay in the lobby until Senator McGovern came down to speak with them.

As the afternoon wore on, the management of the hotel began to regret its willingness to let the demonstrators stay. They had blocked off all of the public elevators and threatened to damage the lobby. Finally, McGovern, who was not fully aware of the sit-in, was brought up-to-date by Mankiewicz, Dutton, and me. When told of the demonstrators' demand, he immediately refused to go down to the lobby on the grounds that it was not "dignified." The others agreed. Eleanor McGovern kept an open mind. I argued strongly in favor of his speaking to the demonstrators because I feared that they would otherwise be removed by force—resulting in unnecessary physical injury and renewed public memories of the 1968 Chicago Convention. McGovern was concerned that talking with the demonstrators might make him seem to be too much of a radical. We urged him to stress his points of difference with them which would show that he shared the concerns of most Americans about such questions. Finally, he agreed, but we planned first for Mankiewicz to speak to the demonstrators to see whether his appearance would be sufficient. They listened politely to Mankiewicz for a few minutes but then renewed their demand that McGovern speak to them before they would leave.

Eventually McGovern came down. We approached the demonstrators from an unexpected side of the lobby, because the Secret Service felt this angle would provide better security. This caused some commotion while the crowd reoriented itself.

As soon as they began making this accommodation to McGovern, I was sure that we would be able to control the situation.

A live television camera was trained on McGovern as he answered the demonstrators' questions, which were no tougher than those he had fielded on many campuses. He was getting national prime time coverage handling a group of demonstrators with firmness and coolness. We thought it could not help but be a plus. Suddenly one of the Secret Service agents called me from McGovern's side to listen to a message coming over their radio. I was told that the Convention floor was asking us to terminate the confrontation. When I stepped up to tell Mankiewicz about the message, McGovern took his cue and ended the meeting. The demonstrators filed out of the hotel.

Later, I was anxious to determine the origin of the message from the floor. After some sleuthing, I discovered that it had come from Pierre Salinger who felt that we were taking too much television coverage away from the proceedings. (So apparently did Mrs. Henry Maier, the wife of the Mayor of Milwaukee, who was reportedly so miffed by her husband's speech having been preempted by the Doral episode that she endorsed Nixon.)

While all of our efforts had been devoted to winning the nomination, the "showdown at the O.K. Doral" was an effort to reach into the general election campaign itself. I had argued, before McGovern came down, that successive Presidents had allowed themselves to be isolated from the people by refusing to deal with demonstrators. As a result, Johnson and Nixon had been unwelcome in many places. I urged McGovern to show that he would be a different kind of President, one who could, once again, move freely in the country. In this way, he would represent a sharp contrast with Nixon. At the same time, he could show average Americans that he did not belong to the "crazies," that he would stand up to them and take issue with them. I felt that the confrontation was perhaps the most successful move we made at the Convention.

Despite his frustrations in trying to line up support from the Regulars and organized labor leadership, the Eagleton affair made it imperative for McGovern to seek the widest possible support from traditional Democrats and from organized labor. To gain this support, he would need the support of those leaders who had been hostile to him. He would have to make some painful compromises on people and positions. Clearly there was no other alternative than to try to induce Democrats to vote for the candidate of their Party. McGovern and the campaign leadership reasoned that if we were sound on the bread-and-butter issues most important to Democrats, we might be able to capitalize on the majority status of the Party in the country. This belief was reinforced by Gallup Poll findings during the summer that a majority of Americans believed that the Democratic Party could better achieve goals they considered important, particularly in the economy, than could the Republicans.

In August, McGovern and Sargent Shriver visited Lyndon Johnson at his ranch in Texas. The former President banned all outside press and cameras because he was not feeling well. Some writers immediately interpreted his action as a sign that his support for McGovern was lukewarm. Perhaps in an effort to counteract this belief and because of his appreciation for Johnson's having seen him when he was not well, McGovern called the visit one of the highpoints of his life.

This praise was topped by a statement by McGovern on the NBC "Today" Show on August 30. Asked about his statement on the former President in view of his bitter opposition to Johnson's war policy, McGovern said that "President Johnson inherited the war." This represented a major change in what McGovern had said over the years about the Johnson war policy especially in view of the escalation that the President had undertaken in 1965. McGovern had always been careful to point out that he had opposed the war under three Presidents—Kennedy, Johnson, and Nixon—and that it was not a partisan matter for him. Now, in what appeared to be an effort to appeal to traditional Democrats, he was turning the war into a narrowly partisan issue. Our Washington headquarters received many calls that day from protesting McGovern workers.

Of equally great symbolic importance was McGovern's coalition with Chicago Mayor Richard J. Daley. Despite the strong anti-Daley sentiments of many of his supporters, McGovern had never seen Daley as his opponent during the Presidential campaign. The South Dakotan realized that without Daley's help in Chicago, he had no hope of carrying that city or the state of Illinois. He believed that Daley cared little about ideology, but that he respected a winner. We had chosen not to run slates against Daley in the Illinois primary and we had sought a compromise when his delegates were challenged by Chicago liberals. In fact, McGovern even refused repeatedly to read Mike Royko's book, *Boss*, because he knew it was critical of Daley.

The Chicago mayor also needed McGovern. His candidate for State's Attorney, Edward Hanrahan, was under indictment for falsifying evidence in the shooting of two Black Panthers in Chicago. While Hanrahan had survived a primary challenge, he faced Republican opposition that might draw on the black and liberal vote in Cook County. Daley reasoned that if he actively backed McGovern, the South Dakotan's "natural" supporters would come out on Election Day and vote for both McGovern and Hanrahan. McGovern backed the entire Democratic slate without mentioning Hanrahan by name. Later, Hanrahan was acquitted of the charges. But the Daley strategy did not work in the end, for McGovern carried Chicago, while Hanrahan went down to defeat. McGovern's supporters had simply spilt their tickets. And they served notice that Dailey was not so invincible as the McGovern campaign leadership had thought he was.

An important part of the effort to attract the support of traditional Democrats was the participation of Senators Kennedy, Humphrey, and Muskie in he campaign. McGovern felt that if it could be demonstrated that these Party stalwarts were not only paying lip service to their support but were actively out on the campaign trail, it would help reassure Democratic voters.

Kennedy campaigned actively at McGovern's side in Chicago, Detroit, Pittsburgh, Philadelphia, New York, and other stops in the industrial Northeast. Muskie was especially effective in Pennsylvania and New Jersey, although at one stop he said that McGovern was fighting against "hopeless odds" and the national press seized on this quote and gave it wide publicity. Humphrey spent two days with McGovern in California, where he had done so much damage in the primaries, but later refused to campaign there on our behalf. As it turned out, he was right to concentrate his efforts on Minnesota, which McGovern had assumed we would be able to carry more easily than California.

O'Brien and Hart issued directives to the field organization to cooperate to the maximum with Regular Democrats. In many cases, this goal was achieved. In Massachusetts, for example, the party officials, who had been defeated by our forces in the primaries, nonetheless worked hard for McGovern's election. In New York, distrust seemed to persist between our campaign, now headed by former Mayor Robert Wagner, and the Bronx and Brooklyn Regulars. In the South, there was obviously little cooperation in many states.

One case will illustrate the problems that persisted until the end. On October 28 a rally was scheduled at the Seattle Center Arena with Senators Warren Magnuson and Scoop Jackson both attending. Magnuson had joined us earlier in the day in Spokane, while Jackson, McGovern's die-hard opponent for the nomination, stayed in Seattle, reportedly to attend a football game. Mankiewicz and I received word that, while Jackson would attend the rally, he would not speak. In part, he was uncertain of the reaction of the crowd, which was made up of McGovern partisans who had long been hostile to their junior Senator. Obviously we wanted Jackson's endorsement of McGovern in his own home state. Then, I found that, in addition to Jackson's own reluctance, the chairman of the meeting, a long-time opponent of the Jackson wing of the Party, did not want the Senator to speak. But he agreed to introduce him when I told him that Senator McGovern insisted. After Senator Magnuson finished speaking, the chairman rushed up to him and told him that he was to introduce Jackson. Magnuson, fully aware of what was happening, cooperated. And in order to avoid a hostile reaction, several campaign workers had stationed themselves at the front of the crowd and at the moment of the introduction had risen to "cheerlead." The result was a good greeting for Jackson and an endorsement from him. But it was hardly the sign of close cooperation between the Regulars and the McGovern forces. It was more like a shotgun marriage and a very temporary one at that.

With Shriver carrying the bulk of the burden, the Democratic ticket tried to build as wide support as possible with the leadership of organized labor. The United Auto Workers, one of the two large independents, was McGovern's strongest ally. There had never been any doubt that because of his anti-war and new priorities proposals, the U.A.W. would find him a natural candidate to support. Indeed, U.A.W. leadership was so progressive that they resisted vigorously when the concept of income redistribution was replaced by a new program. The Teamsters, the other large independent, formally supported Nixon. Their endorsement of the President was generally regarded in our camp as a quid pro quo for the release from Federal prison of their ex-president Jimmy Hoffa. In fact, when the labor members of the Pay Board quit in disgust over its unfairness to working people, Teamsters President Fitzsimmons remained. Only Harold Gibbons, the St. Louis-based director of the Teamsters Central Region, a long-time opponent of the war, remained loyal to McGovern and the Democrats. (In December, Fitzsimmons removed him from his post for this act of disloyalty.)

The situation in the AFL–CIO was somewhat more complex. In April, George Meany had said: "I have no objection to George McGovern at this time." He thought McGovern had no chance. But Meany had since become openly hostile to McGovern. The most important underlying reason was undoubtedly Al Barkan's opposition, based on the exclusion of top union leadership from the Democratic National Convention as a result of the McGovern Commission reforms. These reforms did not prevent the selection of union leaders as delegates, but Barkan felt that, in return for the financial and volunteer support provided by organized labor, its leaders should be exempt from the democratic process and should automatically be given a dominant role in Party affairs.

But Meany also disliked McGovern's foreign policy. The international operations of the AFL–CIO had long been headed by Jay Lovestone, a reformed Communist movement leader. Lovestone had turned against Communism and now professed to see a Communist under every bed. He found McGovern's Vietnam views very suspect. Meany, following the instruction of this tutor, said, on Labor Day 1972: "Frankly, when I read the things that

George McGovern stands for and I find out he's become an apologist for the Communist world, my goodness, doesn't this man know there are no countries in the world where people chose communism?"

In my view, the most significant reason for Meany's coolness was his understanding that McGovern was completely independent of him. While McGovern had an excellent labor voting record and had always enjoyed the support of the South Dakota AFL–CIO, Meany felt that he was essentially a farm state Senator who had not depended on labor in the past and had few debts to it. His stance on Vietnam and even on Nixon's New Economic Policy had been arrived at independently of the unions. So Meany did not really know McGovern and deeply mistrusted him. And he may actually have been led to believe that McGovern espoused the views of some of his supporters on abortion and homosexual relations and marijuana, which he knew were unacceptable to his rank-and-file membership.

Even McGovern's flight from South Dakota to Washington in July, interrupting his vacation in the Black Hills to cast the decisive vote in the Senate on minimum wage legislation, failed to move Meany. He was, he said, "neutral" between McGovern and Nixon and would not vote for either. But his neutrality allowed him to play golf with the President, while he would not speak to McGovern, even on the telephone. Prior to the Convention, McGovern had tried to meet with Meany but had been rebuffed.

The "neutrality" dictum did not extend to the international unions that make up the AFL–CIO, and leaders of most of the larger unions endorsed McGovern. An organization called Labor for McGovern-Shriver was created during the summer, run by Howard Samuel of the Amalgamated Clothing Workers and headed by Joe Keenen, the retired chief of the International Brotherhood of Electrical Workers and Joe Bierne of the Communications Workers. Keenen was selected to head the group because he agreed with Meany on the war, if not on McGovern, and remained a poker pal of the big union chief. He could keep the door open for Meany. Jerry Wurf of the State, County and Municipal Employees Union had been the chief force behind the formation of the group, but had been pushed aside because he was clearly identified as one of the few anti-war members of the AFL–CIO Executive Council and not the least bit afraid to stand up for his views. Other key McGovern backers were Al Grospiron of the Oil, Chemical and Atomic Workers and leaders of other non-industrial unions.

The "neutrality" ban extended to the state labor federations, which were barred from endorsing either candidate. But Herrick Roth, the transplanted South Dakotan who headed the Colorado federation, led his group to an open endorsement. Meany could not tolerate such opposition and moved to take control of the Colorado group. When Roth opposed this take-over in Federal Court, he was vindicated on the grounds that his group's endorsement had nothing to do with the conduct of union functions. In return for this dedicated support, Shriver somewhat hesitantly journeyed to Denver to speak to the state convention, but only after McGovern had directed him to do so.

Other state federations either imitated Colorado's defiance or more often passed resolutions calling on their workers to oppose Nixon's re-election. Despite Meany's protests, powerful federations in Texas and California as well as such disparate groups as Maine and North Carolina, openly worked for McGovern-Shriver.

The rifts within the labor movement indicated the end of the unchallenged reign of George Meany. It was not so much that the labor movement was to undergo a transformation because of the 1972 campaign; it was more that progressive unions were becoming increasingly restive with the dictatorial rule from Washington. Many rank-and-file members felt that Meany was becoming a part of the Establishment they opposed. As a result, a new cohesion was developing among the independent International Union of Machinists, the U.A.W., and the more progressive unions in the AFL–CIO. By his anti-McGovern stance, Meany precipitated the process and weakened his own authority. And, at the same time, the rebellious unions were forced to create Labor for McGovern-Shriver to replace the Committee on Political Education of the AFL–CIO and probably expended more energy for the Democratic ticket than they otherwise would have done.

In the end, McGovern's efforts to win the support of Party Regulars and labor leadership met with mixed success. Some Party leaders, with an eye to their future need for the support of McGovern partisans, gave at least token support to the national ticket. The Labor for McGovern-Shriver organization provided valuable support for the ticket, but Meany's "neutrality" obviously amounted to a tacit endorsement of President Nixon.

But McGovern lost the votes of about one-third of the Democrats who voted and of the majority of members of organized labor. Perhaps, after all of our efforts, their party affiliation or labor union membership (or both because the two groups overlapped) were far less relevant than we had thought. Perhaps McGovern lost their votes because of their perceptions of him as a person and because of weaknesses in our campaign strategy.

6

THE
EAGLETON AFFAIR

"And now a guy named Tom who comes along
and some people say he's going to blow the
whole thing for McGovern"—Senator Thomas
F. Eagleton, July 28, 1972.

A HEARTBEAT AWAY FROM THE PRESIDENCY . . . THE
PRESIDENT OF THE UNITED STATES SENATE . . . PAR-
TICIPANT IN CABINET AND NATIONAL SECURITY
COUNCIL SESSIONS . . . POLITICAL HEIR TO THE PRES-
IDENT . . . THE VICE PRESIDENT OF THE UNITED
STATES.

The person selected to seek this office on the Democratic ticket
would face no primaries, would solicit no votes, would wage
no formal campaign. He would be "elected" by one man—the
nominee of the Party for the Presidency.

What was the state of mind of this "electorate"?

George McGovern wanted Ted Kennedy to be his running
mate and believed that he could convince him to accept the
nomination. Time after time, he had seen Presidential nominees
call their choices to their hotel rooms and, after an appeal on
behalf of the Party and the nation, convince the annointed that

he should accept the assignment. Despite his own preference to remain in the Senate rather than to accept a bid to run for Vice President, McGovern had once told me that it would be impossible for him to turn down such a bid from the Presidential nominee. To that extent, McGovern believed that no man turned down the Vice Presidency. The Vice Presidency has never been considered a political plum, but in recent years there has been a growing awareness that a highly qualified person must stand in the wings in case something happens to the President.

Since 1970, Kennedy had denied both publicly and privately that he would accept either the Presidential or Vice Presidential nomination in 1972. After the Chappaquidick incident, he had pledged to perform faithfully his duties as Senator for the entire term which ends in 1976. He realized that Chappaquidick would be an issue if he ran.

Naturally, there were a great many Kennedy partisans who wanted the last surviving brother of an illustrious family to seek the highest office. But the notoriety he enjoyed as a Kennedy made him the target of more assassination threats than any other man in public life. The Massachusetts Senator felt a strong obligation to his family, and especially to the children of his slain brothers, to protect himself by avoiding the race.

Even so, McGovern was so firm in his belief that he could convince Kennedy when the time came that he paid relatively little attention to the question of the Vice Presidency. In private conversations, he suggested that Kennedy might well accept the offer as a means of rehabilitating himself before the American public. Running as the number two man would be an act of modesty on his part, perhaps even an act of contrition. In addition, McGovern said he would allow his running mate to expose himself to fewer public gatherings and hence to less danger than the Presidential nominee would face. His great strength with working people, blacks, and chicanos could be exploited simply by placing his name on the ballot. In addition, he could devote much of his time to bringing the party leaders back into the Democratic fold.

In June Jules Witcover of the *Los Angeles Times,* who had recently written a book about Spiro Agnew, asked me what

McGovern was thinking about the Vice Presidency. I was forced to admit that McGovern had given little thought to the office. Witcover asked to have a chance to interview McGovern and urged us to attach greater importance to the choice. I passed his views on to McGovern in hopes that they would trigger discussion about the Vice Presidency. Witcover later spoke with McGovern directly.

The conclusion of the primary campaign and the struggle to win the California challenge contest prevented both McGovern and his staff from devoting any time to the consideration of the alternatives to Kennedy. Some staff members knew that McGovern had spoken with Kennedy about the Vice Presidential slot during the spring, and we believed that the candidate might have received a measure of encouragement during his chats on the floor of the Senate. I suspected that McGovern must have some cause to believe that Kennedy would accept, because he raised the question of Kennedy's running several times in our discussions. I noted that we ran the risk of a "tail wags dog" situation, with Kennedy possibly outdrawing McGovern on the campaign trail and getting as much or more media attention. McGovern believed that such a situation would not arise and that he could hold his own as the Presidential nominee.

Yet McGovern was making a few other soundings about possible running mates. He was intrigued with the possibility of Connecticut Senator Abe Ribicoff, who was one of his closest friends in the Senate. Ribicoff was identified with the Kennedy wing of the Party and had been one of the first backers of John F. Kennedy in 1960. He came from the urbanized East, had experience as a governor, Cabinet member, and Senator, and had good ties with the business community. And he was a Jew. McGovern asked me to check on his relationship with the Jewish community. I replied that Ribicoff's nomination would be a source of pride.

During the New York primary, the two spent Sunday, June 18 together campaigning in Brooklyn. At his room in the Biltmore, with me as his witness, McGovern asked Ribicoff to consider accepting the nomination if Kennedy refused. The 62-year-old Senator pleaded that he was too old to play second fiddle to any other person including the President. He asked not to be considered for the job. Had he accepted at that time I have little doubt that he would have been the second choice after Kennedy. And in just that casual way, a Jew would have been named to a national ticket for the first time. McGovern told me that he thought the country was ready.

One other discussion on the Vice Presidency took place a couple of weeks later when McGovern met privately with U.A.W. President Leonard Woodcock in Washington. McGovern asked Woodcock's views on the office and then suggested he might consider the union leader for the job. Woodcock was flattered and clearly interested. Word of the discussion got into the press, probably from U.A.W. sources.

McGovern did go so far as to prepare a list of possible running mates in early July. He told Hart that Kennedy seemed firm in his refusal despite a Boston *Globe* article a couple of weeks earlier that he might consider running if his candidacy could make the difference between winning and losing. But McGovern was not ready for any full-scale discussion of alternatives. He was keeping the matter pretty much to himself.

On Wednesday, July 12, the day he became the nominee of his Party, McGovern took the first formal step in the process of selecting a running mate. He left me with no doubt that he would select his own running mate, although during the primaries he had hinted that he might throw the Convention open. In fact, he was too concerned about being saddled by a Vice Presidential candidate overly identified with the Left to take that course.

He asked me to canvass all the key members of the staff in order to get their first four choices. He wanted to see the list that evening. Throughout the day, I collected bits and pieces of paper. We had no discussion. It was not until I tabulated the preferences from more than a score of people that I obtained any idea of their common leanings.

A vast majority of the staff wanted Kennedy. Beyond that, the names of Minnesota Senator Fritz Mondale, Florida Governor Reubin Askew, Woodcock, Missouri Senator Tom Eagleton, Maine Senator Ed Muskie (the 1968 Vice Presidential nominee),

Idaho Senator Frank Church, Wisconsin Governor Pat Lucey, Ribicoff, and DNC Chairman Larry O'Brien were among the most frequently mentioned. McGovern was interested in the more obvious possibilities. Then he laid the paper aside and said no more about the Vice Presidency.

Later that evening, George McGovern officially became the Democratic nominee for President. After a moment to accept the congratulations of his staff (his family was at the Convention Hall), McGovern retired to his bedroom to take a call from Ted Kennedy at Hyannis.

The newly-named leader of the Democratic Party accepted Kennedy's best wishes and made a valiant attempt to convince his caller that he should accept the number two spot. Using a sheet of notes prepared by Dick Dougherty, McGovern spoke virtually uninterruptedly for 20 minutes and laid out all the arguments—Kennedy's broad appeal, his unique role in the Party and the country, the kind of campaign that could be run to suit his needs. Most importantly, he laid out the case that Ted Van Dyk had succinctly made in his memo listing his four choices earlier that day: "Frankly, I think our chances without EMK are long; with him, they're at least even." McGovern stuck to the practical points and avoided any sentimental call to duty or patriotism.

Now it was McGovern's turn to listen. Kennedy thanked him for the offer but immediately refused. He cited his obligations to his family as his sole reason for refusing. McGovern, who betrayed no surprise at the rejection, pressed on. He reminded Kennedy that the campaign could be designed so that he would not be unduly exposed. But Kennedy maintained that his family obligations, to say nothing of those to the people of Massachuetts, prevented him from changing his mind. McGovern understood and did not ask again.

To show that his refusal did not imply any lack of support for McGovern, Kennedy said he would fly down from Hyannis the following day. He agreed to introduce McGovern to the Convention.

When McGovern hung up the phone, he told those of us in the room what we already knew from following his conversation. Then he added, "You had better get everybody together first thing in the morning to come up with some suggestions."

I was surprised. I felt sure that after the call, McGovern would tell us who his next choice would be and solicit our views on the name, especially after having seen our preference list. So now, with only about 15 hours left, not counting time out for sleep, we were to begin the selection process.

The following morning, July 13, at about nine, a score of the McGovern staff straggled into the Board Room at the Doral. Most of us were weary from loss of sleep, having devoted the three preceding nights to the battles on the Convention floor. We knew that within about two hours, the Senator expected to have our recommendations.

We had no framework for our discussion. McGovern had indicated no preferences. Pat Caddell, who had conducted some polling in June about the impact of various running mates, could only tell us that, with the exception of Kennedy's obvious strength, no other possibility had a significant effect on McGovern's chances.

With nowhere to start, we began throwing out all of the names that any of us thought should be considered. I kept a list which contained these names:

MUSKIE

MILLS   (Wilbur, chairman of the House Ways and Means Committee)

LUCEY

EAGLETON

STEVENSON   (Adlai III, Senator from Illinois)

WOODCOCK

RIBICOFF

HART   (Philip, Senator from Michigan)

BAYH   (Birch, Senator from Indiana)

SHRIVER   (Sargent, former Peace Corps head and Kennedy's brother-in-law)

GILLIGAN   (John, Governor of Ohio)

CHURCH

CRONKITE   (Walter, CBS Evening News Anchorman and reputedly the most respected public figure)

NELSON	(Gaylord, Senator from Wisconsin)
WHITE	(Kevin, Mayor of Boston)
HESBURGH	(Father Theodore, head of the U.S. Civil Rights Commission)
BUMPERS	(Dale, Governor of Arkansas)
HARRIS	(Fred, Senator from Oklahoma)
O'BRIEN	
MONDALE	
LANDRIEU	(Moon, Mayor of New Orleans)
O'HARA	(James, Congressman from Michigan)
FARENTHOLD	(Cissy, defeated candidate for the Democratic Senate nomination in Texas)

These were the 23 names we took under consideration. Askew was taken at his word that he did not want to be considered; Ribicoff was not. Nobody proposed Hubert Humphrey. I suggested we consider a person who could appeal to the disaffected across Party lines, but this proposal was rejected. The consensus was that we must seek a running mate who was compatible with McGovern's views but who would help us patch things up with the Regulars. A black or a Republican running mate would not achieve this purpose.

We then proceeded to eliminate from the list any name for which there was no support. We were able to work quickly and no sharp conflicts emerged because none of the participants had made himself the champion of one of the people on the list.

The final list included: Lucey, Shriver, Nelson, O'Brien, Church, White, Ribicoff, and Eagleton.

Eagleton had a good record in the Senate and seemed personable. Someone mentioned that he had succeeded in knocking the main battle tank out of the defense budget. We recognized that neither McGovern nor the staff knew him well, although one participant questioned whether he was up to the job of President. The Missourian had told a national television audience the preceding evening that he wanted the nomination. This interview had impressed us. Rick Stearns, who had come down to Miami early to line up delegates said that a newsman, from the *St. Louis Post-Dispatch* he thought, had told him that "around Missouri, there are strong rumors of alcoholism or mental illness—or both—in his background." Some said if these charges were true, Eagleton would be elminated from consideration. We all nodded in agreement.

By now it was 11 A.M. We felt we were ready to go to Mc-Govern. As the final list was drawn up, Nelson and Church were removed from those first to be considered. Thus, we had a final list of six (not seven as I erroneously told the press that day). Just before we left the room, there was a brief discussion on how we would proceed. We agreed not to talk with the newsmen hovering outside. Mankiewicz said he would go to McGovern's suite to inform him of our conclusions and to sit in on meetings with leaders of the black, women's, and youth caucuses and of the New Democratic Coalition who had asked to see the candidate. Following these meetings, McGovern would have to make his choice.

Of the six possibilities, four—Lucey, Shriver, O'Brien, and Ribicoff—were either well-known to at least one staff member or to the Senator. Two—Eagleton and White—were relatively unknown to us. I suggested that we should find out what we could about them and volunteered to undertake the check on them while McGovern was meeting with the caucus leaders. In fact, before we left the room, I placed a call to line up one of my possible sources of information on White. He would be available for my call later.

Shortly after this—at about 11:15 A.M.—the meeting broke up, and I went directly to my room on the top floor of the Doral to begin my checking. At the time, I did not believe that either White or Eagleton would be selected because neither of them was particularly close to McGovern. But I went to work to gather what information I could and by 1:20 P.M., I was able to go to the McGovern suite to report on my findings.

On White, I had been able to collect a good deal of information. Generally, our initial impression was borne out. Here was an enlightened, attractive, honest mayor whose most serious failing might have been his defeat in the gubernatorial contest with the popular imcumbent, Francis Sargent. But at least one Cambridge source was critical and rated White as ineffective. This view had to be somewhat discounted because of the known antipathy of the Cambridge academic community to Boston's City Hall and because White had opposed the intellectuals behind McGovern with his own primary campaign for Muskie.

As for Eagleton, I learned that there had been stories about his alleged excessive drinking while he was both Attorney General and Lieutenant Governor of Missouri. Other stories circulated around Washington that he had been seen leaving parties under the influence of too much alcohol. It was known in Missouri that he had been hospitalized, ostensibly for a stomach problem, although it was in fact in connection with drinking. The story I got was that in the hospital it had been determined that he was neither an alcoholic who depended on drink nor a person with too poor judgment to know when to stop drinking. Instead the hospital had diagnosed a physiological problem which gave him a low tolerance for alcohol. As a result, limited drinking could affect him more than a normal person.

My research indicated that Eagleton had not let the matter interfere with his political activities. In fact, during one campaign he had reportedly stuck to milk as his beverage and had avoided any trouble since he came to Washington in 1969 as a Senator.

I interpreted the reference to mental health problems "in his background" to relate to other members of his family. There was no evidence available that any member of his family had any such difficulty. In settling on this interpretation of what was meant by "in his background," I was in error. After the election, in reconstructing those events, I was to learn from Stearns's source that he had been referring to Eagleton himself during his early days in politics.

I also learned that Eagleton was relatively bright and quick. He was considered a good politician with an intuitive grasp of the electorate and the issues.

At the same time as I was checking on Eagleton and White, another key conversation was taking place. We would know nothing of it until long after the election. An old political friend had called Anne Wexler, a Connecticut Democrat who had become active in our campaign after the collapse of the Muskie campaign. He told her that Eagleton had been mentally ill and had been hospitalized. Wexler, who was sick in bed, dressed and went to McGovern's penthouse headquarters to pass the word on. She claims that she told Rick Stearns, who promised he would relay the message to McGovern. But Stearns claims that he was asleep in his room at the time. Had Wexler's message gotten through, I am sure that Eagleton would never have been selected. In any event, McGovern never heard of it.

When I joined McGovern and other staff members in his suite at about 1:20 P.M., I found that the caucus representatives had left. According to Salinger, the caucus representative had suggested Cissy Farenthold and had indicated support for Shriver and White. McGovern and the staff then ruled out Ribicoff on the basis of his refusals and learned that Mondale did not want to give up re-election to the Senate by seeking the Vice Presidency. Salinger and Mankiewicz then urged that McGovern try Shriver. But when Salinger put a call in to his Washington office, he learned that Shriver was in Moscow on business. So he missed his chance at the nomination.

On my arrival, I reported that I had information on both White and Eagleton. There was no interest in the material I had on Eagleton, I was told, because he had been eliminated from consideration. White was of greater interest. This suited me. Although I had remained neutral in the previous discussions, I was now leaning toward White.

I passed on my generally positive report on White and noted that my informants had said that Ted Kennedy would not be likely to stand in the way of his nomination. This confirmed information from Liz Stevens, a close friend of Ethel Kennedy. Yet Kennedy's apparent willingness to let another Massachusetts politician place himself in line for the Democratic Presidential nomination surprised some of us, especially the Senator.

White appeared to be the most likely choice, although both Lucey and O'Brien remained in the running.

Mostly on the basis of the information I had gathered on White, McGovern decided that he would probably invite him to join the ticket. We placed a call to the Mayor, who was vacationing on Cape Cod, to determine if he would be interested in being considered. He was enthusiastic. He could arrange to be with us in Miami that evening. McGovern said he would call him back shortly. It looked as if one of the two unknowns—White and Eagleton—would be the nominee. Stearns was asked to prepare the necessary papers with White's name in order to make the 3 P.M. filing deadline.

At this point, there was a momentary lull in the conversation, and I asked if anybody was interested in my report on Eagleton. McGovern, Mankiewicz, and other staff members listened as I gave a full report of what I had learned. I mentioned that the story about his hospitalization for his physiological problem apparently disposed of the charges of alcoholism. I told the group that I had found no indication of mental problems in his family, which was quite prominent in St. Louis.

McGovern and the others, although somewhat concerned, said that my report took care of the rumors. After all, Eagleton had already survived several campaigns in Missouri, despite these rumors. They could easily be laid to rest during the course of a campaign if Eagleton were the choice. I thought that Mc-Govern was making a political judgment with a small measure of risk, because shooting down a rumor like that could get to be a major annoyance in a campaign. But the possibility of Eagleton's selection seemed slight and we turned to other matters.

McGovern than called Senator Kennedy to make absolutely sure that the choice of White would be acceptable to the Bay State's leading Democrat. Kennedy said he would not object to White but urged consideration of other possibilities, principally Ribicoff, who had already turned us down repeatedly and Mills, who McGovern considered too conservative. Then McGovern suggested that Kennedy reconsider his own refusal in view of his lack of enthusiasm for White and the unavailability of Ribicoff. To our surprise, Kennedy agreed to think it over and said he would call back in 30 minutes. After McGovern hung up, we were jubilant. Perhaps we had stumbled onto the one way to get Ted Kennedy to say "yes."

A second courtesy call went to Ken Galbraith in order to solicit the views of the Massachusetts delegation on White. The Harvard economics professor, a close friend of both McGovern and

Kennedy, was the Senator's own best contact in the delegation. Galbraith, not available, would call back.

While we waited for Kennedy's call, reports of opposition to White filtered in. He was said not to carry enough weight around the country. We used this pause to ask for an extension of the filing time until 4 P.M.

McGovern later told me and other staff members that he regretted that we did not, at this point, ask for the Vice Presidential nomination to be delayed until Friday. In fact, none of us gave any thought to such an extension because we believed that the ultimate decision was in O'Brien's hands and that he would be reluctant to push the Democratic Party $85,000 further into debt just to oblige us. It never occurred to any of us that George McGovern was now the nominee and head of the Party and he could require that the extension be granted. We were thinking like outsiders, not like the leadership of the Democratic Party. It was hard to change roles overnight.

Then came the two calls that sealed White's fate. Kennedy said that he would not reconsider his own decision not to run. McGovern had the clear feeling that he would lose Kennedy's help in the campaign if he went ahead with White. But Kennedy offered his plane to bring White down if we wanted him. Then Ken Galbraith called and delivered a scathing blast at White as an incompetent. He told McGovern that the entire Massachusetts delegation had caucused and had unanimously agreed that all 110 delegates (there were only 102) would walk out of the Convention as a body if White were the choice. He said that Father Drinan, the delegation chairman, was at his side prepared to back him up. Obviously this kind of demonstration would greatly embarrass both McGovern and White. Despite my urgent gestures, McGovern did not ask to speak with Drinan. (Months later, McGovern would say that he was not so much concerned by Massachusetts opposition as by his need to find "somebody better known nationally.")

McGovern hung up the phone obviously agitated. He had thought the search was nearly over. Now he had to begin again. Despite comments by Dick Dougherty, Hart, and me that the Galbraith reaction was the result of the age-old Boston-Cambridge rivalry and perhaps representative of Kennedy's views, McGovern felt he could not defend the choice of White to Galbraith because he hardly knew the mayor. He turned to us and said: "I don't care about the political wisdom of the choice. I want sombody I know, somebody I can work with. Let's get Gaylord Nelson on the phone."

It was now 3 P.M.

While the call to Nelson was being put through, I contacted the Massachusetts delegation to learn more about Galbraith's report. I spoke to a member of the delegation from the extreme western part of the state who said that no caucus on White's selection had been held and that, while there was undoubtedly some opposition from the Boston area to his selection, most members of the delegation would accept McGovern's pick. The caucus, which had been held in the morning, merely urged that the delegation be consulted before any nomination were made. Later that afternoon I confronted Galbraith, who admitted exaggerating the opposition to White.

I returned to the Senator's suite well aware that my new information would not change matters. McGovern obviously did not want to stir up a hornet's nest when he was not sure of himself. He wanted to make a quick selection and then get back to work on the acceptance speech.

Just as I entered, McGovern was ending his conversation with Nelson. He told us that Nelson and his wife had agreed that the Wisconsin Senator would not accept the nomination. With that, McGovern said simply: "Well, I guess it's Eagleton," and asked that a call be placed to the Missouri Senator. I was a little surprised that Eagleton was next on the list, but there was no time left now for discussion.

While he was waiting for the connection, McGovern called Ted Van Dyk to the side to ask for his view of the choice. Van Dyk was better informed on Eagleton's record than any other staff member. But before McGovern was able to get a complete answer, Eagleton came on the line. At that same moment, I received a message that somebody was waiting for me in the hall with more information on Eagleton. I tore from the suite, only to learn that further checking revealed no new information. By the time I returned to the suite the conversation with Eagleton was over and we had a running mate. The second of the unknowns had been chosen.

During my brief absence, both McGovern and Mankiewicz had spoken with Eagleton. The first conversation was extremely brief and has been well documented. In it, Eagleton told McGovern: "George, before you change your mind, I hasten to accept." He had awaited McGovern's call all day.

The Mankiewicz-Eagleton conversation has been subject to controversy. According to the best evidence available—a tape recording by Bob Hardy of St. Louis' KMOX radio of Eagleton's side of his conversation with McGovern and Mankiewicz, the Missourian turned Mankiewicz over to Doug Bennet, his assistant, for biographical information and to discuss the arrangements that evening. Then the tape ends. It appears that Eagleton then came back on the line. He claims that Mankiewicz merely asked him if he had any skeletons in his closet; Mankiewicz says he gave specific examples of the kinds of problems that might have arisen in the past in hopes of drawing an answer relating to the checking I had done. Several staff members back Mankiewicz up on this. It is likely that Mankiewicz ran all these points into a single sentence, eliciting a single negative response from Eagleton. At no time did Eagleton volunteer that he had been hospitalized for any reason whatever.

Mankiewicz then went downstairs in the Doral to announce to the press the selection of Eagleton. I hurried down ahead of Mankiewicz so I would not miss any of the questions. I dreaded that there might be one relating to his hospitalization. At last, we had arrived at our choice. I was afraid that the rumors would begin to plague us immediately. But no one mentioned them.

Later, as I waited in the lobby, Senator Eagleton, Bennet, and other members of his party entered. I met the Senator and took him directly to McGovern's suite. The conversation between the two lasted for about a half-hour, but there was no discussion of matters of substance. Much of the time was devoted to planning the events of that evening. McGovern was impatient to get back to the acceptance speech which was moving toward completion. Eagleton was clearly nervous throughout the meeting, but was agreeable to our suggestions regarding his appearance that evening and left us with the clear impression that we had made a good choice. The next time we would see Eagleton would be at Convention Hall at about 2:30 A.M. By now there was a whirlwind of activity at our Doral headquarters and Eagleton left quickly. We would complete work later on the seconders and on his acceptance speech. Our speechwriters had some suggestions for him.

During the evening while McGovern napped, I watched the interminable nominations of candidates for the Vice Presidency. Shortly after 9 P.M. one of my sources called to say that new rumors were circulating on the floor of the Convention. According to one, Eagleton had a history of alcoholism. I dismissed this charge as being the one we had already run down. The second, reportedly coming from a television newsman from New York's WPIX, claimed that Eagleton had been institutionalized for mental problems.

I immediately phoned this information to our people on the floor of the Convention. We also now knew that the person who had originally spoken with Rick Stearns was Loye Miller of the Knight newspapers. Our people on the floor, led by press secretary Kirby Jones, began trying to track down Miller as well as the others on the floor who might have information on Eagleton.

In retrospect it might have been possible at this point to suggest that McGovern ask for a suspension in the proceedings. If we felt the information was too damaging, we could have, even then, chosen another nominee. Yet, since Mankiewicz's press conference, the process seemed to be inexorably under way. The best we could do, I thought, was to find out all we could in order to deal with whatever stories might arise in the campaign.

It was unfortunate that we could only determine the identity of our original informant at this late date. Miller, it would later turn out, had more information concerning the stories about Eagleton. While he had been the chief of *Time* magazine's Chicago bureau, he had heard rumors of drinking and mental health problems. Then, during the 1968 Senatorial race, a member of his bureau had picked up further rumors about Eagleton having been hospitalized for mental health problems. The *Time* staffer had filed this information with his editors but it had not been printed because these rumors played no part in the campaign.

The nomination and balloting for the Vice Presidency dragged on and the McGovern party did not go to the Convention Hall until about 2 A.M. on Friday.

When we returned to the Doral at about 4 A.M., the McGovern and Eagleton parties went into the nominee's suite preparatory to going to the rooftop restaurant for a reception. I asked Doug Bennet if he would step into my room for a brief chat.

I had not called Bennet earlier that day when I was checking the Eagleton rumors because I felt I had no authority to inform the Eagleton camp that their man was under active considera-tion. Now, without preamble, I told Bennet that we had heard stories of alcoholism and perhaps about mental problems cir-culating on the Convention floor that night and that I thought it best for us to know all we could in order to deal with the inevitable stories that would arise during the campaign.

Bennet replied that it was true that a story had been told in Missouri of Eagleton's having been found slumped over the wheel of his car during the 1960 campaign. Following that cam-paign, Bennet told me, Eagleton had been hospitalized for men-tal exhaustion and depression. But Bennet stressed that Eagleton had not been committed to the hospital, that he had placed himself under medical care. I urged Bennet to tell Eagleton to be forthright about the problem when it came to light because the only way to deal with such matters was by disclosure. I asked Bennet why Eagleton had not told McGovern about his hospitalization earlier. Bennet said that the whole matter had seemed so minor that it had not occurred to them to mention it. I believe that, at that time, Bennet himself did not know the full story.

Bennet reported back to Eagleton. As Eagleton himself later reported: "Even after some of my staff mentioned the rumors that were floating around the Convention floor on Thursday night, I didn't think about it. For one thing those rumors were about booze. And they are simply untrue, flatly absolutely un-true. But there was also the euphoria." Eagleton had already decided that "I would take a calculated risk that the story would not leak out, at least in the form it ultimately did. I thought it would be sort of a general story that I had once suffered from a fatigue problem." Obviously my advice about disclosure was not yet going to be followed.

But Bennet's mere use of the words "depression" and "committed" concerned me and I went up to the reception immediately. I found both Mankiewicz and Hart standing near the door to the Starlight Roof, and I told them both all that I had just learned. I urged Frank to come up with some way of dealing with this 1960 hospitalization. His first reaction was that Eagleton should use a Sunday discussion program, on which he would appear in two days, to say that he was such a hard campaigner that he had to go to the hospital for a rest after an earlier campaign.

None of us informed McGovern at this time, given the hour and the circumstances. For the first time that week, I went for a swim.

At this point, I withdrew from direct involvement in the Eagleton affair. Because my own future status on the campaign was unsettled by the Senator and the object of some controversy among the staff, I had decided to leave Miami Beach the next day for a week's rest. (My departure had nothing to do with the Eagleton case.)

I later learned that, on the following day, *Time* had sent a correspondent to St. Louis on the basis of the information that had been turned up in the files from 1963. This reporter was to draw a blank. Dr. Mark Eagleton, the Senator's brother, denied that there had been any serious problem and said that Tom had neither been in Johns Hopkins for a stomach problem, as the public story had it, nor at the Barnes Hospital in St. Louis for mental exhaustion, where we would later learn he had actually been. Instead Tom had stayed with him, and Dr. Eagleton showed the reporter the room where Tom had been all the time.

Thus the press had already begun to work on the story although it ran into the same kind of stone wall that I had found.*

---

* One reporter, Paul Lewis of the London *Financial Times*, claimed to have learned earlier in the week about Eagleton's mental problems at a British diplomatic luncheon. Either the diplomatic corps and the foreign press were privy to information not yet available to the American press or it was a case of rumor being stated as fact.

Mankiewicz and Bennet talked again on Friday, July 14, and reportedly we learned then of a second case of hospitalization. They arranged to speak another time on Saturday evening before Eagleton's appearance on television. By that time, Mankiewicz was vacationing in the Virgin Islands. He talked with Eagleton who gave him no additional details. Eagleton did not allude to his hospitalization when he appeared the following day. But Mankiewicz was concerned enough to call McGovern. The Senator in turn called Eagleton but gained little information on the seriousness of his illness.

On Monday, July 17, the case took a new turn. An anonymous caller tried to reach both Hart and Mankiewicz at the McGovern campaign headquarters in Washington. Both were in the Virgin Islands, and the message was not relayed because it was like many other crank calls purporting to have important information for the campaign.

Then the same caller is supposed to have contacted John Knight III at the *Detroit Free Press*. He was apparently a young man claiming to be a McGovern supporter. He feared that irreparable damage could be done to the McGovern campaign if information concerning Eagleton's hospitalization for mental illness were made public. The Republicans had the information, he said, and might very well use it. Knight was unable to learn his identity or any further details on Eagleton's background. But the newspaperman was able to extract a promise from him that he would call again. In later calls that week, the informant, obviously young and nervous, gave Knight the name of the hospital in St. Louis and of the doctor and, after some confusion, the dates of hospitalization and the fact that he had undergone electroshock therapy.

Clark Hoyt of the Knight newspapers was then in St. Louis preparing a profile on Eagleton. Armed with the information that had come to Knight, he spoke to the Senator's doctor who remained ethically uninformative. But he was plainly panicked by the question. Another medical source said that he would not deny the story. These reactions lent credence to the anonymous tip.

On Wednesday, July 19, Hart and Mankiewicz had returned to Washington and had found the message from the anonymous caller. The next morning they had breakfast with Eagleton in the Senate dining room. They learned that he had been hospitalized in 1960, 1964, and 1966 for mental exhaustion and depression. They extracted from him confirmation of the electroshock treatment. Hart and Mankiewicz made it clear that McGovern would need to see his medical records. Although McGovern was in town, he was busy with meetings and deferred a session with Eagleton until the next week.

On Friday, the candidate, together with the top leadership of his campaign flew back to Sylvan Lake in the Black Hills of South Dakota for a full dress staff meeting, and to enable the candidate to continue his vacation which had been interrupted for a major Senate vote. I had rejoined the group.

Although I was then unaware of it as we flew west Hart and Mankiewicz filled the McGoverns in on their conversation with Eagleton. For the first time, McGovern learned the full details of Eagleton's illness. While Mankiewicz argued that Eagleton should be dropped from the ticket and Hart urged McGovern to get his medical records, they all agreed to wait to make a final decision until Eagleton and McGovern met on Tuesday in South Dakota.

On Sunday he appeared on "Face the Nation" and mentioned Eagleton several times, commenting at one point on the kind of campaign that Eagleton would run. It seems clear that he was not yet concerned about his running mate.

Knight newspaper reporters, acting according to the highest standards of journalism, had brought their story to Mankiewicz on Sunday. Their memo said that Eagleton had been hospitalized in St. Louis for "severe manic depressive psychosis with suicidal tendencies." Mankiewicz asked for a little time to check and promised to be back in touch.

Late on Monday, July 24, the Eagletons arrived at Sylvan Lake. Almost all of the McGovern staff had returned to Washington. The following morning, George and Eleanor McGovern and Tom and Barbara Eagleton had breakfast together. Here for the first time McGovern came face to face with his running mate's past mental health problems. Eagleton confirmed his treatment for mental depression. McGovern was sympathetic to

Eagleton, but wondered to himself why he had not been told of the hospitalizations earlier. He apparently believed that the revelation of Eagleton's past illness would be an immediate sensation that would soon die away. To those around him, McGovern seemed unhappy but above all compassionate for the ordeal to which Eagleton would be subjected. It was out of this compassion that he immediately turned down Eagleton's pro forma offer to resign from the ticket.

It was unprecedented in American politics to ask the Vice Presidential candidate to step down and then to select his replacement through the National Committee. Clearly McGovern would prefer to wait until we saw the public reaction. But in coming to this initial conclusion, neither McGovern nor Hart and Mankiewicz felt they had received any assurances about seeing the medical records. Hart and Mankiewicz felt that McGovern was allowing himself to be ruled by compassion. But my own understanding of McGovern's reaction, drawn from two long conversations with him later that week, was that he did not believe the political impact of the Eagleton disclosure would be as great as it turned out to be.

The McGovern-Eagleton breakfast was followed by a press conference. There was no doubt that the facts of the case would have to be made public, because the Knight newspapers were ready to publish a story. It was far better for us to break the news ourselves than to let it come from the press. Knight lost its exclusive.

Eagleton told the press about his three periods of hospitalization. He explained that the exhaustion and depression he had experienced had followed periods of intense political activity. It was only in response to questions that Eagleton revealed that he had undergone electroshock therapy during his hospital stays:

REPORTER: During these periods, did you receive any psychiatric help?
EAGLETON: Yes, I did.
REPORTER: Can you tell us what type of psychiatric treatment you received?
EAGLETON: Counseling from a psychiatrist, electric shock.
REPORTER: What were the purposes of the electric shock treatment?

EAGLETON: At that time it was part of the prescribed treatment for one who is suffering from nervous exhaustion and fatigue and manifestations of depression.

Obviously, Eagleton was still holding back as much as he could. Prior to this exchange of questions and answers, he had merely spoken of "fatigue," not "depression." And he had not intended to mention the shock treatments.

In response to another question, Eagleton said he had discussed the matter of revealing his medical history to McGovern with his wife when they were on the way to Miami Beach at the start of the Convention. Barbara Eagleton would later write: "The health matter did not loom large in our discussion because it was so long ago and it's not uncommon knowledge in St. Louis." It was "over and done with so far as we were concerned."

This report did not correspond with the results of my own research on Eagleton during the Convention. And, by Eagleton's own admission later, he wanted to take a "calculated risk" that the story would not come out at all. He had thought about what would happen if the word got around, but he did not let it stand in the way of his accepting McGovern's offer.

As the press conference closed, McGovern gave his full backing to Eagleton. "If I had known every detail that he discussed with me this morning," he said, "he would still have been my choice for the Vice Presidency." There would hardly be an American, including me, who would believe this statement, but McGovern felt that he now owed Eagleton the fullest support he could give him. He also thought that by avoiding any hint of disagreement between the running mates, he could quickly calm the ensuing debate over Eagleton's failure to inform him at the Convention.

Following the press conference, McGovern told Eagleton that he had done well, reinforcing his judgment that we had made a good choice in Miami Beach. Immediately after the press conference, the Eagleton party left for Los Angeles and Hawaii to meet campaign commitments, while McGovern remained in South Dakota.

The Eagletons headed toward Los Angeles in the belief that they could now avoid further questions on his health since they had revealed everything and had gained McGovern's backing. But the pressure continued from the press and on Wednesday morning in Los Angeles, Eagleton held a news conference, where he admitted that if he had it all to do over again, he would have told McGovern about his medical history at the outset.

For the remainder of the week, Eagleton campaigned to retain his own place on the Democratic ticket. His willingness to get out among the public and his personal courage aroused considerable sympathy wherever he went. Then columnist Jack Anderson charged that Eagleton had accumulated traffic violations in Missouri for reckless and drunken driving. But Eagleton knew the charges were false and reacted in righteous indignation. Anderson had succeeded in stimulating more sympathy for the beleaguered candidate. On Sunday, July 30, when Eagleton appeared on "Face the Nation," Anderson apologized but refused to back down on his charge. That kind of half-hearted and half-meant apology built further support for Eagleton. And it hardened Eagleton's resolve to stay on the ticket.

While Eagleton was gliding forward on a wave of sympathy, the McGovern camp was rocked. Phone calls, mail and wires flooded in to me at the Senate office overwhelmingly in favor of dropping Eagleton from the ticket. Among the messages that went to McGovern in South Dakota there were many from psychiatrists who said that on the basis of what they had observed of Eagleton's behavior at the Convention and afterwards, they urged that he be asked to step down. The *New York Post,* the *Los Angeles Times,* and then the *Washington Post* said he should be dropped. Later *The New York Times* joined in. Political pressure, especially from New York, was strong. On Wednesday, July 26, I talked with Matt Troy, the Queens County Democratic leader as he sat in his car outside City Hall. He was strongly in favor of immediate action to drop Eagleton. I asked that he withhold any public statement in order to give McGovern time to decide. But Troy went directly from my call to a City Hall press conference where he said that he had heard that Eagleton's medical profile would not even permit him access to a SAC base.

Henry Kimelman, our national finance chairman, was quoted

in the press as saying that contributions were drying up because of McGovern's decision to keep Eagleton.

To add to the reports of trouble, the process of placing the blame for the Eagleton affair was under way. In response to reporters' questions at Sylvan Lake, Dick Dougherty told the press that I had been detailed to check on Eagleton and left the newsmen with the impression that I had done a "perfunctory" job. I was angered by this attempt to place a part of the blame on me and later told both McGovern and Dougherty. The press secretary denied any intention to place blame on me and Mc-Govern said he understood that I had voluntarily undertaken the checks on Eagleton and White under great time pressure. I refrained from any public comment in an effort to avoid creating still further controversy. (Ironically, Gary Hart was later to ask me to check out the man who became Eagleton's replacement—Sargent Shriver.)

McGovern himself regarded the few days after the Sylvan Lake press conference as a time to judge public reaction. He would have been willing to accept a request from Eagleton to withdraw from the ticket, but outside of the initial pro forma offer on Tuesday when McGovern would have thought it improper to accept, such an offer never came.

McGovern's initial statement of support was weakened, when he told the AP's Carl Leubsdorf that he was waiting to gauge public reaction. He did not want to appear to be pulling the rug from under Eagleton. When some staff members expressed their concern, he gave Dougherty a fresh statement to post in the Sylvan Lake press room. In it, McGovern said: "I'm 1,000 percent for Tom Eagleton."

McGovern was getting no advice from his staff to keep Eagleton. By Friday, July 28, McGovern made it clear to me that he would ask Eagleton to step down even if his running mate would not renew his offer to withdraw. Once he had made the decision, he agreed to wait until Eagleton returned to Washington from his western swing before saying anything. He felt it would be excessively awkward to make the announcement without Eagleton who was then thousands of miles away.

But with his decision made, McGovern chose to talk with

newsmen. Jules Witcover of the *Los Angeles Times* was invited to McGovern's cabin for a chat, probably because of his initial discussion with McGovern on the Vice Presidency. As a result of that meeting, he wrote that McGovern had decided that Eagleton should leave the ticket and still hoped that his running mate would withdraw. It is possible that McGovern hoped Eagleton would read this story the following morning on the West Coast. He wanted to prepare the press for a change in his attitude. On Friday evening he table-hopped in the Lakota Room of the Sylvan Lake Lodge to inform groups of newsmen that some psychiatrists had raised doubts about Eagleton. In addition, he told of defections among contributors and party leaders because of his decision to keep Eagleton and of his own unhappiness over Eagleton's failure to be frank with him at the Convention.

When the word got to Eagleton in San Francisco the following morning, he called McGovern for reassurance. McGovern was reluctant to give him any indication of bad news over the phone, preferring to wait until they met in Washington. So he reassured his running mate.

On Saturday, July 29, Democratic Chairwoman Jean Westwood and Vice Chairman Basil Patterson were preparing for an appearance on "Meet the Press." McGovern sent word that he did not want them supporting Eagleton too strongly because it would make his own later action to remove him that much more difficult. In fact, Westwood agreed to state her own view that Eagleton should withdraw, knowing that she had the full support of the Presidential nominee. The press would not fail to see the handwriting on the wall and so, hopefully, would Eagleton.

The following day, Eagleton himself appeared on television. We did nothing to hinder his appearance because that would have immediately brought the matter to a head. He indicated his desire to remain on the ticket and his belief that McGovern wanted him to remain. He was subjected to considerable pressure from both Jack Anderson, who refused to retract fully his charges about drunken driving, and George Herman, who alluded to the candidate's profuse perspiration. This would arouse more sympathy.

That same day, I was with McGovern in Washington when he spoke with Eagleton on the phone. Only the former patient could release his medical records to any third party, and McGovern asked Eagleton to authorize his doctors to show him those records. Without actually refusing, Eagleton said he was running into difficulties. McGovern felt sure he would not see the records. To me, it was clear that Eagleton did not want McGovern to see them. In effect, he was asking McGovern to keep him on the ticket but still refusing to insure the Presidential candidate against possible trouble later should the records come out.

Monday, July 31, it was all to end. After a flying trip to Louisiana to attend the funeral of Senator Allen Ellender, McGovern returned to Washington to meet Eagleton. The meeting took place in an office just off the Senate floor. Eagleton had asked Gaylord Nelson, whom he knew was a close McGovern friend, to participate. It was virtually settled in McGovern's own mind that Eagleton would have to withdraw because of his lack of candor and because it was imperative to shift the focus of the campaign away from the entire affair. Eagleton called two of his doctors and put McGovern on the phone. He and Nelson withdrew to the other side of the room.

Only McGovern knows what the doctors told him. According to the ethics of the medical profession they pledged him to secrecy. McGovern has abided by that pledge. The two doctors may have told him that Eagleton was now in good health and that there was no reason for concern about his ability to fulfill the duties of the Vice President or President. On the basis of his statement to the press that evening, he may well have received such a message from them. But it is not certain, because he could not convey their diagnosis under the pledge of secrecy, even if it were favorable.

The doctors might have expressed some degree of concern about Eagleton's future ability to serve given the medical prognosis for such illnesses. In this connection, Pentagon sources had leaked word that military personnel with Eagleton's medical history could be denied assignments involving nuclear weapons. If this report were true, it might indicate that fear of possible recurrences was sufficient to merit caution. There is no evidence from McGovern to that effect but again it would not have been excluded by the statement that he later made that Eagleton was in good health.

Finally, the doctors might have described the illness as persisting but have asked that McGovern not let Eagleton himself know. Once again, there is no evidence that McGovern received such a message.

Following his conversations with the doctors, McGovern told Eagleton that he felt that the issue of his health was coming to dominate the campaign. This point was not new to Eagleton; his wife had already raised it with him on Sunday. She later reported that she had said: "It looks like your past health has become the big issue, and I don't think they are going to let up." She pointed out the coverage in the Sunday papers and the three television crews in front of their house. Later she told her son that his father might have to withdraw: "I reminded him that the whole point of the campaign was to make George McGovern President, but that the only issue the press seemed interested in was his Dad's health."

Eagleton admitted that his health dominated the campaign but disagreed with McGovern's prognosis. He believed that the issue would die away in view of the sympathy that he had found around the country. While the mail was now running about even in the McGovern office, his own was overwhelmingly favorable.

Whatever else McGovern might have thought about the Eagleton affair, he believed that the issue could very well cost him the election. We had all seen a Gallup Poll, published on Monday in *Newsweek*, showing that 28 percent of the voters felt that Eagleton's hospitalization would make him unfit for the Vice Presidency with 31 percent saying he should resign from the ticket. Some 80 percent agreed that he should have told McGovern about his past medical problem. As a result of the incident some 23 percent had less confidence in McGovern and 25 percent were less favorable about the Democratic ticket. McGovern knew that he could not afford to lose one percentage point and now he stood to lose as many as 17 percent of the Democrats over this issue. Only through the retrospect of the full campaign might he conclude that he had already lost them and there was no further harm to be done. But nobody, including Eagleton, made that argument.

McGovern and Eagleton prepared separate statements. McGovern considered that Eagleton was now in good health but that his mental health history would dominate the campaign and draw attention away from the issues. Eagleton acceded to the request of the head of the ticket to withdraw but did not indicate that he agreed with his reasons. As Eagleton had told his wife: "If Senator McGovern wants me out, I'll leave. He's the boss. If he wants me to stay, I'll stay." Since Eagleton himself wanted badly to remain on the ticket, he placed the full burden on McGovern who, in theory, had no legal right to remove him if he refused. Before going to the Senate Caucus Room, where McGovern had once hoped to announce his candidacy, McGovern and Eagleton and some of us on the staff joked nervously about the case. The decision was made, and we went to face an unpredictable public reaction.

The following morning Tom Eagleton wrote to Jean Westwood formally withdrawing as the Party's nominee for Vice President. George McGovern began the search for a replacement.

Eagleton had indicated that he would be willing to campaign vigorously for the ticket once a new Vice Presidential nominee had been selected. We appreciated this offer because we thought he would be most effective with those who disagreed with McGovern's decision, particularly in Missouri. We were pessimistic about the future but found some comfort in the belief that memory of the case would fade and that we had enough time to return the disaffected to the fold. Eagleton, by being a good sport, could be a great help.

The Eagleton Affair was to remain with us throughout the campaign. McGovern turned out to be the villain of the piece, while Eagleton was the hero. It was believed that McGovern had failed to check adequately on Eagleton, but even more important he had turned his back on him when the chips were down. The "1,000 percent" support entered into the national political vocabulary as a synonym for betrayal and I could not help but wince every time I heard it. Had McGovern dropped Eagleton immediately, he probably would have suffered less political damage than resulted from his apparent change of mind.

Eleanor McGovern provided us with the best analysis of her husband's reaction. At first, he had reacted with his innate compassion and concern for a man in difficulty. He could not ask Eagleton to step down just as the harsh truth became known. Then, he was forced by the public attention and concern to substitute a political judgment for a personal one. He had only changed his mind about retaining Eagleton in the light of intervening events. Yet one could not help but regret McGovern's use of the "1,000 percent" phrase which could so epitomize the extent of his about-face.

In addition, Eagleton had waged a valiant campaign to remain on the ticket. He had been pushed from the ticket; he would not jump. This placed all of the responsibility for the decision on McGovern. Eagleton would not share it nor would he ever admit that he agreed with it. He disagreed and honesty dictated that he not say something that was not true.

I believe that the greatest damage to McGovern was in the public's perception of him. We had consciously tried to project the image of a non-political man who was opposed to the traditional political practices that were rejected by so many voters. In that respect, we believed that McGovern shared the mantle of protest with Wallace. In addition, McGovern was an unknown. The polls showed that a great many people had known little about him and had been undecided as we went into each primary state. We had turned many of these people into supporters when they realized that here was a man who spoke his mind and shunned the old political ways. We knew that the national electorate generally knew little about this political newcomer and that their relative lack of information about him was the main factor why Nixon, who was naturally better known, led him in the polls. As McGovern gained in public recognition, we felt he would also gain in the polls. That strategy was destroyed by the Eagleton affair.

Eagleton caught the interest of the American people in the six days between the Sylvan Lake Lodge and the Senate Caucus

Room. They came to know George McGovern. And they found him to be a man who had made a major decision strictly on political grounds—the alleged impact of the Eagleton debate on the course of his own campaign for the Presidency.

Once Eagleton had the nomination, this damage was inevitable, as in a Greek tragedy. For McGovern could not reveal anything he might have learned about the state of his running mate's health. To do so would run counter to his own standards of decency. Thus, whether or not he had such information, he could only give a "political" reason for his decision to ask Eagleton to withdraw. Only if Eagleton himself had insisted on withdrawing might some of the weight be taken off of McGovern.

But Eagleton followed the instincts of self-preservation after July just as he had before the nomination. He had campaigned vigorously to be kept on the ticket. On behalf of the ticket from which he had been dropped, he would later make light of the whole affair as if to remind his audience that he was, in fact, in sound health. He even poked jokes at the Shriver nomination. He would refuse to acknowledge that McGovern might have been right about the role his mental health would play in the campaign despite early indications that the Nixon Administration would not be above exploiting it. (The Pentagon report mentioned earlier could have been just the first case.) Finally he would not defend McGovern's initial reaction and his changing his mind because he agreed only with the initial reaction. And all of this, which created sympathy for him, overshadowed his own failure to come clean with McGovern. Soon after the Sylvan Lake press conference, he said that he should have told McGovern: "You just have to try to understand what that phone call [from McGovern] meant to me. You have to understand me. . . . I didn't think it was going to be this big. Frankly, I made a mistake." He would never say that again.

Some members of the McGovern staff became frustrated by what they saw as the injustice of the public's verdict. They believed that McGovern had been told by the doctors that he should ask Eagleton to withdraw because his health was not completely sound. Although McGovern himself could not admit this information, Miles Rubin, the man in charge of soliciting large contributions to the campaign and a devoted McGovern supporter, was quoted in the press as saying that the decision had been made on medical grounds. Mankiewicz hinted as much in his contacts with the press.

I felt that some doubt still remained about Eagleton's health because of his failure to produce his medical records and because of persistent rumors that Eagleton's original illness was even more serious than we had been told. Yet I knew such intimations were bound to be worthless because they were seen to be self-serving. And they made Eagleton furious.

On October 6 and 7, McGovern made his first visit to Missouri during the campaign. He was greeted by enormous turnouts in both Kansas City and St. Louis. He was due to speak at the gathering of the Democratic Party where the Harry S. Truman award would go to Tom Eagleton. The former running mates dined together before the meeting.

I had told McGovern that my own soundings in Ohio where I had campaigned indicated that Eagleton remained the number one problem for us. We needed Eagleton to say that McGovern had been correct in his decision to drop him. McGovern agreed to ask Eagleton if he would make such a statement as part of one of the half-hour television broadcasts we were preparing. Eagleton began the dinner by bringing up Rubin's comments. McGovern, unexpectedly on the defensive, said that such remarks were unauthorized and that he would do his best to make sure they were stopped. In response to McGovern's request for help, Eagleton said he would be willing to appear on the television broadcast, but once again demurred at endorsing McGovern's decision. However, he recited the remarks that he planned to make later at the dinner which went a long way toward calming public concern. While he would not say that he agreed with McGovern's decision, he would not say that he disagreed. His proposed statement was a good response to what McGovern had been saying recently—substantially the approach that Eleanor had suggested.

Eagleton's remarks at the dinner were a distinct dissapointment. He made it explicit that he had left the ticket at McGovern's request and that he did not agree with the reasoning be-

hind the request. His appeal for support for the McGovern-
Shriver ticket was hollow after that. Now it was McGovern's
turn to be angry. The press, too, seemed to feel that Eagleton
had said more than necessary in his own defense, although
they were unaware of what had transpired at the dinner.

Later we learned that John Stewart of Larry O'Brien's staff
had called Doug Bennet the following Monday and asked for
Eagleton to make a radio tape on behalf of McGovern, just as
other leading Democrats had done. Perhaps Bennet, who had
not been at the St. Louis meeting, was unaware of the discussion between the two Senators. He refused on the grounds that
Eagleton was disturbed by what our staff was saying about him.
Stewart let the matter drop, but we were surprised to see reports in the press in late October about Eagleton's refusal to
tape the broadcast. The report did not come from the McGovern
campaign and the Eagleton office issued no denial.

As the campaign headed for its conclusion amidst the revela-
tions that the Republicans had financed a sabotage and espionage
operation against the Democrats, attention focused on the person who had first brought the Eagleton illness to public attention, John Knight's anonymous caller. We learned that the Nixon
Administration knew of Eagleton's illness even before he had
been chosen for the number two spot. Ramsey Clark, who had
served as Attorney General under President Johnson, told Mc-
Govern that the information concerning his hospitalization was
in his FBI file. This file was, of course, available to John
Mitchell, who had moved from Attorney General to service as
the first Nixon campaign manager, and to President Nixon himself.

I learned later that a Detroit doctor had apparently informed
a friend who served on Vice President Agnew's staff about
Eagleton's hospitalizations. The doctor refused to confirm or
deny this report to the press but apparently the fact that he had
written his friend and received an acknowledgment was common knowledge in his community. Hence there was a possibility
that the Agnew office had been the instigator of the call to
Knight.

Knight newspapers believed that the doctor might have obtained his information from a relative who had taken his medical training at Barnes Hospital in St. Louis. They believed that their informant was a genuine McGovern supporter and was probably a personal friend of the original source of the information, perhaps the doctor's son or son-in-law. Because he knew of the doctor's political leanings and perhaps of his letter to his friend in Agnew's office, he might have had reason to worry about the possible impact of a Republican leak later in the campaign.

The Knight theory corresponded with my own to the extent that I had believed all along the source might be someone who had worked at Barnes in the past. No current employee could recently have learned the information, because, as soon as he had heard of Eagleton's selection, the hospital director had placed the Senator's files in his personal safe.

All of us directly involved in the Eagleton affair have looked back over the series of events which began the day McGovern was nominated in search of the one key mistake that brought on the disaster. In my view, there are few points in the story where we could have changed the outcome.

Our first error was to devote so little time to the selection of the Vice Presidential nominee. Although McGovern had remarked on the number of questions he had received during the primaries on the Vice Presidency, he never saw the choice of his running mate for what it was above all else: the only real decision that the non-incumbent Presidential candidate makes in full public view. We all thought that the decision was much easier than it turned out to be, because we believed the myth that no man refuses the Vice Presidential nomination.

McGovern counted on being able to convince Kennedy to accept the nomination. I assumed he had selected an alternate if his first choice refused. Yet, at the Convention where he might have given the matter some consideration, he placed greater emphasis on making an outstanding acceptance speech before what we expected would be a huge national television audience. So the question of the running mate was deferred to the last minute.

Gary Hart, the campaign manager, has said that he was in

error for not setting up a screening process well in advance of the Convention. He, like McGovern, was completely occupied by the California challenge in the days before Miami Beach. It is likely that our doubts about Eagleton would have been allowed to grow to the point that he would not have been selected had his record been before us for more than two hours. But, in my view, Hart's error was merely a reflection of the general attitude among the campaign leadership.

In my opinion, the most fundamental damage, not to McGovern's candidacy, but to the sanctity of the democratic system was caused by Eagleton's failure to tell McGovern about his past mental health problems. I have no doubt that he was aware of the political damage that could be done if they became public. On this point, we have the proof in his own comments in the wake of the Sylvan Lake press conference. In addition, all my own checking was able to reveal was a cover story under a cover story. The true story was largely unknown because most people in St. Louis, including the two major newspapers, believed they had penetrated as far as possible after they learned that the Johns Hopkins hospitalization for stomach problems never took place. Thus Eagleton had taken great pains to cover his past.

By his own admission, Eagleton's ambition held sway over his judgment. He wanted so much to advance politically that he was willing to endanger the ticket. And more important, he was willing to endanger a free and fair choice between the Democratic and Republican candidates if his "calculated risk" did not work out.

Once the story was public, Eagleton devoted most of his efforts to campaigning to save his place on the ticket. In his Los Angeles press conference the day after the announcement in South Dakota, he said that "if my visceral feeling is that my candidacy is untenable and is negative insofar as the McGovern ticket is concerned, I'll not even wait for McGovern to give me the word. I'll give the word myself."

Eagleton maintained until the end that this visceral feeling never came. Apparently he was more impervious than we were to the Gallup Poll that showed 17 percent of the Democrats defecting because of the Eagleton affair.

It is perhaps more understandable, but no more comforting, that, after he had been dropped from the ticket, he let his instinct for self-preservation take precedence over any attempt to erase as completely as possible the ill effects of his actions. He stubbornly refused to admit that McGovern's decision was right, although by so doing he would not have admitted any added failing on his own part.

McGovern's own reaction upon learning of Eagleton's illness has been the subject of the greatest public attention. He has been criticized for backing him "1,000 percent" and then dumping him the next week. The criticism implies that either McGovern should have removed Eagleton immediately or he should not have done so at all.

The removal of the Vice Presidential nominee was without precedent. No Presidential candidate could take hasty action in such a situation. The Eagleton affair, in particular, seemed to McGovern and to his staff to be a matter where public opinion would determine the outcome. While not every policy decision can be made according to the dictates of public opinion, here was one that involved an estimate of the impact on the election of the public's reaction and that alone. So it seemed sensible to wait. The hospitalizations themselves might well have been tolerable, but the electric shock treatment was not. That is what we learned in the following week.

McGovern might have preserved his image as a non-politician and avoided contradicting himself had he kept Eagleton. But he was genuinely concerned about the campaign focusing on Eagleton. The ensuing weeks showed that, while the handling of the Eagleton affair remained one of the major issues, it did not prevent such other issues as the Vietnam war and tax reform from capturing the public interest.

Thus it seems to me that McGovern's error was not his decision to suspend judgment on Eagleton for a few days but his failure to communicate that decision to the public. His expressions of support, designed to demonstrate his sympathy for Eagleton and to deny that he was even considering dropping him, were needlessly extravagant. By doing his job too well at the outset, he made it difficult later to change course gracefully.

I believe, in retrospect, that the role of the doctors is worth consideration. They kept their knowledge about Eagleton's condition to themselves until their former patient himself authorized them to tell McGovern over the phone. They had kept silent in accordance with medical ethics, which are designed to give patients confidence in their relationships with their doctors. If a patient felt that confidential and possibly harmful information might be released by a doctor, he might endanger his own health by refusing to consult a physician.

In my view, once the doctors knew of Eagleton's selection for the Vice Presidency, they ignored a higher duty in deference to their code of ethics. They could reasonably conclude that no patient would lose confidence in his physician simply because they had informed a Presidential candidate about the past disability of his proposed running mate. Patriotism demanded they inform McGovern not because it might help his partisan cause, but because Eagleton had now been placed in line for the Presidency. Since they were aware of the nature of the illness, even if it provided no cause for concern, their message to McGovern might have enabled him better to reassure the American people.

As a result of the Eagleton affair, a number of suggestions have been made for improving the Vice Presidential selection process. Some of them seem too drastic. They imply that the selection of the Vice Presidential nominee should be removed in some measure from the Presidential nominee's discretion.

Such drastic prescriptions are wrong because they ignore the nature of the nomination and election process. Only Presidential nominees are selected by the people through the convention and primary system, and the people vote only for the Presidential nominee in the general election. Vice Presidential candidates are chosen by the man at the top of the ticket and run in tandem with him. Under these circumstances it would be unjust and unwise to saddle a person who had earned his own nomination the hard way with a running mate who might not be fully sympathetic with his candidacy.

But for the same reasons there is no need for the Vice Presidential nominee to be selected in the heat of the National Convention. Despite the votes for some 39 different people at the

Democratic Convention, there was never any doubt that Mc-
Govern's choice would be accepted. The Presidential nominee's
choice could be made within 30 days of the Convention and
confirmed by the National Committee. This would insure an
early session of the National Committee which could also gear
up for the general elections.

The Eagleton case raises the need for one additional safe-
guard: intelligence on the proposed running mate. There is no
reason to presume that any essentially amateur investigation
can turn up harmful information even if given as much as 30
days. It is likely that the FBI has a file on any person who
might be considered. We know they had one on Eagleton and
when I checked on Shriver's background, I managed to speak
with a source who had seen his FBI file. I suggest that, once
the Presidential nominee has made his choice, he alone should
be shown the FBI file. Rules could be laid down preventing
wholesale examination of records. But no Presidential candidate
should be required to make a decision in the dark.

The postscript to the Eagleton affair was the replacement of
Eagleton as quickly as possible by a new running mate. McGovern believed that the Eagleton affair had effectively stripped
him of any chance to run as a non-political figure against the
Establishment. Now it became imperative to find a running
mate that would reassure the Party's leaders that he was indeed
moving toward the center.

McGovern turned to his colleagues in the Senate for advice.
These were men who worked with the Party leaders in their
own states and could be reliable barometers of what would
appeal to the center. The campaign staff was assigned a subordinate role. Our advice on how to placate the center would
not have been as informed as that of McGovern's colleagues.
Yet, our opinions did not differ that much from what McGovern was hearing from his colleagues.

On August 1, I wrote McGovern a memo:

> Obviously the prime consideration remains the person's ability
> to serve as Vice President or President. The next consideration
> must, it seems to me, be the restoration and extension of the kind
> of feeling that this campaign is open, "moral" (in some indefin-

able sense), innovative. Whatever that aura is, we should make every effort to recreate it and the most tangible step would be in the selection of the Vice Presidential nominee.

In our original consideration, there were two categories of possibilities, aside from the special case of Kennedy. First, we could have chosen a person sufficiently out of the ordinary that the choice would have had a certain shock effect. That would have meant a woman or a black or a Republican. Second, we could have chosen a man from the ranks of the good, progressive wing of the Party, probably a Senator or Governor. There was a pool of talent and Eagleton was the choice.

As we approach the choice a second time, the first possibility is clearly excluded. . . . The second group once again seems the obvious choice, but I submit that even this alternative is doubtful given the present circumstances. No member of this group is particularly well-known either in the nation or across the broad spectrum of the Democratic Party. A choice from this group would amount to an effort to find a "clean" Eagleton. But I would maintain that the nomination should be seen as adding a new dimension to the ticket.

That is why I suggest we make a clear step up. Presumably the choices here would be limited to Humphrey, Muskie, O'Brien, Kennedy, Mills, Mansfield, Albert.

McGovern's first step was to determine whether any of those who had been under consideration in Miami Beach would now reconsider their rejection of the nomination. Even before Eagleton stepped down from the ticket, McGovern discussed his replacement with Kennedy as they both flew to the funeral of Louisiana Senator Allen Ellender on Monday, July 31. Kennedy again refused to accept the invitation, as McGovern had expected.

Similarly, both Abe Ribicoff and Gaylord Nelson reaffirmed that they wanted to remain in the Senate and did not want the number two position. Florida Governor Reubin Askew, whom we continued to see as a political personality who would appeal to "protest" voters, refused again on the grounds that he was too new at his present job to think of moving to the national scene. But it was also clear to us in the campaign that Askew did not find it politically wise to be too closely associated with

McGovern. He did not view the Vice Presidential nomination as a way of advancing his own career.

By Wednesday, August 2, McGovern had turned to Hubert Humphrey. At Miami Beach his offer of the Vice Presidential nomination had merely been pro forma and Humphrey had quickly refused. But Ted Van Dyk had learned that Humphrey might be willing to run now. McGovern asked Humphrey to meet him for breakfast in the Senate Dining Room to listen to a serious offer. Humphrey would not again seek the Presidential nomination and was planning to seek a leadership role in the Senate. Thus, he would have nothing to lose by accepting the nomination. But Humphrey's backers wanted nothing to do with the McGovern candidacy. They wanted to pick up the pieces of the Party after what they regarded as McGovern's certain defeat. If Humphrey accepted the number two slot, he would be giving the ticket a seal of approval that many of his supporters opposed.

But Humphrey also had personal reasons for refusing Mc-Govern's request. "Poor old Hubert. He just had to get on [the ticket]. He just couldn't remain off. He smelled the sawdust again and there he's in the ring," Humphrey told reporters in describing the possible reaction to his accepting the nomination. "Well, bullshit. I don't need to be in the ring. That's the way I feel. I'm just not going to leave myself open to any more humiliating, debilitating exposure."

Van Dyk had often warned us that Humphrey took his defeats as personal humiliation and obviously he now wanted to keep his dignity intact. After the way Humphrey had lashed out at McGovern during the campaign, I was afraid that the candidate's own dignity took quite a beating from the public offer and public rejection by Humphrey.

Next, McGovern met with Muskie. The 1968 Vice Presidential nominee was interested in the offer. I thought he would be a good choice because he had been an effective campaigner for Humphrey and, according to the Gallup Poll, shared some of McGovern's positive attributes as a "modern-style moderate" (as opposed to Humphrey, who was seen as "old-fashioned middle of the roader"). Muskie promised to think over the offer, but before he could make a decision he wanted to talk with his wife who had been sorely disappointed when Muskie had failed to get the Presidential nomination.

On Friday, August 4, at Muskie's request, Mankiewicz, Hart, and Kimelman met with the Maine Senator's political and financial advisers. Muskie people asked about everything from the assumption of Muskie's debt to whether their man could have his own campaign aircraft designed to his liking. Our representatives came back from the meeting depressed at the prospect of having Muskie as the running mate. I suggested that if we were having second thoughts, we owed it to both Muskie and McGovern to communicate them to the Mainer. Mankiewicz said he would find some way to let him know.

The following morning, Muskie found on his doorstep a fresh copy of *The New York Times,* whose lead article reported that Mankiewicz had encouraged Shriver, who was also under consideration, to stand by in case McGovern decided to ask him to run and implied that the McGovern camp was not firmly for Muskie. Muskie held a press conference to announce that he would decline McGovern's offer because his wife had opposed another campaign.

Sargent Shriver was playing tennis at the Kennedy compound at Hyannis Port when McGovern's call came on Saturday. Shriver, whose political career had never included a shot at elective office, immediately accepted. With remarkable good humor, he said he would consider himself "lucky seven," since he had been the seventh person asked to take the nomination after the Eagleton affair.

7

WHY I "QUIT" THE McGOVERN CAMPAIGN

> "[McGovern] is so highly admired . . . because of the kind of man he is."—Senator Robert F. Kennedy.

As early as 1969, McGovern began putting together his campaign staff. The work of the McGovern Commission was moving toward completion and he was already considering an early announcement of his candidacy. With his Senate office concerned primarily with South Dakota affairs, he decided to augment it with people specifically assigned to look after his national political interests.

Late that year, he hired Dick Leone, a Princeton political scientist, to coordinate his national political operations. John Stacks, a Washington correspondent of *Time*, came on as press secretary. But in early 1970 both Leone and Stacks left him in part because of personality clashes with the Senate office staff and in part because McGovern was not yet sure how he wanted to shape his campaign.

Through Ted Van Dyk I had first met McGovern in December 1969. As he started again to build a staff, he asked me in February 1970 to join his staff as press secretary, although he was frank to say that he might later want me to move over into legislative work. He told me that he was particularly concerned about gaining more and better television coverage and hoped eventually to line up a video newsman for the job.

At the beginning of April 1970, I joined the staff. I would serve as press secretary for thirteen months and then be named McGovern's executive assistant. In this assignment, I would first —briefly—be in charge of issue development for the campaign. Then I would serve, from July 1971 until the Convention a year later, as McGovern's personal aide as he travelled around the country and around the world. After the Convention, I would become the campaign troubleshooter with an open-ended mandate. I would seek to take charge of the administration of the campaign and, for a brief period, serve as its executive director. Throughout the period between the Spring of 1970 and the election in November 1972, I would, more than any other staff member, be at McGovern's side.

I was attracted to McGovern's office even though I recognized that he was a long shot in the Presidential sweepstakes. I found him totally and deeply committed to ending American military involvement in Vietnam and to insuring that the United States would never again embark on such an adventure. And I sensed that he was an open and considerate man, a person you could feel you were working *with* and not merely *for*.

McGovern appeared to me, as he does to most people at first, to be an uncomplicated man. He is the son of a Methodist minister and a former theology student, and that shows. He is a former professor and that shows. He is from a sparsely settled rural state which has escaped the problems of the cities and that shows.

He is a soft-spoken seemingly moderate man. He keeps a tight rein on his emotions and seldom raises his voice in anger or throws his head back in a good, roaring laugh. He would usually keep his cool in times of stress. He is a politician who does not apologize for being an idealist. He regards as the highest compliment that was ever paid him the words of a South Dakota professor who said: "Mundt [McGovern's former fellow South Dakotan in the Senate] tells us what we want to hear. McGovern shows us what we should be."

Only after I came to know him better did I learn that Mc-Govern is complex and somewhat enigmatic. If there was ever a man who marched to a different drummer, often one that only he can hear, it is George McGovern.

His soft-spoken shyness masked intense ambition and almost no personal doubts. His great personal consideration (I remember once telling some new people in the campaign that the two most important words in McGovern's vocabulary are "thank you") reflected not only his decency but also his belief that a kind word pays off in votes.

A reporter once wrote that McGovern looks and sounds like a YMCA secretary. That appearance gives many people the mistaken impression that he is a milquetoast at worst or a moderate at best. Yet he has little taste for moderation. When he wants something, he will go all out for it, be it a milkshake at midnight or the Democratic Presidential nomination.

His choice of words belies his supposed moderation. He is plainspoken and uses strong language easily. Often he would look questioningly as a person who criticized his harsh statements about Nixon's Vietnam policy or corruption in government. Didn't the person agree with him in his appraisal? If he did, then McGovern could not understand why he could question Mc-Govern's choice epithets.

Yet McGovern's reaction in that situation was symptomatic of a more serious problem which would be the cause of the greatest difficulties in his campaign. Just as he was a difficult man to understand, he found it difficult to understand those around him.

McGovern, like many other people in public life, tries to avoid saying something unpleasant to a person. And the most disturbing result of this approach is that he ends up being indecisive.

For McGovern, almost any decision he might make has a winner and a victim. He seems unaware that many people would often prefer to "lose out" provided they had a clear understanding that a decision had been made that would stick. McGovern believes that indecision is preferable to creating a victim, however willing that victim might claim to be.

Politicians have, in the past, delegated the bulk of the distasteful decision making to a trusted subordinate. Following this practice, McGovern should have designated a campaign manager

and given him an independent power of decision and a direct
delegation of authority.

McGovern never found anybody to whom he could entrust his
campaign for the Presidency. Most of the people around him chose
McGovern and not the reverse. Of course, his choice was not
limited to those in his immediate vicinity, but he seldom reached
out to bring new leadership into the campaign.

Shortly after I joined him, McGovern first spoke with Gary
Hart, a young Denver lawyer who had been active in the Kennedy campaigns and the McGovern reform efforts, and asked
him to serve as his campaign manager. By the summer of 1970,
Hart had moved into this post, although his contact with Mc-
Govern had been limited to several lengthy conversations. In
contrast to most managers of national campaigns, Hart did not
really know his candidate well.

Why did McGovern choose Hart? At the time he was putting
his campaign together, few leading Democrats, if any, conceded
him the slightest chance. They did not want to sacrifice their own
standing by committing themselves early to such a dark horse.
He had no close friends who had the talent, the experience, or
the time to take on the job. Perhaps the only man from South
Dakota who might have been able to move into the slot was Bill
Dougherty, the Lieutenant Governor. But Dougherty, a long-
time Kennedy man who had run Robert Kennedy's successful
1970 primary campaign in South Dakota, was thoroughly occupied with his own political career. As a result, McGovern had
to turn to an untried young man on the make, and Hart's mind
and manner appealed to McGovern. The Coloradan was soft-
spoken, systematic, bright, and shared McGovern's political
views.

Implicit in McGovern's choice of Hart was his decision to run
his own campaign. He had substantial political experience himself, having campaigned five times for public office in South
Dakota and having organized the Democratic Party there under
the most unfavorable circumstances. He was more confident
about his own political judgment than he ever could be about that
of his neophyte manager. In effect, Hart became McGovern's
assistant, and the Senator remained his own manager. Perhaps

this was inevitable in the early stages of the campaign, but it could not justify any long-range plan to have the candidate serve as his own manager. There is virtually no recorded case where that formula has worked. The candidate must function primarily as campaigner which does not leave him enough time to oversee his campaign and make all the necessary decisions in full knowledge of the facts.

McGovern was reluctant to give wide authority to Hart or any other possible campaign manager because he knew that a strong manager would inevitably operate in his own way. The Senator believed that the campaign would hinge primarily on his own personality and character and that if left to a manager, it might well have a style different from his own.

After Hart and I had joined this staff in the spring of 1970, McGovern asked Yancey Martin, deputy minorities director at the Democratic National Committee, to take on the job of building contacts in the black community. Rick Stearns, a Rhodes Scholar who had broken away from his Oxford studies to spend a summer on the Reform Commission staff, also joined the staff. A McCarthy supporter in 1968, Stearns was fascinated by the nuts and bolts of Party operations and especially with the ways in which the Party reforms would take hold. The four of us in the class of 1970 joined Jeff Smith, who had been with McGovern since 1968, keeping track of all the names and addresses that a national campaign would need. This group remained the core of the campaign staff from mid-1970 until the spring of the following year.

In May 1971, McGovern undertook staff changes which would have repercussions for the remainder of the campaign. Frank Mankiewicz gave up his syndicated column and television program and joined the still young campaign. He had told McGovern that he would take whatever assignment the Senator chose, but it was clear to me that Mankiewicz preferred the vague title "senior political adviser" so that he could use it as a base for taking over leadership of the campaign. McGovern wanted him to serve as a broadening influence on the campaign and its chief spokesman, but was reluctant to place him in overall charge.

At the same time that Mankiewicz joined the campaign, Mc-

Govern moved me out of the job as press secretary and asked me to take charge of all issue development. Jeff Gralnick, a young television producer, had impressed McGovern with a feature on the Senator on the CBS program, "60 Minutes." He had lobbied McGovern persistently for the press post. The Senator, still concerned about his television image, decided that Gralnick could help. I would have preferred to remain as press secretary where I had succeeded in establishing good news contacts for McGovern around the country, but I agreed to take on whatever new assignment he wanted to give me. My responsibility for issue development was short-lived. Beginning in July 1971, I travelled regularly with McGovern as his executive assistant and told him that I could not handle that job and the issues work. John Holum, his legislative assistant, then took on issue development and I devoted myself fully to my duties on the road with McGovern.

Ted Van Dyk, who had been a key Humphrey lieutenant, joined the campaign and immediately sought to give it the administrative fiber it lacked. But I cautioned Van Dyk, an old friend, that tightening up on the campaign operation might well run counter to McGovern's style. As I expected, McGovern was uncomfortable with Van Dyk, who he felt placed too high a premium on efficient decision making without sufficiently evaluating the human or material costs. In addition, Van Dyk was used to making decisions under a broad delegation of authority from Humphrey. McGovern had no intention of ceding his authority to anyone in the campaign, and it was often difficult for Van Dyk to know if he had the Senator's approval for actions he wanted to take. Within three months, Van Dyk had moved out of the national headquarters, feeling a keen sense of frustration. McGovern was relieved.

At the end of November 1971, McGovern attempted again to shuffle the staff. Van Dyk agreed to take on special political duties, beginning with surveillance of the problem state of Florida. The Senator asked Hart to get out of the headquarters more and into the states. McGovern wanted him to focus on Illinois and other tough states, aside from New Hampshire and Wisconsin where we had good organizations. At the same time, he called Mankiewicz in off the road to concentrate on political supervision as opposed to organizational activity. Mankiewicz was given the title of national political director and was assigned to develop the kind of activities that would attract more media attention.

This shift would give Mankiewicz the opportunity to take charge at national headquarters. On the road, Hart could have less influence over the campaign except for field operations.

In the press area, McGovern decided to add Dick Dougherty, a former New York *Herald Tribune* and Los Angeles *Times* reporter, to deal with the writing press and to work on his speeches. Gralnick, whose "New York style" had ruffled local McGovern people and who had tried to oust me from my job as executive assistant, was asked to remain in Washington with principal responsibility for the electronic media. Obviously McGovern was still looking for a well-known newsman to serve as his press secretary. Perhaps Dougherty was the man. In any case, McGovern felt he would rather have a man of Dougherty's maturity around him rather than the more unstable Gralnick. Within a month, Gralnick had quit.

The personnel problems that plagued the campaign soon came to a head again, and in March, during the Illinois campaign, we took off one day to assemble the top staff in Milwaukee. Ostensibly, the meeting was to plan the strategy for the last two weeks of the Wisconsin campaign.

Mankiewicz had been pressing for Hart to move out of the headquarters where he had stayed, to work on non-primary states in the field. The two had often differed on decisions regarding field operations. Mankiewicz wanted a clear shot at control of the campaign. Hart, he argued, managed both field operations and the headquarters too casually. In addition, McGovern was deeply disappointed that Hart had not followed his instructions to concentrate more of his time in Illinois.

All of us in the campaign could sense that it was being run with too loose a rein. While we agreed that Hart's plan to decentralize the campaign by giving as much personnel, money, and authority as possible to the state coordinators was sound, we felt the need for better supervision at the center.

Hart naturally resisted being sent to Siberia. He would do

whatever the Senator wanted, but he argued that Mankiewicz could do no better at the helm and there was no other person available. It was clear that because of their inevitable rivalry, each would try to operate independently of the other if he got the chance, so there was no real prospect of a joint command. McGovern did not order Hart to the field and agreed that he could hold on to his managerial role until after the Wsiconsin primary, to which he had devoted so much effort.

McGovern recognized that the staff was gradually expanding and that the campaign would no longer be able to move from one primary to the next after Wisconsin. Several operations would have to be functioning simultaneously. If there were to be any changes in staff, they would have to come immediately after Wisconsin.

The other post of continuing interest to McGovern—the press secretary—had undergone yet another change by the time of the Milwaukee meeting. Gralnick's departure had meant the elimination of certain personality problems in the campaign, but had not solved the problem of the press secretary. Dick Dougherty soon found that he was unable to keep up the pace on the road. A younger man was needed. Mankiewicz sent Kirby Jones, a fellow Peace Corps veteran, out from Washington, and he moved into the job without any formal appointment. Jones tended to the technical aspects of his job with real drive, although his lack of practical press experience was obvious. He did not hesitate to pass on to the candidate the bad news as well as the good. This, I learned, was a rare capacity in a political campaign.

In the flush of the Wisconsin primary victory in April 1972 and the successes which followed, McGovern never returned to the problems of campaign leadership. Because of the decentralized nature of the primary campaign, the need for a decision never seemed urgent.

By the time of the California primary in June 1972, Fred Dutton, a Washington lawyer who had been Robert Kennedy's aide-de-camp and had served in John F. Kennedy's administration, moved into the campaign. An idea man, Dutton had earned his spurs in California politics. He told friends in California that he wanted to take over the management of the McGovern campaign.

Although the Senator studied his lengthy memos with care and adopted some of his proposals (notably one relating to a massive voter registration drive), McGovern never gave him any encouragement to take charge of the campaign. Certainly Hart and Mankiewicz would not step aside unless they received a clear directive from the candidate, and this was never forthcoming. McGovern probably felt that the staff and the organization he had built up over many months would not be responsive to Dutton whose style was more conspiratorial than what we had become accustomed to. While there was unanimity on the considerable creative contribution Dutton could make to the campaign, he had no allies in his quest for overall control.

McGovern had planned to reshape his staff for the general election campaign in the weeks between the New York primary and the opening of the Democratic National Convention. But the California challenge had pushed staff decisions to the side. He could not assign responsibility to anybody else; McGovern had to make the decisions himself. He listened to the counsel of Fred Dutton and Dick Dougherty, who would again assume the job of press secretary. These two men were closer to McGovern's age than many of us who had worked throughout the primaries.

As a result of their advice, McGovern had by early July sketched out his ideas for staffing and had reviewed them with Dick Stout of *Newsweek*, even before he had discussed them in any detail with the people directly involved. Most significantly absent from his thinking was the designation of any single person to take charge of the campaign.

Dutton himself, like Mankiewicz before him, refused any title. Although he would not manage the campaign, he wanted to assume the job of intellectual aide-de-camp—the chief strategist travelling with the candidate. Dougherty wanted a similar role as well as the responsibility for the press which he felt had not been handled with sufficient good humor and bonhomie. Mankiewicz, at his own request, wanted to join the Senator on the campaign plane, because he believed that the focal point would shift from Washington to the Dakota Queen II. In effect, these three men, all contemporaries of McGovern, would be vying for the leadership role on the plane.

If the real decision making shifted to the plane, Gary Hart would be left in Washington, still nominally in charge of the campaign, but limited in fact to dealing with the McGovern organization in the field. Men who had been organizational experts in winning the nomination—Stearns, Pokorny, and Grandmaison —would continue in this area either at headquarters or in the field.

About me, Stout reported: "Gordon Weil, 35, McGovern's executive assistant, who was usually closest to the senator's elbow through the primaries, would likely coordinate issue research from Washington headquarters." In fact, I had always felt that McGovern gave relatively low priority to issues, with the war and military budget-cutting the only matters that really captured his interest, and recognized that I would be relegated to the sidelines. But I told him when we talked briefly on the phone before the Convention that I would be glad to accept whatever assignment he thought appropriate.

By the time of the Democratic Convention in mid-July, Dutton apparently believed that these arrangements had been settled. He saw himself replacing me as McGovern's aide, while I had had no real discussion with McGovern about my duties. I assumed he would make final decisions after the Convention. In the meantime, I thought I should continue as his personal assistant. So friction between Dutton and me at the Convention was inevitable.

Although he would delay most staffing decisions, McGovern was required to choose a new chairman of the Democratic National Committee before he left Miami Beach.

Larry O'Brien had consistently told McGovern that he did not want to remain National Chairman. Whether or not O'Brien really meant what he said, McGovern took him at his word. He finally settled on Jean Westwood, the Democratic National Committeewoman from Utah and member of the Executive Committee of the DNC, who had been committed to his support since his announcement. During the campaign she had moved through the Western states helping our state coordinators and finally took charge of the Oregon primary. She was an able and devoted McGovern supporter and, best of all, she was a woman.

Westwood could be counted on to operate the DNC as an adjunct of the national campaign because of her personal loyalty to McGovern. The candidate was anxious to absorb as many of the DNC functions as practicable into the campaign. Just how far he would want to go became apparent several weeks later when he tried to move the entire operation out of the Watergate complex where it had been for years and where it enjoyed a favorable rent arrangement, and into the dingy campaign headquarters that we had inherited from Senator Muskie.

Pierre Salinger, who had campaigned hard for McGovern during the primaries, also wanted the chairmanship. He could be a powerful anti-administration spokesman and might, at the same time, relaunch his own political career. Although Salinger felt he had a promise from McGovern to be given the post, the Senator never intended to appoint him to more than the vice chairmanship. In fact, DNC rules did not provide for co-chairmen, but did require that the chairman and vice chairman be of the opposite sex. So Westwood, concentrating on organization, and Salinger, serving as spokesman, would make a good team.

McGovern could not reach O'Brien to inform him that he would accept his resignation and appoint Westwood and Salinger. As a result, he could not announce the new officers at the Democratic victory breakfast. When he finally did reach the Chairman later that morning, he was surprised to learn that O'Brien wanted to stay on. His previous statements had not been meant to be taken at face value.

The nominee was in a quandary. He wanted O'Brien to stay on because of his good relations with Party leaders around the country. He certainly deserved reappointment on the basis of his commitment to party reform. But McGovern had already promised the job to Westwood.

O'Brien and his aides came to McGovern's suite at the Doral. He sat on one side of a partition that divided the suite. On the other side were Westwood, Salinger, Eleanor McGovern, Van Dyk, Mankiewicz, Hart, and McGovern. The Senator shuttled back and forth trying to find some way to keep O'Brien in the National Committee job. O'Brien wanted to serve as Chairman of the Committee and campaign chairman. He would not accept the campaign chairmanship alone nor would he accept Westwood as his co-chairman at the Committee since that would violate its rules. He placed the choice of Chairman squarely before the candidate. Of the people in the room with him, only Eleanor Mc-Govern spoke out in favor of O'Brien. Westwood was almost tearful in her insistence that McGovern keep his promise to her. Hart opposed giving O'Brien the chairmanship of the campaign while most of the others took softer intermediary positions. Mc-Govern chose Westwood and told O'Brien that he would want him to play a major role in the campaign. O'Brien was not happy because he believed erroneously, that the staff had vetoed him. He did not immediately recognize that McGovern believed he was already too committed to Westwood simply to drop her.

At the DNC meeting, Westwood was duly confirmed. But when Salinger's name was placed in nomination, Charles Evers, the Mississippi black leader who had never backed McGovern, placed the name of New York's black Democrat Basil Patterson in nomination. McGovern, put in the position of antagonizing the black leadership if he opposed Patterson, announced: "I just wanted you to know that these are both fine men and I would be pleased to have either of them."

Salinger was shocked. He withdrew his name from consideration and immediately left town. McGovern had publicly shown that he would trade off personal loyalty in the interests of the new politics. Once again, he had refused to stand up to one of the forces in his new coalition. Only if he did, could he get its respect and that of millions of people who feared that the coalition controlled him and not the reverse. In addition, political leaders around the country could not help but notice that a Party traditionally headed by white males was now to be run by a woman and a black. If this change rectified past injustices, the change was a bit too brutal for some.

By the time of a staff meeting at McGovern's vacation retreat in the Black Hills on July 22, McGovern was moving toward these assignments and had assured a number of people privately of their new duties. On the plane to South Dakota on July 21, he and I chatted. I was aware that he was having some difficulty in finding an assignment for Van Dyk. He talked about the possibility of assigning Van Dyk to take charge of issue research, because he had had experience in this area in previous campaigns. I knew that he did not want the job if it put me in limbo. I suggested that I might be able to serve as troubleshooter in the campaign, because I could see that with no line of authority and no person assigned responsibility for coordinating the various elements—organization, issues, media, and the candidate's activities—there would be plenty of room for problems to fall between the cracks. McGovern indicated that, if it came to fruition, this job would require me to spend part of my time on the plane and part in the headquarters. Obviously the main task at hand would be straightening out the tax and welfare proposals, after Humphrey's attacks in California.

Despite my effort to discuss the matter with him again the following morning, McGovern refused to talk with me prior to the meeting, because he obviously did not want to be dissuaded from the decisions he had made. As the meeting broke up in late afternoon, he called Van Dyk aside and gave him the issues assignment. He then invited me to join him and his family at his cabin. There, he somewhat nervously tried to sell me on the troubleshooting job. Actually no selling was needed; there was no other assignment available. He tried to convince me of the utility of the job, even though I myself had first suggested it. Perhaps he recognized I had had second thoughts about it. In any case, the troubleshooting assignment was somewhat hollow, I later learned, because the Eagleton affair was at that moment boiling towards its climax. Although I had played a key role in uncovering the problems inherent in his selection at the outset, McGovern did not even hint about the more recent developments to me.

Most significantly, the Black Hills meeting had yielded no new campaign manager. It was unclear who would be in charge on the plane. Hart would be left to manage the headquarters. He had fully expected that, after the nominating convention in Miami Beach, McGovern would receive many offers to help in the management of the campaign from experienced politicians. McGovern had viewed his primary campaign as one *without* the Regulars not one *against* them and might have expected such offers. But few of them liked McGovern well enough to offer their services and most of them were actively hostile. McGovern himself made no effort to reach out and recruit established Party figures to direct his campaign. In part, he must have felt that his personal approach had been successful in the drive for the nomination and that there was no pressing need to alter it.

The question of ultimate leadership began to plague the campaign almost immediately. At a meeting at his Washington home in mid-August, McGovern tried to make it clear that Hart was in charge of the campaign and would be held responsible for it. Notable for his absence from the meeting was Larry O'Brien who had been appointed National Campaign Chairman. While McGovern wanted O'Brien to be a liaison with the Regulars, he obviously did not want him to be in charge of the entire operation. However, he had invited Jean Westwood, now chairperson of the Democratic National Committee. She had been actively lobbying for the assignment as campaign manager, similar to the dual role O'Brien had played in 1968. The designation of Hart was meant to inform her that she would not have that function.

Hart believed firmly in the delegation of responsibility. Kimelman would be in charge of finance, Cunningham of administration, Dougherty of press, Guggenheim and Liz Stevens of media, Robbins of scheduling, O'Brien of Regulars and each would be expected to do his job. The problem with this concept was that it would be difficult for Hart to know who was not performing well and to insure needed coordination among the departments. With the exception of Robbins, each of these people felt he reported to McGovern, not Hart.

At that August meeting, McGovern asked me to return to the travelling party, although he did not specify my duties. I urged him to delay my return. Since the Black Hills meeting, I had been reshaping his tax and welfare proposals. This had turned out to be stimulating and important work, and I wanted to see it through to completion. After the Wall Street Speech on August

29 where he would unveil the new tax and welfare proposals, I told him, I would return to the travelling party.

However, I remained concerned about the problem of coordination as, in fact, did Hart. I determined to make one more attempt to improve the situation. On July 29, I had given McGovern a memo:

> Entirely aside from the Eagleton matter, I feel there is real cause for concern about the campaign more than two weeks after the end of the Democratic Convention.
>
> There is little sign of forward motion in any of the campaign divisions. The headquarters is a shambles. Telephone communications are so bad that we are alienating people who try to reach us.
>
> What the campaign continues to lack is a locus of decision-making. . . .
>
> All of this adds up to a failure to have any single person who can see what needs to be done and then sees that it is done. This is not so much a problem of hierarchy as it might seem. This does not represent a challenge to Gary or Frank. . . .
>
> We still need a person who has recognized authority for requiring that action be taken and that decisions be made. That is not the same thing as making the decisions himself. But at the moment we have a number of autonomous forces, none of them recognizing that it has to take guidance from any source. This procedure worked relatively well in the past (though careful scrutiny suggests it was overrated), but the present state of chaos shows that it is not now adequate. . . .
>
> I suggest that I be appointed to the position I outlined in my earlier memo [while in June I had suggested the creation of the post of executive director, I had not then thought of myself for the job and had not mentioned any specific person]—executive director of the campaign. If I am given full backing by you, which means that all parties concerned know that I have the authority to ask that decisions be made . . . by the end of the week we can be operating at almost full capacity. . . .
>
> This memo may seem unduly pessimistic, critical and self-serving, but I believe we are paying the price for confusion and delay which could cost us the election. Frankly, it would be a better use of my time to deal with this situation than anything

else, but it does require a demonstrated desire on your part that you want the campaign to be organized more tightly than in the past.

At that time, McGovern had shown no interest in naming me to the post and no inclination to close the obvious organizational gap. The matter dropped.

In New York, immediately after the Wall Street speech, McGovern asked me to bring a group of people together at his home the following evening, August 30. Westwood, Hart, Mankiewicz, O'Brien, McGovern, and I attended. Obviously McGovern felt he should have some information about the direction of the campaign and how it was functioning. Ordinarily, a campaign manager would have held such a meeting, but the room contained four staff people who had some claim to leadership in the campaign.

After a surprisingly favorable report on voter registration by Jean Westwood, Larry O'Brien talked about the campaign. He paid high praise to Hart for the field organization and to me for the work on the Wall Street speech. Yet he indicated that he felt better coordination was needed especially in the presentation of the issues. He wanted more "orchestration" as had been done on the Wall Street speech with preparation in the press and among party leaders. There was no opposition to this proposal, which seemed positive and appropriate, and further arrangements were left to be worked out by the staff. Contrary to later press reports, the atmosphere at the meeting was positive.

McGovern and the rest of us at the meeting were surprised the next morning to see a wire service story concerning an interview O'Brien had given prior to the Wednesday night meeting. He quoted as saying: "Labor Day is pretty much D-Day for me. If you see me around here next week, you'll know some thing have been worked out my way. And I think I'll be here." The wire story went on to report that "party insiders say McGovern wanted O'Brien to manage the 1972 campaign against President Nixon but this was opposed by top McGovern aide Frank Mankiewicz and by Mrs. Jean Westwood." (This report probably resulted from what O'Brien had heard through the room divider in McGovern's suite in Miami Beach when Westwood was given the chairmanship.) The interview indicated O'Brien's supposed concern that "McGovern's campaign staff is too free-wheeling and loosely organized to compete effectively with the tightly knit Nixon forces."

O'Brien had given us no hint of this interview nor of that degree of discontent with the campaign. Even if we agreed that the campaign should be tightened up, O'Brien had made no such broad case, but had simply focused on the "orchestration" of new initiatives. McGovern was angry for this open attempt to fight out a power struggle by using the press. In the end, O'Brien's point, a good one, was pushed aside. Hart acknowledged at a press conference that he was "number two" and O'Brien was "number one." O'Brien called a few staff meetings. We "orchestrated" a little better. O'Brien stayed.

On August 31, I decided to raise the matter of improved campaign coordination once again, and McGovern was more receptive. He said that he favored the job and indicated that I should take it on. I stressed that I was not the only person who could handle it, but would be glad to try. I noted that he placed the highest premium on avoiding "rudeness" even above efficiency, and that I operated differently, according to the maxim that: "You can't make an omelet without breaking eggs." He replied, "I guess the time has come for that."

This last remark encouraged me to believe that it might be possible to accomplish what Morris Dees had attempted in late 1970, what Van Dyk had attempted in 1971, and what Mankiewicz had wanted in early 1972—making the campaign operationally efficient. I knew that Hart would have to be willing to accept me in this role in the headquarters, although I felt confident that we could work together without conflict. I asked the Senator to get Hart's agreement to the assignment.

To my surprise, when I met with Hart the next day, I found that McGovern had already spoken with him. The Senator had apparently described the job in line with my own thoughts. I was glad that Hart favored the idea. While he might have viewed my assignment as being a deputy to him, I saw it as more of a complement to him. But I felt that this potential difference of definition was not important, because we knew each other well enough to be sure that we could cooperate. Most important, he agreed with my objectives.

After talking with Hart, I phoned McGovern to tell him that I would go ahead with the headquarters assignment. After again stressing that my methods were likely to be different from his, I told him that I would need his full support, especially when people close to him tried to have him override me. He agreed.

Hart and I drafted a memo to the staff which was cleared by McGovern and distributed late on the afternoon of September 1. It read:

Memo to McGovern-Shriver campaign staff
            cc. Democratic National Committee
From: Gary Hart

Senator McGovern and I have today asked Gordon Weil, the Senator's Executive assistant, to serve as the Executive Director of the campaign.

Gordon's responsibilities will include:

1. Clearance of all statements representing the McGovern position.
2. Assurance of the steady flow of major policy initiatives.
3. Supervision of a campaign operations center which will include:
   —the Clearinghouse operation
   —a campaign situation desk
   —provision for immediate action to deal with urgent situations through improved communications inside the staff
4. Coordination of headquarters operations to insure that campaign objectives are met promptly and efficiently.

In fulfilling these responsibilities Gordon has the full support and authority of Senator McGovern and me.

The first two points were matters of special concern to Mc-Govern. He wanted to be sure that he would not be placed in an embarrassing position by statements which he had not personally cleared. He felt that I was one of the few people completely familiar with his past positions and his frame of reference. On policy initiatives, he was responding both to the success of the Wall Street speech, for which I had been responsible, and

O'Brien's desire for better "orchestration" of our proposals to insure they had maximum impact.

I had already set up the Clearinghouse to maintain constant communications among the principal figures travelling across the country on behalf of the campaign: McGovern, Shriver, their wives, Larry O'Brien, and Jean Westwood. Hart had started the situation desk as a way of monitoring operations of our organization in the states. I proposed this set-up be augmented by a staff person who would insure that when, for example, it was necessary to respond to a statement by the Nixon campaign, all of those in our operation who should take part in the formulation of our answer were fully consulted.

The final point in the memo was the most important for me. It would mean that I could require the necessary decisions from the numerous elements of the campaign—political, administration, scheduling, press, finance, media ,and research and issues— when they were needed. It was not intended to mean that I would make those decisions.

The memo caused an immediate storm. Van Dyk felt that the first point cut into his authority over clearing policy statements. When it was uncertain if he would remain in the campaign, McGovern called him and asked him to stay. The Senator wanted Hart, Van Dyk, and me to work out some *modus vivendi*. Because of my friendship with Van Dyk and my belief that we could hammer out a reasonable working relationship when we got down to cases, I did not point out to McGovern that he had weakened the grant of authority so recently given me. Hart was willing to back me on whatever course I chose.

On Sunday, September 3, just before McGovern went out on the campaign trail, Henry Kimelman went to his house to complain about the memo. He refused to recognize that I should have any authority relating to his control of finances. He did not want me to know what our financial position was, even in the most general terms. He recognized that he exercised some real power over campaign operations to the extent that he could control the pursestrings. McGovern spoke to Hart about Kimelman's position that same afternoon, although I was not to learn the substance of that conversation. In any case, just as with Van Dyk, I thought it was more important to join the issue, if need be, over a specific matter, than to become involved in a dispute of principle. I was confident that, working with Hart, I could make progress toward bringing the finance operation into better harmony with other campaign operations. I understood that in working with the heads of the various campaign sections, some diplomacy and patience would be required.

In the end, whatever authority I had was undermined on a relatively minor matter. Soon after McGovern left Washington, I refused to allow an offset sheet, designed so that weekly newspapers could reprint articles directly from it, to be mailed out. While I was impressed by the technical quality of the sheet, I was concerned that the campaign could be embarrassed by a misstatement of McGovern's position in the sheet. It was prepared by John Wood, McGovern's former public information officer at Food for Peace, who had not been directly involved with the campaign at any stage. Thus, I worried that Wood, whom I had never met, or one of his associates would inadvertently distort a McGovern position. In the first issue, I felt that Wood had misunderstood the thrust of the Wall Street speech and had made it seem anti-business. But because the sheet was already printed and because I was concerned more about emphasis than an error of fact, I told Wood's people that I would clear the first issue on the condition I could get a commitment that Wood would show me future issues prior to publication. Finally, he agreed.

Then, at the last minute, I noticed that the publication had no union label and, on inquiry, learned it had been printed in a nonunion shop contrary to campaign policy. I delayed distribution until I could determine the printing union's attitude which I found to be firmly negative.

On Thursday night, September 7, unknown to me, one of Wood's people flew to Texas, where McGovern was campaigning, to show him the offset sheet and get his approval. The next morning the Senator told George Cunningham, his Senate Administrative Assistant who had originally made the arrangement with Wood to put out the sheet, to go ahead with the mailing. When I learned the mailing was under way, I asked that it be stopped, because of the problem with the union label. But Cunningham told me that the Senator himself had ordered the mailing. At that point, I left the office angrily after informing Holum, who was in the travelling party, that I was leaving the campaign.

My departure was more than a fit of pique over a minor matter. Indeed, because the offset sheet was a minor matter, I had expected that McGovern would back me up in line with the September 1 memo. I could understand that he might not want to give me full backing if he thought that I had seized the authority of one of the key campaign people rather than working with him, but the offset sheet was of such little importance that it demonstrated that he would not, in fact, back me up on any point. I was angry with the Senator for failing to back me up, for reacting just as I had told him he would. And I was frustrated, having failed to get his support just as had others who wanted to improve campaign efficiency.

I was overcome with a feeling of despair about the campaign itself, because McGovern's handling of this problem confirmed what I had really known all along—that he would not permit the campaign to be administered in what I considered to be an efficient manner. For me, the events of the past week came on the heels of my unpleasant experience a week earlier when the Senator had given way to Alvin Schorr's pressure and had, at the last minute, altered his position on income redistribution just before the Wall Street speech. Efficiency and even attachment to principle could be swayed too easily by personal appeals. Perhaps it was futile, by this time, to hope that better campaign administration would be able to turn the tide of the election, but I believed it would have improved our chances and would have helped give us a campaign of which we could all be proud.

I did not mean to harm the campaign by departure from the headquarters. I believed that I could simply leave without it attracting notice until some time later, when it would be of little interest.

But, later on the afternoon of my departure, an official of the McGovern campaign called both the *Washington Post* and the *Washington Star* to tell them that I had left. The *Post* knew its informant and called me. I refused all comment, but they ran the story. The *Star*, which appeared later, did the same, although its caller had been anonymous.

Because I knew the *Post* story had hit the streets and because I had not heard from McGovern, I called him in Rockford, Illinois. He confirmed that he had done just what I had warned would destroy the job; he had overridden my decision without even letting me know and without himself knowing the facts. He said he had not noticed the absence of the union "bug."

At the end of my lengthy phone conversation with him McGovern asked me not to resign. In view of the publicity given to my leaving the headquarters, which both of us deplored, my "resignation" was hurting a campaign already plagued with problems. In this way, it would aid Nixon. For that very reason, I had hoped that I could leave the campaign without public notice. Now this course was closed. I told McGovern I would let him know the following day.

The next morning Cunningham told me that the Senator wanted me back in the travelling party. Obviously, McGovern and I both recognized that I could no longer be effective in the headquarters. In order to put an end to the unpleasant matter and because I did not want to harm the campaign, I decided to stay with the campaign. I issued a statement denying my resignation and indicating my full confidence in the management of the campaign.

Subsequently some campaign "friends" spread the word that I had thrown a tantrum in order to get back on the plane. I could not say, at that time, that the real problem was a staff dispute, which it wasn't. Nor could I indicate the depth and nature of my disagreement with McGovern, so I was forced to accept the erroneous story which Jean Westwood aided by a flippant comment to the effect that I resigned weekly anyhow.

This affair coincided with a major resignation from the campaign that would not be reversed. Congressman Frank Thompson of New Jersey had headed a successful voter registration drive for John F. Kennedy in 1960. Fred Dutton had proposed that we undertake a similar operation among the young and minorities in hopes of gaining their support, and this became the policy of the campaign. McGovern asked Thompson to head the effort which, at one time, we had hoped would be funded at anywhere from one to four million dollars. In August it became obvious that far less would be available. Thompson felt that Hart should earmark all incoming funds, if necessary, to voter registration since it would be completed by early October. Hart felt that some money should be sent to the organization in the field. Whatever the allocation of funds, Thompson felt that he had been told by Mc-Govern that registration funds would be given to him for distribution in the states. Hart felt that he had been told by McGovern that voter registration funds would be distributed directly to our state organizations which would then use them for registration drives.

Inevitably Thompson and Hart disagreed, because of their differing messages from McGovern. The Senator had clearly hoped that they could work out their differences directly and that one or the other would show flexibility, despite what he had been told by the candidate. Unfortunately, neither side felt he could give in on the key issue of money which was the lifeblood of the campaign and the only instrument of control the national campaign manager had over the operations in the states. So Thompson resigned.

McGovern never again intervened in staff matters. At the headquarters, Henry Kimelman, who was the legal head of the entity, McGovern for President, Inc., that had been created to handle campaign finances, thought that this title gave him the authority to direct campaign personnel and, if he wished, to fire them. This absurd interpretation of his functions was a continual cause of friction in the headquarters and kept Hart busy handling personnel problems.

Throughout the entire 1970–72 period, McGovern's desire to manage his own campaign led to confusion about lines of authority. Campaign officials such as Hart, Mankiewicz, O'Brien, Dutton, Van Dyk, Dick Dougherty, the last press secretary, and I were often unclear about our organizational relationship to each other and to the candidate.

An informal campaign structure inevitably built up. Yet McGovern would frequently assign duties without regard to this division of responsibility. The person given a task by the candidate would be held responsible by him, even though another person might consider the matter as part of his own job.

In addition, it was difficult for those who had gained some measure of leadership authority to exercise it. McGovern might assign a job to a subordinate without consulting or informing Hart. Then, when Hart or another supervisor would raise the matter with the Senator, he might easily rescind the assignment without informing the person concerned. That duty would be left to Hart. Thus, the person who had originally received his assignment from McGovern might find his instructions countermanded by Hart or someone else acting on behalf of McGovern. This did not make for a smooth-running operation because considerable time and effort was spent on unravelling such situations.

McGovern accentuated his efforts to keep a loose campaign structure by continually consulting each campaign worker about the others. Once he told an interviewer that if the staff could talk about him with each other, it was no less proper for him to discuss them with their fellows. Indeed, instead of forming conclusions based on his own observations of the people working closely with him, he would rely on the advice of their co-workers. Those asked for their opinions might well use the opportunity to advance themselves. And they could not help but feel a sense of superiority over the person in question.

These practices denied virtually all staff members the feeling that they had McGovern's confidence. A staff member knew that he was the subject of McGovern's conversations with his colleagues. He knew that the candidate would give other staffers information and instructions he should receive. And he knew that any subordinate might go over his head to the Senator and complain about his decisions and that, at worst, he would either be overruled or, at best, a confused situation would result.

The candidate did not seem to understand how much his apparent lack of confidence in his staff members disturbed them. He gave us the impression on occasion that he thought staff members were overly concerned with their own prestige. Because he had so little regard for his own "face," he would not easily tolerate what he regarded as measures to "gain face" by staffers.

His lack of concern about "face" resulted, of course, from his own great self-confidence. One day in September 1972, while campaigning with Ted Kennedy in Philadelphia, McGovern told the crowd that earlier in the day a woman had brushed past him to shake hands with Kennedy and tell him: "Ted, we just can't wait until 1976." Then, she stepped back to reassure McGovern that she was supporting him in 1972. Garry Wills later wrote: "Why, people wondered, did he tell that story on himself? Perhaps because he knew that kind of thing was being whispered. He would be the first to say it out loud—just as he had learned to fly without compulsion. He knows he is the better man; he can do without the glamour." We on the staff felt that this statement was self-demeaning rather than self-deprecating, McGovern seemed completely unconcerned.

While this was an admirable personal quality, McGovern's feeling that his staff should reflect a similar unconcern for "face" complicated administrative problems that were already bad enough. At least in terms of the campaign, McGovern could afford to disregard his own prestige because it was already assured, and he knew he had the respect of his staff. But he apparently failed to appreciate that only he could endow his chief subordinates with authority and, equally as important, the appearances of authority. And his own attitude made it difficult for him to understand why it was necessary for the unknown Hart to seek media exposure to counterbalance the authority Mankiewicz could automatically draw from his popularity with the press.

Yet another facet of McGovern's personality that complicated his relations with his staff in the campaign was his habit of rationalizing an adverse situation in order to view it as a help to his campaign. Once, late in the campaign, he told an obnoxious heckler to "kiss my ass." I was stunned because in a single stroke all our efforts to make McGovern look "Presidential" had been undermined. But the candidate, immediately on the defensive, said that, on the contrary, the remark would help because people really wanted to see hecklers put down and that the salty language might help with blue collar voters. Of course, he may have been right. But, at the time, I felt he was rationalizing an unpleasant situation. Time and again, he would end conversations on problems facing the campaign by rationalizing them rather than solving them.

He would use a similar technique when dealing with clashes

among the staff. He would say what he thought his listener of the moment wanted to hear even if it ran counter to what he had told some other staff member. He would bend the facts to demonstrate how, in his own mind, there was no contradiction. Some might call this lying. "McGovern cannot tell, any more, when he is lying," wrote Wills. Yet I am sure that McGovern never thought of this brand of rationalizing as lying. Instead he wanted to please his listener and strove to eliminate whatever problem seemed to exist by the expert use of his debater's logic.

By the same token, he would frequently put the most favorable interpretation on what people said. He would understand them to say, not so much what he wanted them to say, as what he thought they would want to say if they shared his outlook. This practice would sometimes lead to breakdowns of understanding with his staff who had a differing, and less optimistic, appraisal of what they had heard.

So we have the picture of a man who did not demonstrate great confidence in his staff and who experienced considerable difficulty in communicating with them. His personality could lead voters to believe that he was a different kind of politician, a different kind of man, but it did not make for an efficient campaign operation.

Yet, at the same time, the McGovern style was one of the greatest handicaps to the campaign itself. We never had a manager for the campaign. Confusion, poor communications, misunderstanding, inevitable infighting, a lack of thoroughness, and discouragement plagued it. Because these problems tended to become accentuated over time, they became more critical just as the campaign emerged from the Democratic National Convention.

However much some of us in the campaign hoped that McGovern would recognize the harmful effects of his method of operating, there was in reality no chance for improvement for the simple reason that McGovern would have had to change himself. For that reason, the campaign had a sense of predestination about it. McGovern wanted to run a highly personal campaign and, consciously or unconsciously, did everything possible to insure that result. And because his campaign was so stamped with his personality, it suffered from a fatal lack of organizational strength.

Although he was his own campaign manager, McGovern was a far better campaigner than he was a candidate. Like most people seeking public office, he thought that the most important part of the campaign was what he himself was doing on the campaign trail every day. The most trivial speech seemed more significant than a decision on our objectives in a given state or the kind of media campaign we would run. As a result, McGovern's long and exhausting days stumping the country left him little time or strength to subject campaign strategy or management to a searching review. The campaign coasted most of the time.

Robert Kennedy once said that George McGovern was admired because of "the kind of man he is." He does indeed seem to be a unique personality showing flashes of greatness. But the kind of man he was determined the kind of campaign he would have. And perhaps it was less than he deserved.

8

WHAT HAPPENED
LAST NIGHT?

"I've done everything that it was possible for
me to do."—George McGovern, November 7,
1972.

On Wednesday evening, November 8, a group of campaign
workers gathered at the Capitol Hill home of a staff member
to share a last drink. On television, Walter Cronkite was talking
about the election in which McGovern had been defeated as
badly as Alf Landon in 1936 and Barry Goldwater in 1964.
Cronkite called his program "What Happened Last Night?"

It was a dull program to those of us who had been in the
campaign. And its whole premise was wrong. Nothing had happened on the night of November 7. The outcome of the 1972
Presidential election had been determined many months before.

Indeed, our fall campaign had been a desperation campaign.
McGovern was constantly searching for the winning formula,
hoping for a Nixon mistake. It September, he courted the "ethnics" by an ill-considered announcement that he favored tax
credits for the parents of parochial school children. He courted
the Jews, speaking to rabbinical councils and, as Mankiewicz
quipped, where there were no rabbinical councils, we created
them so that he could speak to them. He sought identification

with the traditional Democratic Party in joint appearances with Kennedy, Muskie, and Humphrey. He wanted big crowds and got them, although he failed to notice that they were the same old anti-war crowds.

He began to hammer away at Nixon's failures as a moral leader. The press was quick to emphasize that he saw his contest with Nixon as a struggle between good and evil. It made for good copy, because of McGovern's religious background. But I always felt that his preoccupation with good and evil toward the end of the campaign was an indication of his desperation rather than a return to what he saw as the fundamental issue.

McGovern undoubtedly felt that the policy pursued by successive administrations in Vietnam was immoral.

McGovern clearly felt on firmer ground with the war issue than with any other because it did contain the important element of pitting good against evil. And as the chances for success in the campaign became dimmer, McGovern became more desperate to strike a clear contrast between himself and Nixon. So he found himself slipping into a gross generality about the morality of everything that Nixon stood for. He singled out those issues where Nixon's "immorality" was most evident.

In his biography of McGovern, Anson quotes the Senator's view of his own behavior in his losing campaign against Karl Mundt in 1960. The White House read this section of the book carefully, we are told, and if they did, it no doubt gave them reassurance about the McGovern campaign in 1972.

Anson wrote:

> McGovern did things and said things that in a calmer context he would never have considered. "It was my worst campaign," he admits today. "I hated him so much I lost my sense of balance. I was too negative. I made some careless charges. When the media in the state turned against me, the television and the radio stations and almost all the newspapers, I got kind of rattled. I got on the defensive. I started explaining and answering things I should have ignored. It was hard to get a hook in Mundt."

This analysis, without any amendment whatever, applied directly to his 1972 campaign. Karl Mundt and Richard Nixon were the toughest opponents he had ever faced. He lost to both of them and both in the same way. He "got kind of rattled."

Pat Caddell, our pollster, confirmed that the national polls were accurate in reporting a wide gap between Nixon and McGovern. He said that the people doubted that McGovern was competent to assume the Presidency, that he was not "Presidential."

The polls were hurting the campaign. They discouraged contributors and workers, which made it tougher to infuse the campaign with the kind of spark that could turn it around. The national polls had been wide of the mark in the primaries because they measured nationwide support at a time when McGovern had only needed the support of the tiny New Hampshire electorate. He was far better known in New Hampshire than he was nationwide. As a result of their misreading of McGovern's chances in the primaries, we downgraded them in the fall. But we were whistling in the dark, because they had almost always been reasonably accurate barometers of national sentiment in Presidential elections.

At Eleanor McGovern's urging, the candidate decided to adopt a more statesmanlike style in October. The focus of our purchased media shifted from the soft-sell spots that had been effective in the primaries but disappointing in the fall to half-hour fireside chats on Vietnam, the economy, and corruption in government. McGovern appeared on a series of statewide telethons to answer questions about distortions of his positions.

Far more creative than our efforts to appeal to the "ethnics" and the Jews was McGovern's campaigning in fundamentalist communities. We discovered belatedly that because of his background as a Wesleyan Methodist and his manner of speaking, he had a unique appeal there. Unfortunately, his efforts among the evangelicals came too late, well after the Eagleton affair had severely and erroneously damaged his image as a man who put principle above political expediency.

Finally, when it was all over, we learned that the political organization which had been so important in the primaries had proved futile in the fall. Traditionally, national campaigns consist of the candidate's activities and the media, and fund raising for both. Field work is left to existing party organizations. To compensate for our weaknesses, we had hoped that a good, independent organization would help in identifying McGovern voters and bringing them to the polls. The Nixon campaign created a very extensive Republican national grassroots operation (to the displeasure of other Republican candidates) in hopes of stimulating a large voter turnout which would counteract the effect of the intensive McGovern effort.

In the mass American electorate, an organization even as good as ours had been in the primaries cannot make the difference in a general election. Even the Nixon organization was unable to stimulate a good turnout. In a Presidential election, the voters are making a direct and personal judgment of the candidates.

Media, which shows the candidate, is far more important than organization. McGovern was a superb campaigner. He actually enjoyed meeting average voters and worked hard at it. But people-to-people campaigning turned out to be far less important than national media coverage. The pervasive influence of the electorate media had made a Truman-style campaign a thing of the past.

I suppose that if everybody who had been on the Titanic had been interviewed, each would have had a different explanation for the catastrophe. Obviously the ship had hit an iceberg— obviously McGovern had not won enough votes—but what was the cause? Each of us will have his own answer.

For McGovern, there seem to be many answers. If George Wallace had not been shot and had come to the Miami Convention to face rejection by the McGovern delegates, he might have been angered enough to run as a third-party candidate. An independent Wallace candidacy, McGovern reasoned would have made the contest a horse-race and he might well have been able to beat Nixon, especially if the President had been forced to campaign out of the White House.

But McGovern understood that Wallace was not the only answer. Perhaps the Eagleton affair could have been avoided, but McGovern feels, quite properly in my view, that the major responsibility lay with Eagleton himself. By taking the "calculated risk" that the story of his hospitalization and electroshock therapy would remain unknown, Eagleton delivered the gravest insult to all of the work that had been done by the McGovern forces to achieve the nomination. He was playing with years of work of thousands of people, all of which he deemed less important than his own ambition.

Just before Election Day, Tom Wicker wrote an article in *The New York Times Magazine*. Although he later rejected its thesis, McGovern called the article to my attention. Wicker suggested that McGovern was a factional candidate who had opted to try to reconcile his differences with the Democratic Party's center while hoping not to disillusion his own supporters. But, Wicker claimed, the Eagleton affair "smashed any possibility of that." To the Regulars, McGovern seemed "incompetent" and "indecisive" in the selection and then the dropping of Eagleton. To the new national constituency that McGovern was trying to build, the candidate seemed "ruthless" and "political." As a result, he was never able to convince the Regulars' that maybe he knew something about the electorate they had missed and that, as a result, they ought to support him. And he lost whatever chance he had to appeal to the disaffected on the grounds that he was not a traditional politician.

McGovern also believed that the American public, so imbued with cold war propaganda, was not yet ready to accept a shift in national priorities away from excess military spending to meeting domestic needs. Because they were not ready for this shift, did not want it badly enough, they were susceptible to scare tactics which said they would lose their jobs if they voted to reduce the defense budget.

Probably unaware that the specific alternative defense budget that he had proposed provided ammunition to his opponents rather than making his own case for new priorities any stronger, McGovern remained faithful to his budget throughout the campaign. He was concerned about the reaction if he seemed to retreat from his commitment to every last detail of the proposal. As a result, he found the debate focused more on specific cuts and on lost jobs than on new priorities.

In addition, McGovern came to the conclusion that he stood little chance of appealing to Wallace supporters. Although in Florida he had said that Wallace's vote was "not entirely a racist vote" and that his supporters sought "to register a protest against things as they are," he later saw the Florida, Michigan, and Maryland primaries as indications that racism still runs deep in the United States. White resentment of black demands has not died away, he said, and Wallace was the candidate of that racist sentiment. McGovern, running on a platform of social justice and embracing, however reluctantly, the busing of school children, could never win that vote.

McGovern placed part of the blame on the income redistribution proposal which became, perhaps in his mind and certainly in the public's mind, the $1,000 proposal. Undoubtedly our handling of that concept raised questions about his competence and that of his staff. He certainly questioned the capacity of the people around him to run his campaign, but he never took action to strengthen the campaign leadership or to replace those he thought less competent.

Add to the infamous $1,000 plan the charges of radicalism, so carefully nurtured by Humphrey. The result was that McGovern's own ability to perform the duties of the Presidency were brought into question.

On amnesty—the epitome of his "radicalism"—McGovern had mixed feelings. He sincerely believed in his proposal of a grant of amnesty for those who have fled the country or who have gone to jail to avoid service in Vietnam. This was not a calculated political proposal and it was not the invention of his staff. Undoubtedly, it was a major help in recruiting the dedicated campaign workers from campuses all over the country who helped make McGovern's primary successes possible. But McGovern knew that it was highly unpopular with a majority of Americans whose votes he needed in the fall.

The press were, for the most part, McGovern's villains. He worried about their lack of coverage in the early days of the campaign, but later felt that they paid too much attention to the mechanics of his campaign and to him personally, especially to such irrelevancies as his voice and his appearance. If they had only paid greater attention to what he was saying, to his proposals, he would have stood a better chance of winning. He did not regard close press coverage as a kind of testing and did

not understand that Nixon and Muskie had been similarly ex-
amined. Consequently, he did not recognize that once a candidate passed that testing, the press and the public could make a
judgment about him as Presidential material. Instead he lamented
the obvious double standard that existed between his treatment and that of Nixon. Even if it was understandable in the
media's own terms, it ignored the obvious and, for McGovern,
the important differences between the two candidates on issues
such as the Vietnam war.

The McGovern campaign had a particular problem, because
we had fostered the candidate's image as a man of special virtue.
On every campaign letterhead had been printed the words
from McGovern's announcement address of January 18, 1961:
"I make one pledge above all others—to seek and speak the
truth." (It was by no accident that we dropped this logo at the
time of the Convention.) The press and many politician saw in
this a claim that McGovern adhered to a higher standard of
honesty than most politicians. Issues he raised—debates among
candidates and full disclosure of campaign contributions—
strengthened the impression that he professed to subscribe to a
higher code of conduct than his competitors. He created an
aura of honesty, openness, and rectitude, although a close examination of what he actually said would probably show that
his claims to a special corner on honesty were not so grand as
the press remembered them to be. He knew he could draw a
distinction between himself and other candidates by running an
open campaign and by stressing his willingness to take the unpopular side of major public issues as he did in the case of
Vietnam.

But in an interview in the fall of 1972, Bill Greider of the
Washington Post noted:

> The things that have come clear to the people this summer were
> not secrets to those who knew him before then. McGovern wants
> you to believe that he's direct and always expressing his true
> thoughts; that he's not like other guys—that he doesn't shift and
> make tactical omissions and maneuver. But a lot of people sud-
> denly discovered, gee whiz, maybe he does those things differ-
> ently and less often, but he's still one of the same breed—you

know, takes a position, gets burned, changes it the next day. Well, they made a big deal of it and it broke the myth, the White Knight thing.

Greider's analysis is essentially correct. But McGovern never consciously saw himself as having changed; he always thought he was speaking the truth (except when he said he would have chosen Eagleton as his running mate even if he had known about his shock treatment). He told a *Life* interviewer: "The quality I treasure most is my credibility. I haven't told a lie or a falsehood in this campaign to anybody, but things that had to be done were made to look devious."

What did McGovern mean by this last qualification? If "things that had to be done" meant his handling of the Eagleton affair, then the candidate may be justified in his defense of his approach of giving the Missourian his full support before dropping him. His effort to avoid hurting Eagleton while the reconsideration of his candidacy was under way may have seemed "devious" to many voters.

But McGovern may have been alluding to his habit of saying the same thing two different ways, depending on the audience. For example, when asked about amnesty by students, he would begin: "Yes, I am for a general amnesty," and then delimit his pledge later. With a group of workers, he would begin his answer: "No, I'm not for amnesty until after the war is over." There was no actual shift in his position, and he was merely using a technique common to many candidates. But that was just the point, because he claimed to be different from other candidates. The simple recasting of some of his positions did undermine his credibility.

In short, McGovern sincerely set a higher standard for himself than for other candidates. When he failed to reach that standard, however much more honest he might be than President Nixon, the press pounced on his fall rather than his relative probity. McGovern, who was unaware that he was creating his own credibility problem, could not understand the press reaction.

Greider and many of the other newsmen who covered McGovern will admit that a double standard was applied in the general election campaign. Much was known about Nixon's weaknesses that the newsmen never chose to write or broadcast. In what was either unabashed self-justification or incredible confidence in the voters' collective memory, Dick Harwood of the *Washington Post* later explained, "A campaign is an opportunity for people to discover a politician, what he believes, what he stands for, and how he performs under pressure. In Nixon's case, we've been observing this man for 25 years. . . . I don't think the country was deprived of knowledge of Richard Nixon this year."

Jules Witcover, writing in the *Columbia Journalism Review*, found that many newsmen felt that the Nixon noncampaign had led them to cover the entire campaign inadequately. Certainly it led to an unwarranted manifestation of the double standard. Speaking of coverage of Nixon, Lawrence O'Rourke of the *Philadelphia Bulletin* said: "It's a tough system to crack, but we had an obligation to try to crack it. We fell for the Nixon technique: You don't ask a question you anticipate you won't get an answer to; you get a nonanswer and there is great reluctance to press hard on substantive issues. We did do it a few times, but my experience with Nixon was we just let him get away.

"Because McGovern was the only Presidential candidate in the field," Witcover wrote, "not only the man but all aspects of his campaign underwent examination beyond that to which most previous candidates had been subjected."

Even when Nixon's spokesmen contradicted themselves on just what he was going to do in the way of property tax relief, no newsman followed up and kept pressing. When the oratory of Nixon or his surrogates became overly extravagant, only one reporter challenged them. One September evening NBC's Cassie Mackin stunned us by taking on a Nixon speech and highlighting three specific distortions of McGovern's positions in it. This one news item was the only time that Nixon was subjected to the same kind of treatment as McGovern. The White House called NBC even before the newscast was off the air, and that was the last of such reports.

Of course, Richard Nixon, the incumbent President whose record was, after all, supposed to enter into the campaign, felt that coverage by the *Washington Post* on the Watergate break-in and by CBS on that and the Soviet grain deal, which the administration tailored to the benefit of the big grain exporters, was unfair and partisan involvement in the campaign.

The press was remarkably soft on Nixon in part because it was intimidated. This was the administration that had unleashed Agnew on television news, and had striven for full disclosure of reporters' sources, and that would not mind stooping to petty harassment in order to show their disapproval of their coverage in the *Post* or other publications. Greider admits the double standard: "After all, most editors thought Nixon was going to win, so why go out of the way to alienate him."

Not all of the slanted coverage was due to anything as innocent as intimidation. In a survey of 30 newspapers representing 23 percent of daily circulation, Ben Bagdikian of the *Columbia Journalism Review* found definite bias in the placement and even the use of news stories by papers that had endorsed Nixon. Their editorial views clearly carried over into their news columns. Bagdikian also found that the television networks avoided problems by sharply reducing or even eliminating their traditional election year specials.

In addition, as Adam Clymer of the *Baltimore Sun* pointed out, "the inexperienced reporter [and we had many of them on the Dakota Queen] shows that he's tough, not snowed" by writing unfavorably about McGovern. Editors saw the trouble-plagued campaign as going steadily downward. It was hard for a reporter to sell his editor or his news desk on a positive McGovern piece. That reporter had to show a great deal of self-confidence. As Mankiewicz noted at the time, most reporting was aimed at a self-fulfilling prophecy.

Mankiewicz also hit on another problem with the coverage of McGovern when he noted that Theodore White and his series on the *Making of the President* had made it fashionable to cover the minutiae of the campaign. All through the primaries the media had focused on the strategy and tactics of winning delegates, a matter of relatively little interest to most voters to judge from our own contacts with them, instead of discussing the issues and the contrasts among the candidates. Much the same was true in the autumn as the newsmen practiced what Mankiewicz called "fuselage journalism," a kind of daily gossip column about what was happening on the campaign plane.

In part, this type of coverage was the price we had to pay for an open campaign. We had few campaign secrets. Mankiewicz, Dutton, Dick Dougherty, Hart, and other campaign officials spoke to the press without inhibition, despite an unusually sharp appeal from McGovern for restraint. Often these press conversations were not well motivated. A campaign official would seek to insure that he was given proper credit for a new or planned turn in campaign tactics, so he leaked it to newsmen. Or he would want to protect himself from responsibility for a mistake and would discuss the shortcomings of other people in the campaign with the eager reporters. Or he might simply trust too much that a newsman would regard a conversation as small talk, not for publication, until he saw it in print. In short, an open campaign requires more self-discipline and coordination among its leaders than the kind of closed operation run by the Republicans where the discipline was imposed from the top. So headline-hunting and ego-tripping cost us dearly and hurt our experiment with open campaigning.

Finally, and even more disappointing for McGovern than his treatment by the media, was finding that his moral outrage over American military involvement in Vietnam was not shared by most Americans. While the vast majority wanted the complete withdrawal of American forces from Southeast Asia as soon as possible, they believed that President Nixon's policy had been designed to achieve that end. Against McGovern's rhetoric and even his obvious sincerity, voters could weigh Nixon's accomplishment in reducing the number of Americans involved in combat. Many were ready to trust him to complete the process of withdrawal.

McGovern's criticism of the war implied a criticism of the nation itself. He would often speak of "our great, but deeply troubled, land." Perhaps most Americans did not feel troubled by the war and what it had done to American society. Indeed, with campus and ghetto disorders having quieted down, they may have felt that the worst was over for American society. The perversion of American values embodied in our continuation of the war was not apparent to them or, at least, they did not want to admit it. They did not want to hear the voice of their consciences, and that was what McGovern tried to be. We learned once again that it would be easier to say later, "I didn't realize what was going on."

This, then, is McGovern's catalog of causes.

I would submit that, at best, McGovern had only a slight chance of being elected President of the United States.

Richard Nixon, as an incumbent President, would be a hard man to beat. Out of the 21 times an incumbent had stood for re-election to the Presidency, he had been defeated on only six occasions. In the twentieth century, Taft lost because of Theodore Roosevelt's third party movement, and Hoover lost because of the Great Depression. Clearly there was no such factor at play in 1972. Nixon had reversed most of the failures of his first three years in office in his last year and had compiled a record that was hard even for his opponent to criticize in foreign policy and in some areas of domestic policy such as agriculture.

It may well be that the election was lost on May 22, the day that the mining of North Vietnamese ports by the United States was completed and the day that Richard Nixon arrived in Moscow to sign a series of agreements on matters ranging from trade to disarmament. How could the American public accept the McGovern view of Vietnam and world affairs when the Soviets were placing their seal of approval on Nixon's Vietnam policy? At the same time that McGovern and Humphrey were slugging out the California primary, Nixon, who had earlier made his triumphant visit to Peking, was being feted in Moscow. What more did he need to demonstrate his competence as President? And if the Soviets had been forced to swallow a Vietnam situation they did not like in order to obtain needed grain imports from the United States, what better vindication of Nixon's view of a world based on practical necessity and power, not idealism? Here was masterful use of the incumbency. And it received the ultimate blessing when the U.S. Conference of Mayors in June reversed its 1971 stand calling for complete withdrawal from Vietnam in six months and instead backed Nixon.

Nor should we forget that the Committee for the Re-election of the President, which we tried to ridicule by calling CREEP, actually was a well-run and well-financed campaign.

Of course, with virtually unlimited financing, the Nixon campaign was tempted to make mistakes such as the Watergate incident. But, on the whole, the Nixon high command made good use of its resources. Much effort went into neutralizing any advantage we might have. The phone and mail canvassing we had developed in the primaries was met by a Nixon operation costing more than $10 million. Wherever McGovern appeared, one of the Nixon surrogates would appear to garner his share of television time. When McGovern was due to make a statewide telecast, newspaper advertisements would be placed by the Republicans. When he visited a plant, Nixon canvassers had been there first. When we launched our effort to reach the evangelicals, the Republicans followed suit. Our media expenditures were matched. Perhaps the only parts of our campaign which were not duplicated (and exceeded in the process) were foot-canvassing, which required dedicated volunteers, and candidate travel, which represented a conscious policy of the President.

The Nixon campaign was thorough. In September, an anonymous messenger delivered to columnists Evans and Novak a copy of one of my books charged out of the Library of Congress by Senator Goldwater. Passages were marked, presumably to show that McGovern had a radical working for him. The columnists declined to use the story, because they found the material was nothing more than "liberal."

Using the Democrats-for-Nixon front organization, most of the Nixon media money went for spot announcements attacking McGovern for changing his mind, for reducing the military budget, and for wanting to spend too much on welfare. Due to the Eagleton affair and the California debates, many people were more familiar with these aspects of the McGovern campaign than they were with the more positive elements of it. Nixon, on the other hand, did not expose himself prior to the Republican Convention because he was virtually unchallenged for the nomination and then he prudently took the course of playing President rather than running for the job. In this effort, the Republicans must be credited with taking the fullest advantage of the asset of incumbency of any modern-day campaign for the Presidency.

In short, we recognized that while we were making errors, the Nixon campaign was essentially a well-run and thorough operation. If the people would not respond to the evidence of corruption or failure to end either inflation or the war, we could make little headway against the Republican strategy. And the fact that people did not respond indicates that the Republican campaign leaders had a better understanding of the people than we did.

But Nixon also represented the Establishment, the cold, unresponsive, and political cabal that sought to keep power merely for its own sake and to perpetuate its control rather than as a means of responding to the needs of the people. If McGovern were to have a chance, he would have to offer the electorate some hope that he stood against that Establishment.

That was the offer he made when he announced his candidacy in January 1971:

> [T]oday, our citizens no longer feel that they can shape their own lives in concert with their fellow citizens. Beyond that is the loss of confidence in the truthfulness and common sense of our leaders. The most painful new phrase in the American political vocabulary is "credibility gap"—the gap between rhetoric and reality. Put bluntly, it means that people no longer believe what their leaders tell them. . . . The kind of campaign I intend to run will rest on candor and reason. . . .
>
> I believe the people of this country are tired of the old rhetoric, the unmet promise, the image makers, the practitioners of the expedient. The people are not centrist or liberal or conservative. Rather, they seek a way out of the wilderness.

In order to win the Democratic Party's nomination, McGovern had to draw on the support of the liberal wing of that Party— the peace activists, the young, the women's rights movement, the minorities. He believed that in order to convince these people of his commitment to their objectives and to demonstrate his superiority over other candidates, he had to lay out a specific program. He argued that a campaign of candor required him to talk in specifics, not, as Muskie, to ask people merely to trust

him. "I think the American people want me to say what I believe," he told an interviewer in June 1972. "You can't straddle
the issues anymore."

McGovern did not try to *lead* that constituency of the left; he
tried to *use* it to achieve the nomination. He wanted their votes
and their work, and he paid their price by espousing their causes.
But never would he tell them directly that theirs was not the
path to ultimate victory in November. He did not tell them that
the new constituency that he hoped to weld together would not
agree with their left-wing, liberal, or progressive causes, because "the people are not centrist or liberal or conservative.
Rather, they seek a way out of the wilderness."

As the liberal wing of the Democratic Party moved him closer
to the nomination, McGovern was faced with a three-way choice
about the future course of his own campaign.

First, he might seek to maintain the ideological purity of his
march toward the White House. In that sense, he would be the
Goldwater of the Left. In September in a commentary on CBS
television, John K. Jessup, a man who opposed McGovern, appealed to him to follow this course:

First, he should stop trying to reunite the Democratic Party.
The old Roosevelt coalition was cracked wide open in Chicago
in '68 and has now come apart at the seams. McGovern won the
nomination, not by uniting his party, but by splitting it. And he
can only mount a national challenge the same way.

Second, he should not duck but welcome the cliché that he is
the Barry Goldwater of the Left. I'm not a centrist, he once said
proudly. He should say that again and again. He needs to re-
capture the freshness and candor that attracted people to him in
the first place. He can't do that by shaving and retracting his
views on the issues.

Third, he should make one central issue of the honesty and
morality of American politics and its institutions. . . . What this
country needs and might just welcome is a good scolding.

Am I kidding? Not altogether. I don't think McGovern can
win in any case, but he could perform a needed service by testing
the limits of cynicism in this Republic.

Are we just a pluto-democracy of selfish interest groups, or is
there still a sense of the public interest to be awakened in each

of us? The secret desire to be good citizens of an ethical country may be more widespread than is thought. Such a campaign at least would leave a cleaner taste in the national mouth than the claptrap we've been getting.

Jessup was asking that McGovern remain the refreshingly un-inhibited candidate that he had been at the outset, saying what he thought was right rather than what he thought was expedient. As much as anything else, he meant that McGovern should stop catering to all the interests which had come together to form the Democratic coalition and appeal directly to the people to perform their civic duty.

A second option would have required McGovern to seek a delicate balance between the interests of the ideological constituency that could deliver the nomination to him and the mass of the disaffected across the country. We knew that many of the Wallace voters were expressing a protest against the unresponsiveness of their government. Millions of others, both young and old, had not voted in Presidential elections because they repudiated the entire political apparatus. I remembered well a New York subway conductor during the New York primary in June who was asked whom he supported. "I don't care," he answered. "McGovern, Nixon. It's all the same. And you still end up paying."

Could we break through to this man and tell him that it was not all the same, that George McGovern would be different? If so, McGovern would have to be a different candidate. He would have to avoid a close association with the traditional Democratic Party. He would have to try to build a new coalition, drawing on progressive and moderate Democrats, on the young, on the disaffected, those who supported Wallace and those who didn't. He would have to openly avow that the new coalition was not the old Democratic coalition.

If this was to be McGovern's course of action, he would have to avoid becoming too much of an ideological candidate. He would have to say to those who would give him the nomination: "We in the progressive wing of the Democratic Party have a common cause—the end of the war in Vietnam. And we agree that government must be more open, more honest, more responsive. But I cannot espouse your particular causes and you must not ask me to do so. If you do, it will be political suicide and you will not have advanced your causes."

V.O. Key, Jr., a great old man of American political science, once wrote: "The bewildered citizen could listen to the speeches by Messrs. Roosevelt and Dewey in 1944 and conclude that the principal issue was which party could do the same thing better. Indeed, in the nature of American politics, this is invariably one of the major issues." Translated into the 1972 context, this would have meant that McGovern should try to convince the electorate that he should be chosen over Nixon, not because his proposals were different, but because *he* was different. He would have had to represent change without excess ideological baggage—admittedly a difficult task.

The third option before McGovern was to try to recreate the Democratic coalition. He would try to bring to his support the Party leaders and traditional Party voters who had opposed and scorned him during the primaries. He could try to reunite them around the ideas that all Democrats share, especially the idea of a better life for working men and women. At the same time, he would expect his ideological supporters to understand that he would have to soft-pedal his espousal of their causes in the effort to achieve the ultimate victory. If he were to succeed in this effort, he would have to be able to reassure traditional Democrats that much of what he had said to please the liberals was not seriously meant or at least not properly understood and that he was no wide-eyed radical. In the process, he would have to be willing to disappoint the disaffected who thought he represented something new in American political life. He would have to move toward the center and in the process he would have to change his positions or seem to change them (it didn't make much difference which). But by acting out of political expediency, he would lose any chance he had of appealing to those who despised expediency.

As Wicker wrote in his November 1972 article: "The problem was that, while the Democratic left might dominate the party long enough to nominate McGovern over divided opposition, it would not necessarily dominate the country when McGovern faced the far different problem of defeating President Nixon.

Classically, in that dilemma, the factional candidate should turn to the rest of his party, conciliate it, compromise where necessary, and unify it as much as possible."

In April, long before the Eagleton affair would make it seem imperative for McGovern to seek reconciliation with the traditional Democrats, McGovern opted for the third choice. This decision was made immediately after he had made a strong appeal to the disaffected and had won the Massachusetts primary.

On April 20, he delivered an address at Catholic University in Washington in which he blasted what he called "the establishment center." In his remarks, he threw down the gauntlet and criticized the policies and attitudes of those who had governed the country since John F. Kennedy. He said:

> Most Americans see the establishment center as an empty decaying void that commands neither their confidence nor their love.
> It is the establishment center that has led us into the stupidest and cruelest war in all history. . . .
> The establishment center has persisted in seeing the planet as engaged in a gigantic struggle to the death between the free world and the Communist world. . . .
> The establishment center has constructed a vast military colossus based on the paychecks of the American worker.

In place of this establishment center, McGovern pledged "a new coalition at the center." His message was that the center had in fact moved from these policies to a more progressive view of society's needs. "In short," he said, "I want all of us to have the assurance that we live in a nation where we care deeply about each other." This was the ultimate appeal to the disaffected. While his rhetoric was still built around the concept of "the center," he was clearly putting distance between himself and the kind of people and policies identified with the traditional Democratic (or Republican) party.

On April 25, McGovern won his biggest victory of the primary season, carrying more than half of the vote in Massachusetts. The Regulars had been swept aside. McGovern was looking forward to the nomination and was feeling infallible and magnanimous.

His victory caused him to reverse course suddenly and repudiate the Catholic University speech. In an interview with David Broder published in the *Washington Post* of April 28, McGovern said he would reject the counsel of the "more rigid purists" in his campaign and move to broaden his base. He had never talked with his campaign leadership before making this decision.

"I think I've got the skill and the common sense to quiet the fears of those people [traditional Party and labor leaders] and bring them on board at some point." He had always thought that his ideological supporters had no real quarrel with Regulars and would follow him in this gesture. Mistakenly he thought they would be no problem.

At the time, I could only wonder who the "more rigid purists" were. The man who spoke of the "establishment center" might be "a rigid purist." It seemed that McGovern was rejecting the first option—Goldwater of the Left—in favor of the third. Perhaps he had never put very much stock in the forces of alienation and disaffection as a political reality. In that case, he would see no hope of putting together a winning majority in the second option while the third option would be the only possible course.

In effect, McGovern turned his back on what Evans and Novak called his "oil and water blend" which drew on the Democratic left's ideological support and the votes of those who sought an honest, new politician, regardless of his specific views. Perhaps the balance between the liberal Democrats and the disaffected would have been impossible to maintain because the liberal positions he had already taken would displease the alienated. I believe that, at that moment, a tough talk with his own hard-core supporters would have made the creation of the new coalition possible. But on April 28, that possibility was lost forever.

The reconciliation with the Regulars was doomed to failure. As the California challenge and the "Anybody But McGovern" movement indicated, their alienation from McGovern was already complete. They disagreed with his programs or what they thought were his programs, and they disliked his methods which seemed to exclude them. His attempts to placate them and to demonstrate that he was a candidate of the center failed because he seemed so insincere. McGovern had shunned making promises to each conceivable interest group and had avoided watering down his proposals when they were criticized. Now, he resorted to this kind of brokenfield running, and it did not persuade the Regulars.

It infuriated his own supporters who felt that he was "selling out." Admittedly one could suggest that they now had nowhere else to go, but they did not need to go anywhere. They could stay home and not canvass and not run the storefronts and not make the phone calls and not vote. They might not have understood if he had told them that the coalition he sought meant that he could not explicitly fight for their causes. But they certainly did not misunderstand when he made his move toward the center—"Lyndon Johnson *inherited* the Vietnam war."

The debates with Humphrey in California and the Eagleton affair, however unjustifiably, broadcast to the nation as a whole the truth about George McGovern. Humphrey showed that McGovern was seeking to place his proposals closer to the center rather than remembering that New Hampshire billboard, "McGovern . . . if you *really* want a change." He made what seemed a "political" decision to drop Eagleton.

Yet we should be careful not to blame the defeat on Humphrey or Eagleton; we can only blame the disaster on them. The choice of the third option—reconciliation with the very people who had been the brunt of his campaign—pushed victory out of reach (unless Nixon himself had already done so). McGovern could never count on Wallace's running, however rejected he might have felt by the Convention. For Wallace was busy making himself into a solid Democrat, and doing a good job of it. Wallace could look ahead to 1976 by which time he might appear to be sufficiently cleansed of his past racism especially if he remained loyal to the Democrats in 1972. Without Wallace's defection, the weaknesses in his own strategy would certainly deny McGovern the election. A Wallace endorsement in itself was made more unlikely by his April 28 move, because McGovern was joining forces with the same opponents that he and Wallace had both challenged. To endorse McGovern, Wallace would have to have been willing to lose much of his own appeal among the alienated.

If defeat was certain, Humphrey and Eagleton deserve the

credit for making it of such record-breaking magnitude. When Eagleton said his case had been only one rock in the landslide, Washington wags countered, "Oh yes, but he was up on top of the mountain pushing the rocks off." Perhaps the Humphrey attacks were the revenge of the Democratic Right on the Democratic Left for having sat out 1968. More likely, I think, they were the irrational actions of a man, who, as McGovern said, was "bent on further self-destruction." He wanted to be the President too much.

Given the way McGovern had launched his campaign, I would have hoped for him to have chosen the second option—that delicate balance between the ideologues and the disaffected. Perhaps millions who did not vote would have voted. Perhaps McGovern would have won some of the Wallace votes that went to Nixon. (In fact, despite his ultimately pessimistic view of Wallace supporters, he got many of their votes in the North.) Perhaps the McGovern workers and voters would not have been dispirited but buoyed as the general election campaign began.

Perhaps not. But the McGovern campaign and McGovern himself would have kept some of that integrity that was so much a part of it when it began. McGovern could have remained "pure," not ideologically pure in the eyes of his Democratic left backers, but true to himself, seeking and speaking what he knew were his long-standing beliefs about America and its people rather than the panicked half-truth [5] of a political style that repudiated all that he had said and stood for in the early days of the campaign. If nothing else, McGovern might have been a happier man on November 8.

Every candidate must assume the burden of responsibility for his campaign. For George McGovern this was particularly true, because he alone had determined the strategy and the style of his campaign. He had decreed the "why" and the "how" of the campaign. In the primaries, his ability to capitalize on Party reform and his penchant for a decentralized campaign structure had worked. But McGovern had recognized that the general election would demand a fresh approach. In developing his strategy for the fall, McGovern disregarded the impact of his primary campaign both on his own supporters and on the Party

Regulars whose help he sought. By underestimating the legacy of conflict between these two forces, he made what may well have been a fatal error in strategy.

Once, early in my association with McGovern I accompanied him to a Senate hearing at which he was to testify on a piece of legislation that I had drafted for him. Instead of asking me to sit beside him at the witness table as most Senators would have done, he indicated that I should sit in the audience. When I remarked on this to John Holum, who knew McGovern well, I was told that McGovern liked to be "the man alone." At the time, I romanticized this habit as a part of the carefully cultivated image of the South Dakota "cowboy" come to Washington. But, as I came to know McGovern better, I realized that he never gave his full confidence to any person, perhaps because he did not want to become dependent on him. As a result, he stood above his campaign, yet remained not only its leader but its manager. That was why, especially after the early successes, it was often chaotic and disjointed. And that was why the most important decision on strategy was made by McGovern—alone.

Wicker wrote that McGovern wanted the Presidency badly and should have recognized that he could not achieve it by being " 'above' the politics he thought would win it." McGovern never believed that there was a "new politics" which was somehow different from the old. But he had believed that there could be a "new coalition" to be the successor of the old. The tragedy of the McGovern campaign of 1972 is that it was never a fair test of that "new coalition."

Speaking to a bittersweet reunion of his campaign workers on December 10, 1972, McGovern told them that, after all, he was only "disappointed, but not defeated." He had forgotten that he had been a long shot. He had forgotten that in 1970 he had written: "How . . . exciting it is to have an opportunity to educate an entire nation and to learn from an entire nation over the period of the next two years. That is its own reward."

INDEX

1963   **Sept. 24** • First Senator to criticize American involvement in Vietnam.

1970   **Aug. 10** • Announces candidacy for Democratic nomination. Short campaign nets 146½ delegates, mostly Kennedy supporters.
April 28 • Report of the McGovern Commission on Party Structure and Delegate Selection.
April 29 • Introduction of the McGovern-Hatfield Amendment "to end the war."
May 12 • National telecast for the McGovern-Hatfield Amendmen
Sept. 1 • Senate votes on McGovern-Hatfield, defeating it 55–39.
Nov. 1 • Muskie delivers Election Eve address, undermining McGovern's hopes.

1971   **Jan. 18** • Earliest announcement in U.S. history of candidacy for Presidential nomination.
Sept. 11 • Meets in Paris with North Vietnamese delegation to peace talks.
Sept. 14 • Target of fire-bombing and rock-throwing crowd in Saigon.

1972   **Jan. 23** • Low point in Gallup Poll, which shows McGovern favored by only 3 percent of Democrats.
Feb. 18 • Tours Manchester, New Hampshire, and discovers strong support among blue-collar workers.
Feb. 19 • Incident in front of Manchester *Union Leader*, where Muskie allegedly cries over insults to his wife.
Mar. 7 • Strong second-place showing in New Hampshire primary with 37 percent of vote to Muskie's 46 percent. Muskie, from Maine, had expected more than half.
Mar. 14 • Weak sixth-place finish in Florida primary, but McGovern learns lesson and says not all Wallace supporters should be called racist.
Mar. 16 • Secret discussion in Milwaukee motel as staff split becomes complete.
Mar. 21 • Finishes distant second to Muskie in Illinois delegate race, while McCarthy fails to make strong showing in popular vote contest.
April 4 • Wins Wisconsin primary. Wallace second; Humphrey third; Muskie fourth. Lindsay quits race.
April 25 • Smashing victory in Massachusetts primary. Finishes behind Humphrey and Wallace in Pennsylvania, but again